PROBLEM SOLVING
Step by Step
Teacher's Edition

Metropolitan Teaching and Learning Company
33 Irving Place
New York, New York 10003

Printed in the United States of America

ISBN: 1-58120-675-5

Problem Solving, Step by Step

Program Author: Jack Beers

Edited and Designed by Curriculum Concepts

Editor: Michael Ellis

Illustrated by Michael Hortens

Cover Design: Charles Yuen

Cover Photograph: Joseph Sohm;ChromoSohm, Inc./CORBIS

Metropolitan Teaching and Learning Company
33 Irving Place
New York, New York 10003

Printed in the United States of America

ISBN: 1-58120-675-5

10 9 8 7 6 5 4 3 2 1

INTRODUCTION

This book is designed to help your students become better problem solvers and to score higher on the problem solving portion of standardized tests. It is built on a teaching approach that uses a few powerful thinking strategies over and over. Repeated use of these strategies helps students to make them part of their permanent problem solving toolkit and improve their test scores. These strategies are:

- **Decide What to Do First**
  For problems that have more than one step or where a misstep is common, students are given real help in deciding what the first step is.

- **Find Needed Information**
  Students learn how to find information in graphic displays such as tables, graphs, diagrams, and complex word problems.

- **Show Information Another Way**
  For many problems, it is useful to show the information in another format such as a diagram, a table, a drawing, a word sentence, word equation, or equation. Both visual and algebraic tools are stressed.

- **Decide on the Kind of Answer You Need**
  Students learn to decide what form the answer should take: whether or not it is a number, what kind of unit it has, and whether an estimate will suffice.

LESSON STRUCTURE

Each lesson has four parts that move students from initial instruction to test preparedness.

- **Instruction** includes several examples and is interactive.

- **Guided Practice** focuses on process skills and each step of the solution process.

- **Practice** provides several problems to be solved from start to finish.

- **Test-Taking Practice** provides multiple-choice items and writing tasks to prepare students for all items that they will see on standardized tests.

HOW TO USE THIS BOOK

The sequence of chapters in this book closely parallels the sequence of topics in a mathematics textbook for Grade 7. Each problem solving lesson contains math content that is normally taught in that chapter. For example, the lesson on Using Part-Part-Whole Percent Diagrams in Chapter 8 requires some familiarity with solving proportions. This is indicated in the running foot at the bottom of each page in the lesson. Four specially prepared lessons, titled "Choosing a Strategy for Solving Problems," provide students with practice in deciding to use a particular strategy for solving a particular kind of problem.

Here are two ways of using the book that the author recommends:

1. Use about one lesson per week in the sequence in which they are listed in the book. The Table of Contents will help you match up the math content with your textbook.

2. For more intensive work on particular problem solving topics, such as bar graphs, have students work on topical lessons in order. The list of Topics on page 4 will help you find the lessons you need.

ASSESSMENT

Each lesson contains both multiple-choice items and writing items that can be used to assess students' progress in problem solving. In addition, these assessments will help prepare students for the style and content of items found on current state and standardized tests.

The multiple choice items include questions that ask about the process used to solve a problem — without asking for the answer. Many states currently require that students can exhibit understanding in this way.

The WRITE ABOUT IT item or items that appear in each test are also similar to those on many state and standardized tests. Students need help developing the skills to do well on the writing assessments. The TEST-TAKING SKILLS lessons that appear after chapters 4, 8, and 12 provide instruction and practice for writing assessments. They will help students learn to describe their plans and methods for solving problems. There are also additional TEST-TAKING SKILLS lessons at the end of chapters 2, 6, and 10. These skills relate to multiple-choice items.

TEACHING SUGGESTIONS—STEP 7

Chapter 1

Lesson 1

In this lesson, students **Show Information Another Way** by making a diagram to show the relationships in a problem and then use the diagram to solve the problem.

Instruction: Make sure that students understand how the diagram shows all of the information in the problem. By breaking the problem into steps, students should be able to see which step they need to solve first. Students should realize that the equations in Steps 1, 3, and 4 isolate the unknown quantity by using the inverse operations of those shown in the diagram.

Guided Practice: If students have difficulty, show them how they can use parts of the diagram individually. For example, Step 1 uses the relationship shown among the costs of the items and the cost of the order.

Test-Taking Practice: For problem 5, students should realize that the customer might have bought only bookcases, only worktables, or a number of each.

Extension: Have students make a diagram to show the relationship among the information given in problem 5 of Test-Taking Practice, using variables for the number of each item bought.

Lesson 2

In this lesson, students **Show Information Another Way** by making a diagram that they can use to make a solution plan for a problem. The diagram helps students to see the algebraic solution to the problem.

Instruction: You may want to review the method of finding a mean, using simple numbers such as 1, 2, and 6. Students will then understand more clearly how they can use the inverse operation to solve the first step of the problem.

Practice: For problem 3, make sure that students understand that w represents the number of ounces in a glass of water.

Test-Taking Practice: For problem 5, make sure students understand why they do not need to know the size of the audience for each of the first three nights—the total of 324 is a completed step of the problem.

Lesson 3

In this lesson, students **Decide on the Kind of Answer Needed** to determine whether to use an exact quotient as the solution to a problem, or to round the quotient up or to round it down.

Instruction: Make sure that students understand that in these sorts of problems, rounding up or down does not follow a rounding rule, but is determined by the kind of answer that will make sense.

Guided Practice: Problem 2 asks for the remainder of the quotient; discuss with students what happens with the remainder in problems 1 and 3. In problem 1, the remainder *will* take up space in a tank; in problem 3, the remainder *will not* be downloaded.

Test-Taking Practice: For problem 7, you may need to explain that 1 spin is the same as 1 revolution; the problem can be solved as a simple rate problem, even if students are not familiar with 45-rpm records.

Lesson 4

In this lesson, students **Decide on the Kind of Answer Needed** to determine whether they can estimate or need to find an exact number to solve a problem.

Instruction: You may wish to use simple numbers to demonstrate why the method of rounding suggested in the two boxed items will result in better estimates.

Guided Practice: For problem 2, discuss with students why they cannot depend on the estimate being close enough. Make sure that students do not mistakenly think that rounding each factor by the same number—in opposite directions—will result in an exact answer.

Test-Taking Practice: Problem 2 requires students to compensate as they round each addend—the best estimate is *not* found by rounding each number according to whether its unit place is greater or less than 5.

Extension: You may want to ask students to come up with a rule about when they should estimate "high" and when they should estimate "low."

Lesson 5

In this lesson, students **Find Needed Information** in tables and then use the information to solve problems.

Instruction: If students highlight Spanish-speaking nations for Example 1, they can simply use those entries that are *not* highlighted for Example 2.

Guided Practice: Students may answer problem 2 incorrectly if they estimate the sum of the populations; make sure that they understand that their estimate is too close and that they should find the exact total.

Test-Taking Practice: For problem 4, students will need to add integers; they should also realize that the greatest range will not necessarily be that of the city with the highest average temperature.

Chapter 2

Lesson 1

In this lesson, students **Show Information Another Way** by making a table from data shown in a line graph and then use the table to derive new data to solve a problem.

Instruction: Make sure that students read the labels of the graph shown, and that they understand that the values shown on the y-axis are cumulative. Some students may want to simply find the steepest segment of the line graph. This is also a reasonable method of solving the problem.

Guided Practice: Students may simply compare the distances between marked points on the graphs at each time interval to solve these problems; making a table will reinforce their understanding of reading line graphs.

Lesson 2

In this lesson, students **Find Needed Information** in a line graph and use the information to solve rate problems.

Instruction: Make sure that students understand that they can use any point on a straight-line graph to find a rate. If necessary, find the rate using several points to demonstrate that it is always the same.

Test-Taking Practice: The graph shown cannot be directly read to find the unit cost of carpeting; for problem 2, students can most easily find the unit rate by dividing the cost of 10 square feet by 10. They can use the unit rate to solve problem 4.

Lesson 3

In this lesson, students **Find Needed Information** by reading a continuous line graph and interpreting changes in the graph.

Instruction: Students should note that, although there are no labels on the y-axis of the graph, each interval represents the same (unknown) quantity. For Example 3, students should realize that the faster a car travels, the more distance it covers in a given period of time—this is why it uses more gasoline each hour.

Practice: Make sure that students realize that the days marked on the x-axis are represented by the intervals *between* numbers shown on the scale. Students will need to use common sense to infer what changes will be shown on the graph by the situations given in problems 6–9.

Test-Taking Practice: Discuss students' solutions for problem 6. Point out why they would not be able to determine from the graph that the train was standing still if the problem had not so stated—for example, the train could simply be traveling across flat land.

Extension: Ask students to come up with other ideas for meaningful graphs in which they would not need values shown on the y-axis.

Chapter 3

Lesson 1

In this lesson, students **Decide What to Do First** when they have to rename a number in order to solve a problem.

Instruction: For Example 2, make sure that students understand why they can use the reciprocal of the divisor. If necessary, use simple whole numbers and fractions—such as $4 \div \frac{1}{2}$ or $1 \div \frac{1}{4}$—to demonstrate.

Guided Practice: Point out that there is no single correct method to solving these problems, but that students will find the computation in certain methods easier than in others. Some students may want to solve problem 3 by renaming $8\frac{3}{4}$ as an improper fraction and then multiplying 12.95 by the reciprocal. This method is also reasonable.

Test-Taking Practice: For problem 6, some students may find it easier to rename both measures as decimals, and give the solution as 163.875 square feet.

Lesson 2

In this lesson, students **Show Information Another Way** by making a diagram to show the steps they will need to follow to solve a problem.

Instruction: Most students will find it easier to first make the simple diagram showing the general information in the problem. They should then be able to complete the diagram with the specific information. Because the problem gives the additional charge per minute, students should rename hours as minutes, rather than renaming minutes as a decimal or fraction of an hour.

Guided Practice: Students may want to make a diagram before following the steps of problem 2.

Test-Taking Practice: Students need not be familiar with kilowatt-hours to solve problem 2; point out that they can manipulate kilowatt-hours as they would any rate.

Lesson 3

In this lesson, students **Decide on the Kind of Answer Needed** to estimate products and quotients with fractions and mixed numbers.

Instruction: Some students have difficulty estimating products of fractions and mixed numbers because the meaning of multiplication with these numbers is still unclear to them. Suggest that they write word equations for the examples before they round the numbers, so that they understand how to solve the problems.

Guided Practice: For problem 2, students should realize that dividing by a fraction is the same as multiplying by its reciprocal, and that they need round only the whole number, 32. For problem 3, make sure that students understand why they need to find a number compatible with the denominator of the fraction.

Test-Taking Practice: Students should take care to round for compensation when they answer problems 1 and 2.

Lesson 4

In this lesson, students **Decide on the Kind of Answer Needed** to estimate with measures given in mixed units.

Instruction: Make sure that students understand why 1 lb 5 oz is renamed differently in Example 1 and Example 2; stress that the denominator should be rounded to a compatible number to make the estimation easier.

Practice: Students should use two steps to solve problem 8: add an estimate of $6 for the first quart to an estimate of 7×2 for the second two quarts. The remaining pint can be ignored as it compensates for each of the estimates being rounded up.

Test-Taking Practice: Students should take care to round for compensation to find the best estimates for these problems. In problem 4, students will round three factors to find an estimated product.

Lesson 5

In this lesson, students multiply by reciprocals to **Show Information Another Way**.

Instruction: If students have trouble understanding how reciprocals "undo" multiplication, give them some additional examples with unit fractions or intermediate products that are easy to find. For example, $3 \times 4 \times \frac{1}{4} = 3$. Also, $3 \times \frac{5}{3} \times \frac{3}{5} = 3$.

Test-Taking Practice: Some students may need a hint for problem 5—remind them that a decimal can be expressed as a fraction.

Chapter 4

Lesson 1

In this lesson, students **Show Information Another Way** by making a table that shows the relationships among given data in a problem and then use the table to write algebraic expressions that they can use to solve the problem.

Instruction: The first example on this page shows students how to write an algebraic expression as a solution; the second example shows them how to substitute values in the algebraic expression to determine a quantitative answer.

Guided Practice: For problem 2, students should take care to follow the order of operations correctly.

Practice: Students should realize that the answers to problems 4–9 are algebraic expressions.

Test-Taking Practice: As on the Practice page, the answers to these problems are algebraic expressions. Some students may write the expressions without first using numerical values; encourage them to check their expressions by substituting numbers.

Lesson 2

In this lesson, students **Show Information Another Way** by rewriting a formula to isolate a particular variable.

Instruction: In the first example, students solve a formula for substituted values; in the second example they determine which variable they are solving for, and rewrite the formula to isolate that variable.

Guided Practice: For problem 2, draw students' attention to the boxed note, and make sure that they understand the relationship between decimals and percents.

Test-Taking Practice: For problem 6, students may want to draw diagrams of the figures. They should realize that the larger dimension of the first rectangle determines whether or not it can fit into the second, regardless of the smaller dimension.

Lesson 3

In this lesson, students **Show Information Another Way** by making a diagram that allows them to write an equation that will solve a problem.

Instruction: On this page, students make a diagram that they then use to write a complete equation to solve a problem.

Guided Practice: Students should note that they must follow the correct order of operations in these two problems. You may want to review the use of parentheses in an equation.

Practice: For problem 3, part b, tell students that they should complete the equation using operation signs ($+$, $-$, $\times$, or $\div$).

Lesson 4

In this lesson, students will further their ability to choose an appropriate strategy to solve a problem.

Instruction: Make sure students connect the strategy of showing information another way with the need to rename measures so that all the quantities in the problem are expressed in the same unit of measure.

Guided Practice: For problem 2, make sure students recognize the need to interpret a quotient that includes a remainder. The question asked by the problem needs to be answered by finding the remainder.

Test-Taking Practice: For problem 4, students should understand that the solution requires a combination of addition and multiplication.

Chapter 5

Lesson 1

In this lesson, students **Show Information Another Way** by drawing a number line that can be used to solve problems that contain positive and negative integers and rational numbers.

Instruction: Some students may not understand absolute value. Point out to them that the absolute value of a number is simply the number itself, without a plus or minus sign in front of it. Make sure that students understand that they should add absolute values of numbers that have the same sign and that they should subtract absolute values of numbers that have opposite signs.

Practice: If students have difficulty solving problem 7, point out that if there is a loss, "net earnings" will be negative.

Test-Taking Practice: Students may solve problems 2–5 by writing equations directly, without using number lines. Students may also solve equations by using the rule of like and unlike signs (like signs make a plus; unlike signs make a minus).

Lesson 2

In this lesson, students **Show Information Another Way** by drawing a number line, which they can then use to write an equation to solve problems that contain comparative values.

Instruction: Ask students why the 0 point is placed at the right end of the number line in this problem. (Every event in the problem took place *before* the museum opened.)

Guided Practice: Draw students' attention to the boxed note in problem 1, and make sure that they understand why they cannot mark 0 on the number line: until they complete the problem, they cannot tell where the other points will lie relative to 0.

Practice: Encourage students to read the problems carefully to identify correctly the direction in which they should move along the number lines. Remind students to look for words such as *above, below, up, down, climb, descend, before,* and *after.*

Chapter 6

Lesson 1

In this lesson, students **Show Information Another Way** by writing proportions to find unit rates.

Instruction: Make sure that students set up parallel proportions; most errors in writing and solving a proportion result from setting up the proportion incorrectly. Including words in proportions and unit rates will let students know that they are setting them up correctly.

Guided Practice: In problem 1, point out that the British pound is a unit of currency, not a unit of weight.

Practice: Encourage students who have difficulty with these problems to write the unit rate including words for the units; by canceling like units in a product, they can check that they have set up the unit rate correctly.

Lesson 2

In this lesson, students **Decide What to Do First** in problems which can be solved by first calculating a unit rate.

Instruction: Point out to students that, when they have several questions about one rate, it is easier to find and use the unit rate rather than setting up a proportion for each question.

Guided Practice: For problem 3, make sure that students understand that lightning and thunder originate at the same time, but the sound of the thunder travels more slowly than the light of the lightning.

Test-Taking Practice: To solve problems 4 and 5, students will need to rename 1 hour as 60 minutes.

Lesson 3

In this lesson, students **Show Information Another Way** by renaming rates as equivalent rates with different units.

Instruction: Students should take care to use the appropriate form of each conversion, especially in cases such as that in Example 2 when they are using two conversions. Stress that canceling like units will allow students to check that they have used the appropriate conversion.

Guided Practice: As on the previous page, stress that canceling like units will allow students to make sure that they have used the appropriate conversions.

Test-Taking Practice: For problem 3, students will need to know that there are 8 pints in a gallon and 16 ounces in a pound. Some students may solve problem 7 by multiplying $0.10 per ounce by 16 to find the price per pound at the Blue Grocery Store: $1.60.

Chapter 7

Lesson 1

In this lesson, students **Show Information Another Way** by converting between customary and metric units.

Instruction: As in the previous lesson, most student errors will result from using the inappropriate form of the conversion. Making sure that students include units in their conversions, and then cancel like units, will prevent them from this error.

Practice: In problem 6, students need only convert one of the measures. It doesn't matter which measure they rename, but most students will find it easier to multiply 26 by 1.6 than to divide 40 ÷ 1.6.

Lesson 2

In this lesson, students **Show Information Another Way** by writing proportions to solve problems that involve scale models.

Instruction: Point out to students that they should make sure that the proportions they write are equivalent. When they write a proportion in words, they can be sure that the proportion is correctly written.

Guided Practice: These problems involve rates—ratios of more than one kind of unit. The comparison for proportions of equal rates is not always of the part:whole type. In these problems, for example, point out that the units in each side of the proportion are inches/feet. Students should realize that the units on both sides should match. This concept can also help students determine the units for answers to proportion problems.

Practice: In problems 5 and 10, students should understand that the scale can be used as one side of the proportion. For example, 1:60 can be written as $\frac{1}{60}$.

Test-Taking Practice: Students may need a hint on how to solve problem 5. Tell them that they can find the scale by writing one side of the proportion $(\frac{15 \text{ in.}}{60 \text{ ft}})$ and reducing it to its lowest terms. Although it wouldn't be incorrect to write the scale using only inches $(\frac{1}{48})$, they can keep the mixed units $(\frac{1 \text{ in.}}{4 \text{ ft}})$.

Lesson 3

In this lesson, students **Show Information Another Way** by drawing diagrams and writing proportions to solve problems involving similar figures.

Instruction: Point out to students that drawing a diagram to show the information in a problem of this kind will help them discover that the problem involves similar triangles. Students should have had enough experience writing proportions to set up proportions for similar figures correctly.

Guided Practice: For problem 1, you may want to have students draw the two triangles as separate figures. Students may also want to draw diagrams for problem 2.

Practice: If students have difficulty with problem 4, point out that the two triangles are similar, even though they have a different orientation.

Test-Taking Practice: Students may need to draw diagrams for problems 2–4.

Lesson 4

In this lesson, students will further their ability to choose an appropriate strategy to solve a problem.

Instruction: Students should understand that the two strategies illustrated here are alternatives; they can use either one to arrive at the answer to the question. Using either method will finally lead students to realize the need to write an equation to solve the problem.

Guided Practice: Encourage students to choose strategies with which they feel comfortable. Some students may find that strategies involving visual presentation make solving problems a relatively simple process.

Practice: You might want to ask students to explain the vertical line in the middle of the fourth hour. They should conclude that that is the point at which the driver puts more gasoline into the tank.

Test-Taking Practice: For problem 1, students should recognize that the solution requires a combination of multiplication, addition, and division.

Chapter 8

Lesson 1

In this lesson, students **Show Information Another Way** by drawing diagrams to show part-part-whole percent relationships and then using the diagrams to set up proportions.

Instruction: Make sure that students understand that each side of the proportion shows the same relationship. The proportions are set up to show the relative sizes of the boxes drawn in the diagrams.

Practice: If students have difficulty, point out that the diagrams are drawn to show relative sizes; this will give them a hint as to how to complete the diagrams and thereby set up the proportions.

Test-Taking Practice: Make sure students understand the part-whole relationships and how to correlate the percents to the numbers presented in the problems.

Lesson 2

In this lesson, students use diagrams to **Show Information Another Way** for percents greater than 100; they use the diagrams to set up and solve proportions.

Instruction: Make sure that students understand the concept of percents that are greater than 100 percent. Students should see that the diagrams are set up to show the relative sizes of the quantities involved.

Practice: Remind students to set up their diagrams, if they use them, to show the relative sizes of the quantities involved in the problems. This technique enables students to see more clearly the relationships between the numbers that are involved.

Lesson 3

In this lesson, students **Show Information Another Way** by writing proportions to solve percent problems that involve measures.

Instruction: It is important that students understand that the problems on this page involve the dimensions of the figures, not the areas. Although the dimensions can be described in percents, the areas will not have equivalent increases or decreases.

Guided Practice: Point out to students that percent problems can involve measures that are not linear; the measures can be weights, masses, or even amounts of time.

Test-Taking Practice: For problem 5, make sure that students remember not to confuse dimensions (length and width) with area.

Lesson 4

In this lesson, students **Show Information Another Way** by drawing diagrams setting out the relationships in multi-step problems.

Instruction: Make sure students understand that the additional 10% off means that 10% should be taken off the already discounted sale price.

Practice: Remind students to be careful, when they are setting up their diagrams, to keep close track of the accuracy of the steps in these multi-step problems.

Test-Taking Practice: For problem 5, students should come to realize that an additional 10% off a price that has been discounted by 25% does not result in a final price that is equal to a full 35% off the original price.

Lesson 5

In this lesson, students **Show Information Another Way** by drawing diagrams to show percent increases; they use the diagrams to find interest.

Instruction: Make sure that students understand that the repeated factor produces a new total each time it is applied. The factor is not simply applied to the original total multiple times.

Guided Practice: Remind students that when they are dealing with increases, they are dealing with percents that are greater than 100. Some students may continue to first find the repeated smaller percent and then add that amount to the base total. They may need some help to see their way toward using percents that are greater than 100.

Practice: For problem 6, students need to recognize that they are dealing with a percent decrease as a repeating factor. This means using a percent less than 100.

Test-Taking Practice: For problem 6, students should recognize that the repeated increase of 10% will yield a greater result than the one-time application of a 20% increase.

Lesson 6

In this lesson, students **Decide on the Kind of Answer Needed** for percent problems that require estimation.

Instruction: Students should realize that one of the main reasons to estimate percents is to work with familiar benchmark amounts, which makes mental calculation simpler.

Guided Practice: Point out to students that the table of equivalents at the top of the page provides a useful guide to benchmarks that are helpful in estimating percents.

Test-Taking Practice: Remind students to use benchmarks for both quantities in the problems, the base amounts and the percents.

Chapter 9

Lesson 1

In this lesson, students **Find Needed Information** from diagrams or descriptions to solve problems involving similar figures.

Instruction: Make sure that students do not confuse the relationships between the dimensions of figures and the relationships between the areas of figures.

Guided Practice: Make sure students remember that area is expressed in squared units and that volume is expressed in cubed units.

Test-Taking Practice: For problem 6, make sure that students understand the ratio of the areas of two figures is the ratio of the two figures squared.

Lesson 2

In this lesson, students **Show Information Another Way** by drawing diagrams to show the relationships in geometric problems.

Instruction: Make sure students understand the need to find the area of each whole figure in the problem so that they can find the answer called for by the problem.

Guided Practice: Remind students to be careful to find all of the values that they need so that they can perform the operations necessary to find the answers to the questions.

Practice: Make sure students find the dimensions of the figure in problem 4 correctly. Point out to them that the yard has five sides.

Test-Taking Practice: Point out to students that for problem 4, they can treat the two half circles as one circle and then find the circle's circumference.

Lesson 3

In this lesson, students **Show Information Another Way** by breaking solid figures into parts to solve geometric problems.

Instruction: Students might need help in developing the ability to visualize the parts of the figure that they cannot see. Help them to interpret the diagrams.

Guided Practice: For problem 1, you might want to point out to students that the easiest way to solve the spatial relations puzzles is to separate the figures made of cubes into layers.

Practice: For problem 5, remind students to separate the figure into layers, noting that the length of the bottom row of the back layer is 1 cube shorter than the length of the bottom row of the middle layer.

Lesson 4

In this lesson, students will further their ability to choose an appropriate strategy to solve a problem.

Instruction: Remind students that problems that involve diagrams should normally be approached first by analyzing the diagrams for any necessary information contained in the diagrams.

Guided Practice: Some students might naturally lean toward representing the elements of a problem visually. Encourage them to keep track of the elements of the problem to ensure that they perform all the steps necessary to solve the problem.

Test-Taking Practice: For problem 4, make sure students remember to rename the centimeters correctly.

Chapter 10

Lesson 1

In this lesson, students **Show Information Another Way** by using tree diagrams to show outcomes and find probabilities.

Instruction: Point out to students that the outcomes of the second draw are dependent on the outcomes of the first draw.

Guided Practice: For problem 2, clarify for students, if necessary, that in this case, the second draw is not dependent on the first draw, because each card drawn is replaced, thereby maintaining the original pool of cards.

Practice: Remind students to distinguish between outcomes that are independent of a previous outcome and outcomes that are dependent on a previous outcome. For problem 1, the second draw is a dependent event. For problem 2, the second draw is an independent event.

Lesson 2

In this lesson, students **Show Information Another Way** by using Venn diagrams to solve probability problems for finite sets.

Instruction: For Step C, make sure students realize that they should not count the numbers in the C part of the diagram twice.

Practice: Remind students that numbers that meet none of the requirements should be recorded in the space outside of the circles of the Venn diagram.

Test-Taking Practice: Some students might need to be reminded not to count the numbers in the C part of the diagram twice for certain parts of the problems.

Lesson 3

In this lesson, students **Show Information Another Way** by using Venn diagrams to solve probability problems for universal sets.

Instruction: Remind students that in Step 3, they must subtract the overlapping amount.

Test-Taking Practice: Remind students that the numbers that fall into part D of the diagrams must meet none of the requirements to be included in parts A, B, or C.

Chapter 11

Lesson 1

In this lesson, students **Find Needed Information** from data in function tables.

Instruction: Make sure students understand that they might have to try two or more possibilities when they are trying to determine the rule that governs a "function machine."

Guided Practice: Remind students that they must find a rule that holds for each ordered pair in any given "function machine" problem.

Practice: For problem 6, students might need help in determining that the rule involves more than one operation.

Test-Taking Practice: Encourage students to recognize that whether the result of applying a rule produces a greater or a lesser number can help in testing the rule. Addition or multiplication is often involved in giving a greater number; subtraction or division is often involved in giving a lesser number.

Lesson 2

In this lesson, students **Show Information Another Way** by making straight-line graphs that allow them to extrapolate the data given.

Instruction: Explain to students that by setting up a line graph based on the data given in the problem, they can quickly and easily find the answer to the question.

Guided Practice: Remind students to be careful to include the zero value of their graphs in their visual thinking. Simply because the line on a line graph begins at a value greater than zero does not mean that all calculation begins at that point.

Practice: Make sure students construct the line of the graph correctly.

Chapter 12

Lesson 1

In this lesson, students **Show Information Another Way** by drawing number lines to compare and order items in logic problems that involve linear order.

Instruction: Students should find that whenever the items in a set have a spatial or temporal order, they can be represented on a number line.

Guided Practice: Make sure that students position each member of a set of data appropriately, according to the clues given in the problems.

Test-Taking Practice: Students might need help extrapolating the information from the table in problem 3.

Lesson 2

In this lesson, students **Show Information Another Way** by making logic tables to solve deductive logic problems.

Instruction: Make sure students understand that in these logic tables, each column or row can have only one box checked.

Guided Practice: Make sure students are correctly using marks to identify checked boxes and other marks to indicate boxes than can be eliminated.

Practice: Remind students that these logic problems cannot be solved by using number lines, because the problems do not involve location or spatial relations. These problems can be solved only by using deductive reasoning.

Test-Taking Practice: Point out to students that, even though the information includes four groups of elements, the problem can be solved in steps, using only two sets of elements at a time.

Lesson 3

In this lesson, students will further their ability to choose an appropriate strategy to solve a problem.

Instruction: Make sure that students understand that certain probability problems are best solved by constructing tree diagrams. Remind students that in coin-toss problems, the first pair of the letters *H* and *T* (Heads or Tails) indicates the first outcome or toss and must be included in figuring probability.

Guided Practice: Make sure students complete the logic table correctly. For problem 2, if students have difficulty doing the required estimation, encourage them to break 15% into 10% and 5%. Doing this may make the mental computation easier for students.

Practice: For problem 10, make sure students understand how to find the missing dimension of the figure. Also make sure that students recognize that they must find the volume of each part of the crate separately.

Test-Taking Practice: If students have difficulty with problem 6, suggest that they draw a number line to help to visualize the data in the problem.

PROBLEM SOLVING
Step by Step

Metropolitan Teaching and Learning Company
33 Irving Place
New York, New York 10003

Cover Photograph: Joseph Sohm;ChromoSohm, Inc./CORBIS
Printed in the United States of America

ISBN: 1-58120-673-9

10 9 8 7 6 5 4 3 2 1

STEP 7 • Table of Contents

STEP 7 • Topics

TABLES, GRAPHS, AND CHARTS
1.5   Reading Information from a Table or a Chart
2.1   Using Sample Data to Interpret Graphs
2.2   Reading a Rate Graph
2.3   Interpreting Changes in Line Graphs
4.1   Making a Table to Generalize

MULTI-STEP PROBLEMS
1.1   Making a Diagram to Solve Multi-Step Problems
1.2   Making a Diagram to Plan a Solution to Multi-Step Problems
3.2   Making a Diagram to Solve Multi-Step Problems
8.3   Solving Percent Problems Involving Measures
8.5   Using a Repeated Factor to Find Interest
9.2   Using a Diagram to Solve Multi-Step Problems

ESTIMATION/NUMBER SENSE
1.4   Deciding Whether to Estimate
3.1   Deciding What Kinds of Numbers to Use
3.3   Estimating Products and Quotients
3.4   Estimating with Mixed Expressions
3.5   Using Reciprocals to Solve Problems
5.2   Using Zero as a Benchmark
8.6   Estimating Percents

REPRESENTING PROBLEMS DIFFERENTLY
1.1   Making a Diagram to Solve Multi-Step Problems
1.2   Making a Diagram to Plan a Solution to Multi-Step Problems
2.1   Using Sample Data to Interpret Graphs
4.2   Solving a Formula for a Desired Variable
4.3   Using a Diagram to Write and Solve an Equation
5.1   Drawing a Number Line
6.1   Using Unit Rates
6.3   Renaming Measures That Are Rates
7.1   Using Rates to Write Measures in a Different System
7.3   Writing Word Proportions for Similar Figures

ANSWER INTERPRETATION
1.3   Interpreting Quotients
2.3   Interpreting Changes in Line Graphs
11.2   Interpolating and Extrapolating Data by Making a Graph

PROPORTIONAL THINKING
6.1   Using Unit Rates
6.2   Calculating Unit Rates
6.3   Renaming Measures That Are Rates
7.1   Using Rates to Write Measures in a Different System
7.2   Writing Word Proportions to Solve Scale Models
7.3   Writing Word Proportions for Similar Figures
9.1   Comparing Perimeters, Areas, and Volumes of Similar Figures

ALGEBRAIC THINKING
4.1   Making a Table to Generalize
4.2   Solving a Formula for a Desired Variable
4.3   Using a Diagram to Write and Solve an Equation
7.2   Writing Word Proportions to Solve Scale Models
11.1   Using a Function Rule to Solve Problems
11.2   Interpolating and Extrapolating Data by Making a Graph

VISUAL THINKING
3.2   Making a Diagram to Solve Multi-Step Problems
4.3   Using a Diagram to Write and Solve an Equation
8.1   Using Part-Part-Whole Percent Diagrams
8.2   Using Percents Greater than 100
8.4   Using a Diagram to Solve Multi-Step Percent Problems
9.3   Breaking a Figure into Parts

LOGICAL THINKING
10.1   Using a Tree Diagram to Compute Probabilities
10.2   Using Venn Diagrams
10.3   Using Venn Diagrams to Show Probabilities
12.1   Using a Number Line to Order a Set
12.2   Using Logic Tables to Solve Problems Deductively

Making a Diagram to Solve Multi-Step Problems

Sometimes a problem will take several steps to solve. Drawing a diagram of the problem can help you decide what steps you need to follow.

Example

From a catalog, Eden ordered 3 shirts, a pair of pants, and a skirt. The pants cost $39 and the skirt cost $35. She paid $9.95 for shipping and handling. Before tax, the total order came to $140.95. How much did each shirt cost?

A. **Make a diagram to show the problem. Use a variable for the cost of one shirt, the amount you are trying to find.**

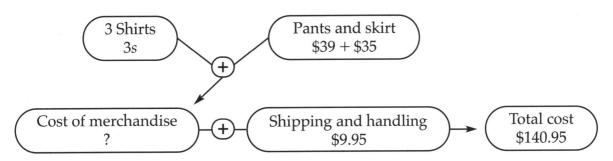

B. **Use the diagram to help you decide which piece of information you can find first.**

Step 1: **Find the cost of the merchandise.**

Total cost − Shipping and handling = Cost of merchandise

$140.95 − $9.95 = $131.00

Step 2: **Find the cost of the pants and skirt.**

$39.00 + $35.00 = $74.00

Step 3: **Find the cost of 3 shirts (3s).**

Cost of 3 shirts = Cost of merchandise − Cost of pants & skirt

$3s = \$131.00 - \$74.00$

$3s = \$57.00$

Step 4: **Find the cost of 1 shirt (s).**

$s = 3s \div 3$

$s = \$\underline{\ 57.00\ } \div 3$

$s = \$\underline{\ 19.00\ }$

Each shirt cost $\underline{\ 19.00\ }.

1. At the Ice Cream Shoppe, the Presbury family bought 4 ice-cream cones for $1.25 each. They also bought a root beer float for $2.50. All items were taxed. Ms. Presbury paid for the order with a $10 bill and received $2.12 in change. How much did the Presburys pay for tax?

Step 1: **Complete the diagram to show the problem.**

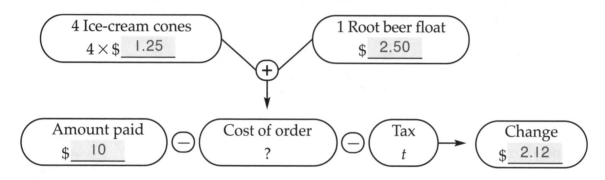

4 Ice-cream cones
$4 \times \$\underline{1.25}$

1 Root beer float
$\$\underline{2.50}$

$+$

Amount paid
$\$\underline{10}$

$-$

Cost of order
?

$-$

Tax
t

Change
$\$\underline{2.12}$

Step 2: **Use the diagram to help you decide which piece of information you can find first.**

THINK: I can find the cost of the order first. Then I can subtract the cost of the order plus the change received from the amount paid to find the tax.

a. **Find the cost of the order.**

4 Ice-cream cones + 1 Root beer float = Cost of order

$4 \times \$\underline{1.25} + \$\underline{2.50} = \$\underline{7.50}$

b. **Add the cost of the order to the change received.**

$\$\underline{7.50} + \$\underline{2.12} = \$\underline{9.62}$

c. **Subtract that number from $10 to find the tax paid (*t*).**

$t = \$10 - \$\underline{9.62}$

$t = \$\underline{0.38}$

The Presburys paid $\$\underline{0.38}$ for tax.

2. Darcel bought 2 shirts for $29.95 each and a pair of shoes for $75.99. After he paid for his purchases, he had $9.11 left. How much money did Darcel begin with?

   a. Complete the diagram to show the problem.

   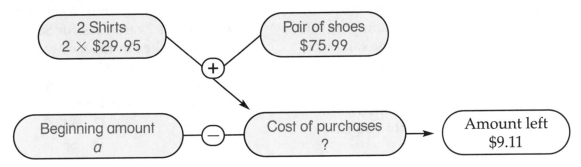

   b. Solve. How much money did Darcel begin with?

   Cost of purchases = 2(29.95) + 75.99 = $135.89

   $a - 135.89 = 9.11$; $a = 145.00$; Darcel began with $145.00.

3. Aurianna bought a toolbox for $47.99 and 10 tools, each at the same special price. The tax on her purchases was $8.27. She gave the salesclerk $160 and received $13.84 in change. What was the cost of one tool?

   a. Complete the diagram to show the problem.

   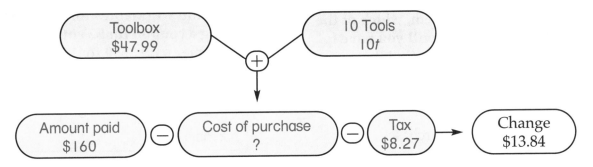

   b. Solve. What was the cost of one tool?

   Cost of purchases = 160 − 8.27 − 13.84 = 137.89;

   $47.99 + 10t = 137.89$; $10t = 89.9$; $t = 8.99$; one tool cost $8.99.

Choose the best answer for each problem. Fill in the answer box of your choice in the section at the bottom of this page.

1. Jeff bought 3 books from an online bookstore. Two of the books cost $18.50 each. The cost for shipping and handling was $2.50 per book. If Jeff's total order came to $66.25, what is the cost of the third book?

   To solve the problem, which of the following values should you find first? A

   A The cost of the first 2 books
   B The cost of the third book
   C The cost of the total order before shipping and handling
   D The cost of the total order after shipping and handling

2. At the music store, Cassie bought 2 compact discs for $12.95 each and 3 cassette tapes for $10.95 each. After she paid for her purchases, she had $12.15 left. How much did she have to begin with?

   To solve the problem, which of the following values will you have to find before you can find the amount Cassie had to begin with? M

   J Cost of 2 compact discs
   K Cost of 3 tapes
   L Total cost of purchases
   M All of the above

3. Star bought 3 paintbrushes at the art store. She also bought a set of paints for $25 and 2 canvases for $6.25 each. The tax on her purchases was $3.20. She gave the salesclerk $50 and received $1.05 in change. What was the cost of one paintbrush? B

   A $1.50   C $4.83
   B $2.75   D $8.25

4. Li bought a movie video for $39 and 2 video games for $19.95 each. He also bought a set of headphones for $24.99. The tax on his purchases was $7.27. If he received $3.84 in change, what amount of money did he give the salesclerk? L

   J $103.08   L $115.00
   K $111.16   M Not given

Write About It

5. A catalog offers bookcases for $108 each and worktables for $364. After using a coupon for $25 off, a customer paid $650 for his order. What other information do you need to figure out how much he paid for shipping and handling?

   Sample answer:

   You need to know how many

   bookcases and/or worktables the

   customer bought.

© 2000 Metropolitan Teaching and Learning Company

---

1. A ☒ B ☐ C ☐ D ☐   3. A ☐ B ☒ C ☐ D ☐

2. J ☐ K ☐ L ☐ M ☒   4. J ☐ K ☐ L ☒ M ☐

Making a Diagram to Plan a Solution to Multi-Step Problems

You can use a diagram to plan a solution to a problem with two or more steps.

Example

Raymond has test scores of 83, 93, 99, and 79 this quarter. He has one more test to take. What score does he need to get an average of 90 for the quarter?

A. **Make a diagram to show the problem.**

THINK: To find a mean (average) for a set of numbers, first add all the numbers. Then divide the sum by the number of addends.

$$\boxed{\begin{array}{c}\textit{Sum of test scores}\\ 83 + 93 + 99 + 79 + t\end{array}} \longrightarrow \div \longrightarrow \boxed{\begin{array}{c}\textit{Number of tests}\\ 5\end{array}} \longrightarrow \boxed{\begin{array}{c}\textit{Average}\\ 90\end{array}}$$

Division and multiplication are inverse operations, so you can also draw the diagram to show multiplication.

$$\boxed{\begin{array}{c}\textit{Sum of test scores}\\ 83 + 93 + 99 + 79 + t\end{array}} \longrightarrow \div \longrightarrow \boxed{\begin{array}{c}\textit{Number of tests}\\ 5\end{array}} \longleftarrow \times \longleftarrow \boxed{\begin{array}{c}\textit{Average}\\ 90\end{array}}$$

B. **Use the diagram to solve the problem.**

Step 1: **Find the sum of the test scores.**

Average $\times$ Number of tests = Sum of test scores

$$90 \quad \times \quad 5 \quad = \quad 450$$

Step 2: **Find the sum of the four known test scores.**

$$83 + 93 + 99 + 79 = \underline{\quad 354 \quad}$$

Step 3: **Find t (the test score Raymond needs).**

t = Sum of test scores – Sum of four known scores

$t = 450 - \underline{\quad 354 \quad}$

$t = \underline{\quad 96 \quad}$

Raymond must get a $\underline{\quad 96 \quad}$ **on his last test.**

GUIDED PRACTICE

1. At the amusement park, 4 members of a group entered for the children's price of $14.50 each. The other 2 members had to pay the higher adult price. If the group spent a total of $102.00, what is the price of one adult ticket to the amusement park?

   Step 1: **Complete the diagram to show the problem.**

   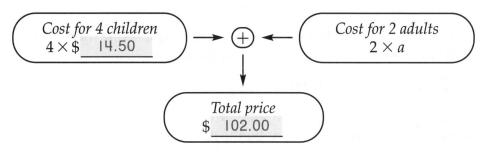

   Cost for 4 children
   $4 \times \$$ __14.50__ → (+) ← *Cost for 2 adults*
   $2 \times a$

   Total price
   $\$$ __102.00__

   Step 2: **Use the diagram to make a plan for solving the problem. Then solve.**

   a. **Find the cost of admission for the 4 children.**

   __4__ $\times \$$ __14.50__ $= \$$ __58.00__

   b. **Find $2 \times a$.**
   $2 \times a + $ Cost of children $=$ Total price
   So, $2 \times a = $ Total price $-$ Cost of children

   $2 \times a = \$$ __102__ $- \$$ __58__ , so $2 \times a = \$$ __44__

   c. **Find a.**

   $\$$ __44__ $\div 2 = \$$ __22__

   The price of one adult ticket is $ __22__ .

2. Richelle worked 4 days this week. The first day she made $18.50, the second day she made $25.25, and the third day she made $30.00. How much did she make on the fourth day if she earned an average of $25.00 per day for the week?

   Step 1: **Find the total amount Richelle earned.**

   Average pay $\times$ Days worked $=$ Total pay

   $\$25.00 \times$ __4__ $= \$$ __100.00__

   Step 2: **Find the sum of Richelle's earnings for the three known days.**

   $\$18.50 + \$25.25 + \$30.00 = \$$ __73.75__

   Step 3: **Find f (Richelle's earnings for the fourth day).**

   $f = $ Total pay $-$ Pay for three known days

   $f = \$$ __100.00__ $- \$$ __73.75__ , so $f = \$$ __26.25__

   Richelle earned $ __26.25__ on the fourth day.

3. For a science project, Jorge kept track of his liquid intake for one week. Over the week, he drank 112 ounces of milk. Each day, he also drank a 6-ounce can of juice and 5 glasses of water. Jorge drank a total of 434 ounces of liquid during the week. How many ounces did each glass of water contain?

a. Complete the diagram to show the problem.

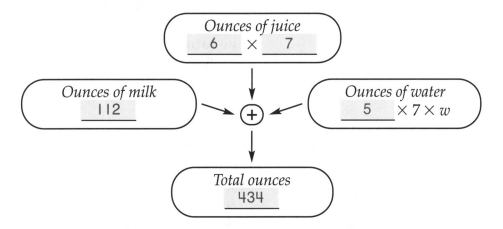

b. Solve. How many ounces were in 1 glass of water?

Ounces of water = Total ounces − Ounces of milk − Ounces of juice
Ounces of water = 434 − 112 − 42 = 280
$5 \times 7 \times w = 35 \times w$; so $35 \times w = 280$; $w = 8$. Each glass contained 8 ounces of water.

4. The Pappas family paid $22.50 to see a movie. The 3 children got children's tickets, and the 2 parents had to pay $6 each. What is the price of a child's ticket to the movie theater?

a. Make a plan to solve the problem.

Subtract the cost of the parents' tickets from the total cost to find the cost of
3 children's tickets. Divide that number by 3 to find the cost of 1 child's ticket.

b. Solve. How much did 1 child's ticket cost?

Parents' tickets = 2 × $6 = $12; Children's tickets = $22.50 − $12 = $10.50;
1 child's ticket = $10.50 ÷ 3 = $3.50. A child's ticket cost $3.50.

Choose the best answer for each problem. In the answer section at the bottom of the page, fill in the box of your choice.

1. Jamie has test scores of 82, 87, 86, and 88 so far this semester. She has one more test to take. What score does she need to get an 86 average for the semester?

   Which of the following equations shows the problem? C
   A $82 + 87 + 86 + 88 = 86 \times t$
   B $82 + 87 + 86 + 88 + t = 86 \times t$
   C $82 + 87 + 86 + 88 + t = 86 \times 5$
   D $82 + 87 + 86 + 88 - t = 86 \times 5$

2. **At a basketball game, 3 members of a group bought children's tickets for $9.50 each. The other 3 members of the group bought adult tickets. If the group spent a total of $73.50, what is the price of 1 adult ticket?** K
   J $12.25   L $22.50
   K $15.00   M $28.50

3. **In one week, a puppy ate 56 ounces of dry dog food. Each day, she also ate a 3-ounce treat and 2 cans of wet dog food. If the puppy ate a total of 133 ounces of food that week, how many ounces are in 1 can of dog food?** A
   A 4 ounces   C 56 ounces
   B 8 ounces   D Not given

4. **Mr. Kearny earned an average of $825.00 per week last month. He earned $875.00 the first week, $782.50 the second week, and $800.25 the third week. How much money did he earn in the last week?** L
   J $800.25   L $842.25
   K $825.00   M $852.50

Write About It
Write a plan for solving the following problem. Then solve.

5. **A play ran for 5 nights. Over the first three nights, 324 people saw the play. The auditorium was full on the last two nights. If the average size of the play's audience was 114 people, how many people does the auditorium hold?**

   | Find the total number of people by |
   | multiplying the average by the number |
   | of performances. Subtract the known |
   | number from the total, and divide that |
   | number by two. |
   | $114 \times 5 = 570$; $570 - 324 = 246$ |
   | $246 \div 2 = 123$ |
   | The auditorium holds 123 people. |

© 2000 Metropolitan Teaching and Learning Company

1. A ☐ B ☐ C ☒ D ☐   3. A ☒ B ☐ C ☐ D ☐
2. J ☐ K ☒ L ☐ M ☐   4. J ☐ K ☐ L ☒ M ☐

Interpreting Quotients

Sometimes the answer to a division problem is not a whole number. You will have to decide what kind of answer you need to match the question you have been asked.

Example 1

A jeweler uses 5.2 grams of silver for each ring she makes. How many rings can she make with 63.7 grams of silver?

Step 1: **Read the problem carefully to determine what you are being asked.**
Each of the following is a possible solution to $63.7 \div 5.2$.

Decimal	Rounded Up	Rounded Down
$63.7 \div 5.2 = 12.25$	$63.7 \div 5.2 \rightarrow 13$	$63.7 \div 5.2 \rightarrow 12$

THINK: The problem asks how many <u>rings</u> the jeweler can make—so the answer will be a whole number, and there may be some metal left over.

Step 2: **Divide, rounding down to the nearest whole number.**

$63.7 \div 5.2 \rightarrow$ __12__

Step 3: **Include the units in your answer.**

The jeweler can make __12__ rings.

Example 2

A chef bought 5.2 kilograms of salmon for $63.70. What is the price of salmon per kilogram?

Step 1: **Read the problem carefully to determine what you are being asked.**

THINK: The problem asks how much money a kilogram of salmon costs—so the answer will be a decimal.

Step 2: **Divide. Write the answer as a decimal.**

$63.7 \div 5.2 =$ __12.25__

Salmon costs $__12.25__ per kilogram.

GUIDED PRACTICE

Use the table to solve each problem.

Whole Number with Remainder	Decimal	Rounded Up	Rounded Down
$99.84 \div 9.6 \rightarrow 10 \text{ R } 3.84$	$99.84 \div 9.6 = 10.4$	$99.84 \div 9.6 \rightarrow 11$	$99.84 \div 9.6 \rightarrow 10$

1. In the laboratory, Dr. Smith is pouring a solution into tanks. Each tank holds 9.6 liters. How many tanks will he need if he has 99.84 liters of the solution?

   a. Read the problem to determine what you are being asked.
   The problem asks how many <u>tanks</u> are needed—so the answer will be a whole number, and the last tank may not be full.

   b. Divide, rounding up to the next whole number.

   $99.84 \div 9.6 \rightarrow$ __11__

   Dr. Smith will need __11__ tanks.

2. Dr. Smith is setting up as many experiments as he can. Each experiment requires 9.6 grams of sulfur. If he has 99.84 grams of sulfur, how much will Dr. Smith have left over after setting up the experiments?

   a. Read the problem to determine what you are being asked.
   The problem asks how many grams of sulfur will be <u>left over</u>—so the answer will be a remainder.

   b. Divide. Write the answer as a whole number and remainder.

   $99.84 \div 9.6 \rightarrow$ __10 R 3.84__

   c. The answer to the problem will be the remainder.

   Dr. Smith will have __3.84__ grams of sulfur left over.

3. Dr. Smith's galactic-web-wonker uses exactly 9.6 megabytes of memory to download a chicken from outer space. If his web-wonker has 99.84 megabytes of memory left, how many chickens can Dr. Smith download?

   a. Read the problem to determine what you are being asked.
   The problem asks how many <u>chickens</u> Dr. Smith can download—so the answer will be a whole number, and there may be some memory left over.

   b. Divide, rounding down to the nearest whole number.

   $99.84 \div 9.6 \rightarrow$ __10__

   Dr. Smith can download __10__ chickens.

4. Complete the chart to show the answer to 15.3 ÷ 4.5 in four different ways.

Whole Number with Remainder	Decimal	Rounded Up	Rounded Down
15.3 ÷ 4.5 → __3 R 1.8__	15.3 ÷ 4.5 = __3.4__	15.3 ÷ 4.5 → __4__	15.3 ÷ 4.5 → __3__

Use the completed chart to answer Problems 5–10.

5. Mrs. Morris's truck can hold 4.5 cubic meters of sand at a time. How many trips must she make to move 15.3 cubic meters of sand?

   She must make 4 trips.

6. Mr. Nugent spent $15.30 when he bought 4.5 kilograms of plaster. How much does a kilogram of plaster cost?

   A kilogram of plaster costs $3.40.

7. Marcelo has 15.3 meters of canvas, which he is using to make canoe covers. If each cover requires 4.5 meters of canvas, how many covers can Marcelo make?

   He can make 3 covers.

8. Olga is in a walk for charity. Her average walking speed is 4.5 miles per hour. Will it take her more or less than 3 hours to cover the 15.3 miles of the walk?

   It will take her more than 3 hours.

9. Lupe is cutting lengths of electrical wire from a spool that has 15.3 meters of wire left on it. If each length she cuts is 4.5 meters long, how much will she have left over?

   She will have 1.8 meters left over.

10. Archie and his friends had a pet snail race. Archie's snail lost the race. It only traveled 15.3 millimeters in 4.5 seconds. What was the speed of Archie's snail in millimeters per second?

    Its speed was 3.4 mm/sec.

Choose the best answer for each problem. In the answer section at the bottom of the page, fill in the box of your choice.

1. **One table can seat 8 people. How many tables would you need to seat a group of 99 people?** D

   A 8 tables   **C** $12\frac{3}{8}$ tables

   B 2 tables   **D** 13 tables

2. **A carpenter is cutting 18-inch shelves from a 96-inch board. How many inches of the board will be left over?** K

   J 5 shelves   **L** $6\frac{1}{3}$ inches

   K 6 inches   **M** 18 inches

3. **For the Pumpkin Festival, the Millers baked a pie using 52 kilograms of pumpkins. If there were 16 pumpkins in the pie, what was the average weight of each pumpkin?** C

   A 3 kg   **C** 3.25 kg

   B 3 R 4 kg   **D** 4 kg

4. **A box of 50 envelopes costs $6.50. What is the cost of 1 envelope?** K

   J $0.10   **L** $0.20

   K $0.13   **M** $1.30

5. **Mr. Lippson cut 67.25 cm of wire into 5 equal lengths. How long is each piece of wire?** B

   A 13 cm   **C** 14 cm

   B 13.45 cm   **D** Not given

6. **Jackie is pouring 369 liters of oil into drums that each hold 18 liters. How many drums will she fill?** J

   J 20 drums   **L** 21 drums

   K 20.5 drums   **M** 351 drums

Write About It

7. **Explain what kind of answer is best for the following problem. Then solve.**

   A 45-rpm record spins at a rate of 45 revolutions per minute. If the record spins 153 times, how many minutes of music will it play?

   The problem asks for an exact

   measurement in minutes, so the

   answer will be a decimal.

   $153 \div 45 = 3.4$

   It will play 3.4 minutes of music.

1. A ☐ B ☐ C ☐ D ☒   4. J ☐ K ☒ L ☐ M ☐

2. J ☐ K ☒ L ☐ M ☐   5. A ☐ B ☒ C ☐ D ☐

3. A ☐ B ☐ C ☒ D ☐   6. J ☒ K ☐ L ☐ M ☐

Deciding Whether to Estimate

Before you begin calculating, decide what kind of answer a problem requires. You can solve some problems by estimating rather than finding an exact number.

Example 1

A swim team plans to have 67 T-shirts printed at a cost of $5.25 each. The team has $560. Is that enough money to pay for all the T-shirts?

A. **Read the problem carefully, and decide whether or not you need to find an exact number.**

You need to find out whether the T-shirts will cost more or less than $560. The answer will be a *yes* or a *no*. You don't need an exact number.

B. **Estimate.**

Round 67 up to 70, and $5.25 down to $5.

The T-shirts will cost about 70 × $5, or $350.

C. **Compare the estimate to the amount the team has.**

$350 < $560

Yes, the team has enough money to pay for the T-shirts.

> You'll often get a better estimate in an addition or multiplication problem if you round one amount up and one amount down.

Example 2

The Pool Club is open 52 weeks a year. It costs $421 a year to join the club. About how much does it cost per week?

Step 1: **Decide whether or not you need to find an exact number.**

The question asks for __about__ how much money it costs, so you don't need an exact number.

Step 2: **Estimate.**

Round 421 down to 400, and 52 down to 50.

400 ÷ 50 = 8

It costs about $8 per week.

> You'll often get a better estimate in a subtraction or division problem if you round both amounts up or both amounts down.

GUIDED PRACTICE

1. During the first week of the month, Dennis swam 188 laps. He swam 204 laps during the second week, 172 laps during the third week, and 268 laps during the last week. Did Dennis swim farther during the first half of the month or during the second half of the month?

   a. Decide what you need to find.

   Is 188 + 204 greater than or less than ___172___ + ___268___ ?

   b. You don't need an exact answer, so estimate.

   THINK: This is an addition problem, so I'll round one number up and the other number down to get a better estimate.

   Round 188 up to 200, and 204 down to 200.

   200 + 200 = ___400___

   Round 172 up to 200, and 268 down to 250.

   200 + 250 = ___450___

   c. Compare the estimates.

   ___400___ < ___450___

   Dennis swam farther during the ___second___ half of the month.

2. The swimming coach figures there will be about 270 people at the annual picnic. He has 32 packs of hot dogs, with 8 hot dogs per pack. Does the coach have enough hot dogs so that each person gets one hot dog?

   a. Decide what you need to find.

   Is 32 × 8 greater than or less than ___270___ ?

   b. You don't need an exact answer, so estimate.

   Round 32 packs down to 30, and 8 hot dogs up to 10.

   30 × 10 = ___300___

   c. Check the estimate.

   THINK: The estimate is too close to 270. I do need to find an exact answer.

   32 × 8 = ___256___

   d. Compare your answer to the number of people at the picnic.

   ___256___ < ___270___

   So, the coach ___doesn't___ have enough hot dogs.

Decide whether you can use estimation to solve each problem. Then solve.

3. Leanna swam 58 laps in a 50-meter pool on Tuesday. On Wednesday, she swam 130 laps in a 25-meter pool. On which day did she swim farther?

She swam farther on Wednesday.

4. Odd, Inc. earned $717,135 last year, while the Even Company earned $466,284. About how much more than the Even Company did Odd, Inc. earn?

about $250,000

5. Nolan's average score last year was 3.8 points per game. This year, he played in 27 games and scored 117 points. Has his average score improved?

yes

6. During the first week of Keiko's cross-country drive, she drove 2,620 miles. During the second week, she drove 1,870 miles. About how far did she drive in all?

about 4,500 miles

7. Ada May bought 88 lb of Swiss cheese for a total of $360. About how much was the cheese per pound?

about $4 per pound

8. The baseball team bought a box of 24 baseballs at a cost of $3.15 per ball. About how much money did the box of baseballs cost?

about $75

9. Which is the better deal per ball: 3 tennis balls for $5.95 or 18 tennis balls for $29.95?

18 tennis balls for $29.95

10. Carlton cut a 75-inch board into 18 identical pieces. About how long was each piece?

about 4 inches long

11. Lawrence ran 19 laps around a 400-yard course. His partner Gish ran 6 laps around a 1,000-yard course. Which of the two ran farther?

Lawrence ran farther.

12. At birth, a goldfish weighed 13 g. After one year, it weighed 42 g. After two years, it weighed 78 g. During which year did the fish gain the most weight?

during the second year

● Estimating with Whole Numbers and Decimals

Choose the best answer for each problem. In the answer section at the bottom of the page, fill in the box of your choice.

1. The 67 families on the swim team each paid $42 to join the team. Which expression can best be used to estimate the amount that the team received? C

A 60 + $42
B 60 × $40
C 70 × $40
D 70 ÷ $40

2. Pam bought in-line skates for $67.95, a helmet for $35.50, and pads for $37.89. Which expression can best be used to estimate the amount that Pam spent? L

J $60 + $30 + $30
K $70 + $40 + $40
L $70 + $35 + $35
M $75 + $50 + $50

3. A baseball team traveled 1,912 miles in 9 days. What was the average distance they covered each day? A

A about 200 miles
B about 300 miles
C about 400 miles
D about 500 miles

4. The two top runners in a race finished with times of 32.86 seconds and 32.62 seconds. Which estimate best expresses how close their times were? L

J less than 0.1 seconds apart
K less than 0.2 seconds apart
L less than 0.3 seconds apart
M less than 0.4 seconds apart

5. Juanita bought hats and gloves for the 18 people who came to her party. The hats cost $3.35 each and the gloves cost $2.80 each. About how much did Juanita spend? C

A about $60   C about $120
B about $90   D about $200

Write About It

6. Gina ordered 34 dance programs that cost $3.15 per program. She rounded the amounts to 30 and $3, and took $90 to the store.

Did Gina have enough money to pay for the programs? Explain.

Sample answer: Gina did not have

enough. She rounded both amounts

down and multiplied, so her estimate

was lower than the actual product.

1. A ☐ B ☐ C ☒ D ☐   4. J ☐ K ☐ L ☒ M ☐
2. J ☐ K ☐ L ☒ M ☐   5. A ☐ B ☐ C ☒ D ☐
3. A ☒ B ☐ C ☐ D ☐

Reading Information from a Table or a Chart

Some problems require you to use information that is presented in a table or a chart. Here is a table about nations in South America.

The Nations of South America			
Nation	Population	Area (sq mi)	Principal Language
Argentina	36,265,463	1,073,518	Spanish
Bolivia	7,826,352	424,162	Spanish
Brazil	169,806,557	3,286,470	Portuguese
Chile	14,787,781	292,528	Spanish
Colombia	38,580,949	440,762	Spanish
Ecuador	12,336,572	105,037	Spanish
Guyana	707,954	83,000	English
Paraguay	5,291,020	157,046	Spanish
Peru	26,111,110	496,223	Spanish
Suriname	427,980	63,039	Dutch
Uruguay	3,284,481	68,039	Spanish
Venezuela	22,803,409	352,143	Spanish

Example 1

Which Spanish-speaking nation has the greatest area?

Step 1: **Make a plan for solving the problem.**
First, you'll need to find which nations are Spanish speaking. Then, you can compare their areas.

> It may help to highlight or circle the nations that speak Spanish. Then you can focus on the highlighted nations as you solve the problem.

Step 2: **Use your plan to solve the problem.**

The Spanish-speaking nation with the greatest area is <u>Argentina</u>.

Example 2

What is the area of the least populated Spanish-speaking nation?

Step 1: **Make a plan for solving the problem.**
First, you'll need to find which nations are Spanish speaking.
Highlight those nations.
Next, find which of these nations has the lowest population. Mark the row.
Lastly, find the area of the nation in the marked row.

Step 2: **Use your plan to solve the problem.**

The area is <u>68,039</u> **square miles.**

The Nations of South America			
Nation	Population	Area (sq mi)	Principal Language
Argentina	36,265,463	1,073,518	Spanish
Bolivia	7,826,352	424,162	Spanish
Brazil	169,806,557	3,286,470	Portuguese
Chile	14,787,781	292,528	Spanish
Colombia	38,580,949	440,762	Spanish
Ecuador	12,336,572	105,037	Spanish
Guyana	707,954	83,000	English
Paraguay	5,291,020	157,046	Spanish
Peru	26,111,110	496,223	Spanish
Suriname	427,980	63,039	Dutch
Uruguay	3,284,481	68,039	Spanish
Venezuela	22,803,409	352,143	Spanish

1. Which nation has the greatest population density—Brazil, Ecuador, or Suriname?

> Population density shows the ratio of people to space. To find a nation's population density, divide the nation's population by its area.

   A. **Write the amounts to compare.**

   Brazil $\dfrac{169,806,557}{3,286,470}$ Ecuador $\dfrac{12,336,572}{105,037}$ Suriname $\dfrac{427,980}{63,039}$

   B. **Use mental math to eliminate any clearly wrong answers.**

   Compare the number of digits in the numerators and denominators.

   Which nation's fraction obviously has the least value?   Suriname

   C. **Compare the remaining amounts by rounding.**

   $\dfrac{169,806,557}{3,286,470}$ → $\dfrac{200,000,000}{3,000,000}$ which equals about   70

   $\dfrac{12,336,572}{105,037}$ → $\dfrac{10,000,000}{100,000}$ which equals about   100

   So,   Ecuador   has the greatest population density.

2. What language is spoken by the most people in South America?

   Which two languages are possible answers?   Spanish   and   Portuguese

   Add to find the solution.

   The language spoken by most people is   Portuguese .

3. Complete the final column of the table. The factor of increase is found by dividing the 1998 population by the 1900 population.

Area and Estimated Population of the World				
Continent or Region	Area (sq mi)	1900 Population	1998 Population	Factor of Increase of Population
North America	9,400,000	106,000,000	305,000,000	2.88
South America	6,900,000	38,000,000	504,000,000	13.26
Europe	3,800,000	400,000,000	729,000,000	1.82
Asia	17,400,000	932,000,000	3,586,000,000	3.85
Africa	11,700,000	118,000,000	748,000,000	6.34
Oceania	3,300,000	6,000,000	30,000,000	5.0
Antarctica	5,400,000	0	0	0

4. **Which region with an area of less than 10 million square miles has the greatest population?**

    Europe

5. **What is the area of the region whose population did not change between 1900 and 1998?**

    5,400,000 square miles

6. **What is the approximate population density of the world's most populated region?**

    about 206 people/sq mi

7. **Which region's population increased by the greatest factor between 1900 and 1998?**

    South America

8. **What was the approximate total population of the world in 1900?**

    about 1,600,000,000

9. **What was the approximate total population of the world in 1998?**

    about 5,900,000,000

10. **What was the population density of the smallest region in 1900?**

    1.82 people/sq mi

11. **By how many people did the population of the smallest region increase between 1990 and 1998?**

    24,000,000 people

● Reading a Table

Use the table below to choose the best answer for each problem. In the answer section at the bottom of the page, fill in the box of your choice.

City	April T	April P	May T	May P	June T	June P	July T	July P	August T	August P	September T	September P
Barrow, AK	-2	0.2	19	0.2	34	0.3	39	0.9	38	1.0	31	0.6
Galveston, TX	69	2.4	76	3.6	81	4.4	83	4.0	84	4.5	80	5.9
Oklahoma City, OK	60	2.8	68	5.2	77	4.3	82	2.6	81	2.6	73	3.8
Omaha, NE	52	2.7	62	4.5	72	3.9	77	3.5	74	3.2	65	3.7
San Diego, CA	62	0.8	64	0.2	67	0.1	71	0	73	0.1	71	0.2

Monthly Average Temperature (T) in Degrees Fahrenheit and Precipitation (P) in Inches

1. **In which row and column would you find the highest average temperature of the data shown in the table?** D
   A   84°F, 4.5 inches
   B   Galveston, September
   C   Barrow, July
   D   Galveston, August

2. **By how many degrees does the monthly average temperature in Omaha differ between May and September?** J
   J   3°F   L   13°F
   K   7°F   M   65°F

3. **In August, how much more precipitation than San Diego does Barrow get?** B
   A   0.4 inches   C   1.1 inches
   B   0.9 inches   D   35°F

4. **Which city shows the greatest range of temperatures during the months shown?** J
   J   Barrow   L   Omaha
   K   Galveston   M   San Diego

5. **Which of the cities shown has the greatest difference in its average temperature between July and August?**
   A   Barrow   C   Oklahoma City
   B   Galveston   D   Omaha   D

Write About It

6. How could you find which city has the most precipitation over the 6-month period shown in the table?

   Write a plan for solving the problem, and then solve.

   Eliminate cities that clearly don't have

   the greatest amount of precipitation.

   Then add the precipitation readings

   for other rows.

   Galveston: 24.8 in.

   Oklahoma City: 21.3 in.

   Omaha: 21.5 in.

   Galveston has the most precipitation.

1. A☐ B☐ C☐ D☒
2. J☒ K☐ L☐ M☐
3. A☐ B☒ C☐ D☐
4. J☒ K☐ L☐ M☐
5. A☐ B☐ C☐ D☒

● Reading a Table

Using Sample Data to Interpret Graphs

Sometimes it's helpful to make a table showing the information that is presented in a graph.

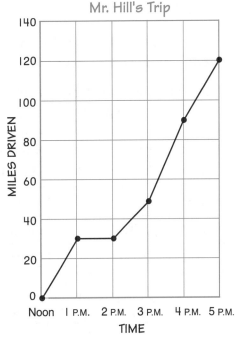

Mr. Hill's Trip

Example

The line graph shows the miles driven each hour by Mr. Hill during a recent trip. During which hour did he drive the most miles?

A. To solve the problem, you need to find the distance Mr. Hill drove each hour. You can show the data from the graph in a table.

Time	Noon	1 P.M.	2 P.M.	3 P.M.	4 P.M.	5 P.M.
Total Distance	0	30	30	50	90	120

B. Add a row to the table, and calculate the distance Mr. Hill drove each hour.

Time	Noon	1 P.M.	2 P.M.	3 P.M.	4 P.M.	5 P.M.
Total Distance	0	30	30	50	90	120
Distance in Past Hour	0	30	0	20	40	30

C. Use the table to solve the problem.

The table shows that the greatest distance traveled in one hour was ___40___ miles.

Mr. Hill drove this distance between ___3 P.M.___ and ___4 P.M.___ .

Mr. Hill drove the most miles between ___3 P.M.___ and ___4 P.M.___ .

● Making a Table

GUIDED PRACTICE

The line graph shows how far from the start of a dogsled race two competitors were at the end of each day of the race.

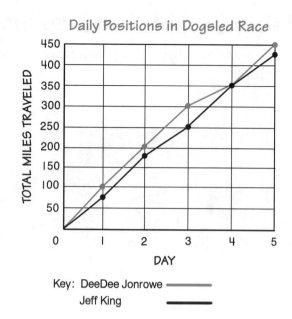

Daily Positions in Dogsled Race

Key: DeeDee Jonrowe ———
Jeff King ———

1. On what day did DeeDee Jonrowe have the biggest lead over Jeff King?

   a. Complete the table below to show the data in the graph.

Day	Miles Traveled		Distance Between
	Jeff	DeeDee	Jeff and DeeDee
1	75	100	25 miles
2	175	200	25 miles
3	250	300	50 miles
4	350	350	0 miles
5	425	450	25 miles

   b. Use the table to solve the problem.

   The greatest distance between DeeDee and Jeff is ___50___ miles.

   This distance occurred on Day ___3___.

   DeeDee Jonrowe had the biggest lead on Day ___3___.

2. On what day did DeeDee Jonrowe have the smallest lead over Jeff King?

   The shortest distance between DeeDee and Jeff is ___0___ miles.

   This distance occurred on Day ___4___.

   DeeDee Jonrowe had the smallest lead on Day ___4___.

3. At the end of Day 5, what was DeeDee Jonrowe's lead over Jeff King?

   At the end of Day 5, the distance between the racers was ___25___ miles.

   At the end of Day 5, DeeDee Jonrowe's lead was ___25___ miles.

PRACTICE

The line graph at right shows the amount of water used by the Turner family one morning.

Complete the table below to show the data in the graph. Then use the table to solve the problems.

Turner Family Water Usage

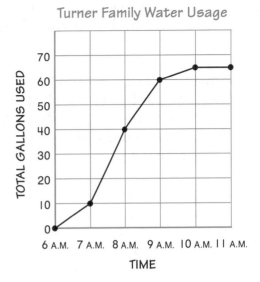

TIME

4.

Time	6 A.M.	7 A.M.	8 A.M.	9 A.M.	10 A.M.	11 A.M.
Total Gallons	0	10	40	60	65	65
Gallons in Past Hour	0	10	30	20	5	0

Solve . . . .

5. **During which hour did the Turner family use the most water?**

between 7 A.M. and 8 A.M.

6. **During which hour did the Turners use the least water?**

between 10 A.M. and 11 A.M.

7. **How many gallons of water did the Turners use between 8 A.M. and 9 A.M.?**

20 gallons

8. **How many gallons of water did the Turners use during the period shown?**

65 gallons

9. **During which period did the Turners use only 5 gallons of water?**

between 9 A.M. and 10 A.M.

10. **During which period did the Turner family use no water at all?**

between 10 A.M. and 11 A.M.

● Making a Table

Choose the best answer for each problem. In the answer section at the bottom of the page, fill in the box of your choice.

A scientist tracked the calories burned over a single hour by two people doing the same activities. The graph shows the total number of calories burned at 10-minute intervals.

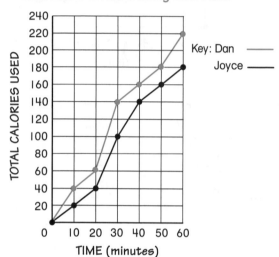

Calories Burned During One Hour

Key: Dan ——
Joyce ——

1. The scientist wants to find the 10-minute period when Joyce used the most calories.

   Which points should the scientist consider to solve the problem? B
   A The points at 10 and 20 minutes
   B The points at 20 and 30 minutes
   C The points at 30 and 40 minutes
   D The points at 40 and 50 minutes

2. **How many calories did Joyce use between 50 minutes and 60 minutes?** J
   J 20 calories   L 160 calories
   K 40 calories   M 180 calories

3. **During which 10-minute period did Dan burn fewer calories than Joyce?** D
   A Between 0 and 10 minutes
   B Between 10 and 20 minutes
   C Between 20 and 30 minutes
   D Between 30 and 40 minutes

4. **How many more calories than Joyce did Dan burn during the hour?** J
   J 40 calories
   K 180 calories
   L 220 calories
   M None of the above

Write About It

Write a plan for solving the following problem. Then solve.

5. **How could the scientist find out in which 10-minute period both people burned the most calories?**

   Sample answer:

   Make a table to show the data for

   each person at each 10-minute period.

   Then make a row or column to

   subtract the calories burned during

   the period, and compare. Both people

   burned the most calories between 20

   and 30 minutes.

1. A ☐ B ☒ C ☐ D ☐
2. J ☒ K ☐ L ☐ M ☐
3. A ☐ B ☐ C ☐ D ☒
4. J ☒ K ☐ L ☐ M ☐

● Making a Table

Reading a Rate Graph

Sometimes, the information you need to solve a problem will be given in a rate graph.

Miles Traveled and Gasoline Used

Example 1

The graph on the right shows the amount of gasoline a truck uses. How many miles can the truck travel per gallon of gas?

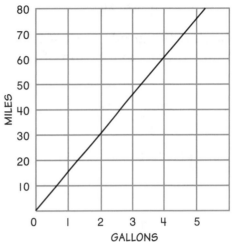

A. The truck travels the same distance for each gallon, so you can use any point on the graph to find the solution.

THINK: It will be easiest to use the point showing the miles traveled on one gallon of gas.

Use the graph. Find how many miles the truck travels on 1 gallon of gas.

The graphed line passes through the point (1, 15).

This means the car travels 15 miles on 1 gallon of gas.

So, the truck travels 15 miles per gallon of gas.

Check your solution using another point on the graph, such as (2, 30).
30 mi/2 gal = 15 mi/gal
It checks.

Example 2

How far could the truck travel on 4.6 gallons of gasoline?

Step 1:   **Use the graph to estimate the answer.**

THINK: 4.6 gallons is about halfway between 4 and 5 gallons. On the line graph, that point comes between 60 and 75 miles.

The answer will be between ___60___ and ___75___ miles.

Step 2:   **Solve the problem. Use the rate you found in Example 1.**

4.6 gal × 15 mi/gal = ___69___ mi

The truck could travel ___69___ miles on 4.6 gallons of gas.

● Reading a Graph

GUIDED PRACTICE

The graph at the right shows the price of gasoline at Phil's Fill 'Em Up.

1. How much does a gallon of gas cost at Phil's Fill 'Em Up?

   Look at the graph. Find out how much money one gallon of gas costs.

   The graphed line passes through the point (1, __1.75__).

   So, a gallon of gas costs $__1.75__.

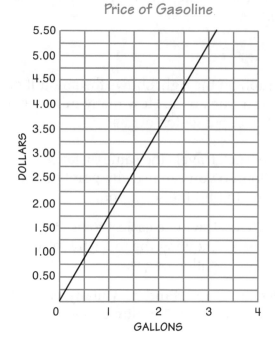

Price of Gasoline

2. How much money will 2.4 gallons of gas cost?

   Step 1: **Use the graph to estimate.**

   THINK: 2.4 gallons is between 2 and 3 gallons, but a little closer to 2 than to 3. On the line graph, that point is about $__4.00__.

   So, the answer will be about $__4.00__.

   Step 2: **Solve the problem. Use the rate you found in Problem 1.**

   2.4 gal × __1.75__ dollars/gal = $__4.20__

   So, 2.4 gallons of gas will cost $__4.20__.

3. How many gallons of gasoline could you buy for $11.55?

   THINK: The line graph doesn't give any information beyond $5.50. I can't use it to estimate.

   Solve the problem using the rate you found in Problem 1.

   $11.55 ÷ __1.75__ dollars/gal = __6.6__ gal

   You could buy __6.6__ gallons of gas for $11.55.

PRACTICE

In 1769, French Army Officer Captain Nicolas Joseph Cugnot built what has been called the first automobile. His three-wheeled vehicle carried four people and was powered by steam.

The line graph shows how fast Cugnot's automobile traveled. Use the graph to solve the problems.

4. **How many kilometers per hour did the steam-powered automobile travel?**

   3 kilometers per hour

   Which data pair did you use?

   Sample answer: (1, 3)

5. **Check your solution by using another data pair. Which data pair did you use?**

   Sample answer: (2, 6)

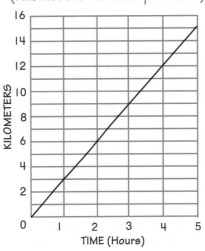

Solve..

6. **How far could the automobile travel in 3 hours?**

   9 kilometers

7. **How many hours would it take the automobile to travel 12 kilometers?**

   4 hours

8. **How far could the automobile travel in 2 $\frac{1}{2}$ hours?**

   2 $\frac{1}{2}$ hours × 3km/hour = 7 $\frac{1}{2}$ km

9. **How many hours would it take the automobile to travel 8 kilometers?**

   8 km ÷ 3 km/hr = 2.67 hr or 2 $\frac{2}{3}$ hr

10. **How far could the automobile travel in 6 hours?**

    6 hours × 3km/hour = 18 km

11. **How many hours would it take the automobile to travel 30 kilometers?**

    30 km ÷ 3 km/hr = 10 hr

● Reading a Graph

Choose the best answer for each problem. In the answer section at the bottom of the page, fill in the box of your choice.

The line graph shows the sale price of carpeting at Under the Ceiling, Inc. Use the graph to solve the problems.

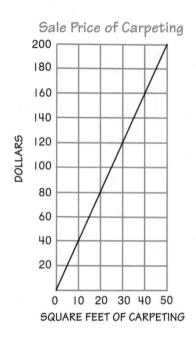

Sale Price of Carpeting

1. **Which of the following points shows the price of 20 square feet of carpeting?** D
   A (20, 20)   C (80, 10)
   B (80, 20)   D (20, 80)

2. **What is the price per square foot of the carpeting?** M
   J $10   L $40
   K $20   M Not given

3. **How much money would 25 square feet of carpeting cost?** D
   A $6.25   C $25
   B $10   D $100

4. **How many square feet of carpeting could you buy for $280?** J
   J 70 sq ft   L 276 sq ft
   K 140 sq ft   M 1,120 sq ft

5. **How much money would 200 square feet of carpeting cost?** C
   A $50   C $800
   B $200   D $1,600

Write About It

Write a plan for solving the following problem. Then solve.

6. **Use the graph to estimate the cost of 46 square feet of carpeting.**

   Sample answer:

   46 is a little more than halfway

   between 40 and 50. On the line graph,

   the corresponding dollar amount is

   more than $180 but less than $190.

   The point will be about (46, 185).

   The price will be about $185.

1. A ☐ B ☐ C ☐ D ☒

2. J ☐ K ☐ L ☐ M ☒

3. A ☐ B ☐ C ☐ D ☒

4. J ☒ K ☐ L ☐ M ☐

5. A ☐ B ☐ C ☒ D ☐

● Reading a Graph

Interpreting Changes in Line Graphs

Sometimes, the information you need to solve a problem is in a line graph.

The direction and steepness of the line connecting the points in a line graph can provide the information you need to solve a problem.

- A horizontal line shows no change.

- A line sloping upward shows an increase.

- A line sloping downward shows a decrease.

- The steeper the line, the faster the change.

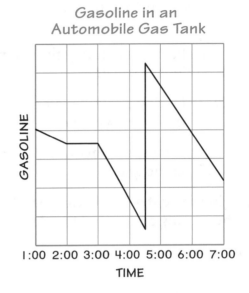

Gasoline in an Automobile Gas Tank

GASOLINE

1:00 2:00 3:00 4:00 5:00 6:00 7:00

TIME

Example 1

The driver of the car stopped for an hour at a restaurant. When?

THINK: There will be no change in the amount of gasoline if the car is parked. I'll find where the graph is horizontal.

The car was stopped between ____2____ o'clock and ____3____ o'clock.

Example 2

When did the driver of the car refill the gas tank?

THINK: The steeper the line, the faster the change. Filling the tank is an extremely fast increase. I'll find where the line goes up vertically.

The driver refilled the tank at about ____4:30____ .

Example 3

The faster a car travels, the more gas it uses each hour. When was the car traveling the slowest?

THINK: The steeper the line, the faster the change. I'll need to find where the line slopes downward the least.

The car traveled the slowest between ____1____ o'clock and ____2____ o'clock.

● Reading a Graph

GUIDED PRACTICE

Use the line graph to find the information you need to solve the problems.

The graph shows the amount of inventory—the stock that a store has to sell—at a computer-game store during six weeks in the summer.

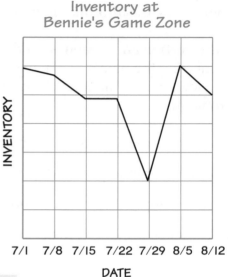

Inventory at Bennie's Game Zone

1. The store held a sale during the summer. When did the sale take place?

   THINK: During a sale, people buy more, so the inventory would decrease the fastest.

   a. Find the steepest downward slope for one week on the graph.

   b. Find the dates that correspond to the beginning and end of the slope.

   The sale took place between ___7/22___ and ___7/29___.

2. The store closed for a week during the summer. When was the store closed?

   THINK: There would be no change in inventory when the store was closed.

   a. Find the part of the graph showing no change—a horizontal line.

   b. Find the dates that correspond to the beginning and end of the horizontal line.

   The store was closed between ___7/15___ and ___7/22___.

3. The store received a large delivery of new games during the summer. During which week was the delivery?

   THINK: After a delivery of new stock, the inventory would increase very quickly.

   a. Find a steep upward slope on the graph.

   b. Find the dates that correspond to the beginning and end of the slope.

   The store received the delivery between ___7/29___ and ___8/5___.

PRACTICE

Use the line graph to find the information you need to solve the problems.

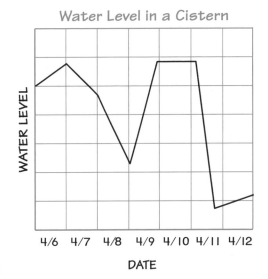

Water Level in a Cistern

WATER LEVEL

4/6 4/7 4/8 4/9 4/10 4/11 4/12

DATE

A cistern is used to catch rainwater. The water can then be used to water a garden when it isn't raining. The graph shows the changes in the water levels of a cistern during one week.

4. **When was the water level of the cistern the highest?**

   April 10

5. **When was the water level of the cistern the lowest?**

   April 11

6. **On which day didn't anyone water the garden?**

   April 10

7. **On which day did it rain the most?**

   April 9

8. **One day during the week the cistern sprang a leak. When did this happen?**

   April 11

9. **On how many days did it rain during the week? (Include every day on which it rained.)**

   It rained four days.

● Reading a Graph

Choose the best answer for each problem. In the answer section at the bottom of the page, fill in the box of your choice.

The graph shows the height above sea level of the Sky Express—a train traveling through the mountains—at different times during the day. Use the graph to solve the problems.

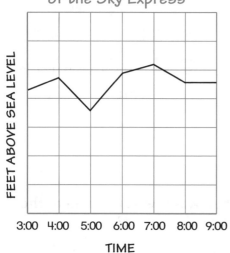

TIME

1. **At what time was the Sky Express the most feet above sea level?** C
   A 5:00   C 7:00
   B 6:00   D 8:00

2. **During which hour did the Sky Express climb the most feet?** K
   J between 4:00 and 5:00
   K between 5:00 and 6:00
   L between 6:00 and 7:00
   M Not given

3. **At what time was the Sky Express the closest to sea level?** B
   A 3:00   C 7:00
   B 5:00   D 9:00

4. **During which hour did the Sky Express descend the most feet?** J
   J between 4:00 and 5:00
   K between 5:00 and 6:00
   L between 7:00 and 8:00
   M between 8:00 and 9:00

5. **Which of the following describes the Sky Express's position at 6 o'clock?** D
   A higher than at 7 o'clock
   B lower than at 4 o'clock
   C the same height as at 4 o'clock
   D higher than at 4 o'clock

Write About It
Write a plan for solving the following problem. Then solve.

6. **The Sky Express stood at a station for over an hour. How could you use the graph to find out when it was at the station?**   Sample answer given.

   Find a part of the graph that shows no

   change in height above sea level— a

   horizontal line. The Sky Express was at

   the station between 8 o'clock and

   9 o'clock.

1. A ☐ B ☐ C ☒ D ☐   4. J ☒ K ☐ L ☐ M ☐
2. J ☐ K ☒ L ☐ M ☐   5. A ☐ B ☐ C ☐ D ☒
3. A ☐ B ☒ C ☐ D ☐

Test-Taking Skill: **Use Estimation**

Multiple-choice tests often contain estimation problems. You can use estimation strategies to choose a reasonable number from the answers provided.

Example 1

Over the course of last year, Liz paid about $75 for milk. The price varied between $2.29 and $2.79 per gallon. About how many gallons of milk did Liz buy last year?

A about 10 gallons   **C** about 30 gallons
B about 20 gallons   **D** about 40 gallons

Step 1: **Decide what you need to find.**
You need to find the quotient of $75 and a price per gallon. Try to find compatible numbers.

> You can estimate a quotient by using compatible numbers.

THINK: The price per gallon varies between $2.29 and $2.79. A price of $2.50 is compatible with $75, and it's also just about in the middle of these prices. I'll divide $75 by $2.50.

Step 2: **Use the compatible numbers to estimate.**

$75 ÷ $2.50 = 30, so Choice C is correct.

Example 2

To repair the pipes in his house, Frank needs 46.3 ft of pipe priced at $11.65 per foot. About how much will the pipe cost?

A about $400   **C** about $600
B about $500   **D** about $700

Step 1: **Decide what you need to find.**
You need to find the product of the amount of pipe and the price per foot. Try rounding each factor to its greatest place.

> You can estimate a product by rounding to the greatest place of each factor, or by rounding one factor up and one down.

$46.3 \times \$11.65$
$\downarrow \qquad \downarrow$
$50 \quad \times \quad \$10$

Step 2: **Use the rounded factors to estimate.**

50 × $10 = $500, so Choice B is correct.

● Test-Taking Skill

Choose the best answer for each problem. In the answer section at the bottom of this page, fill in the box of your choice.

1. A computer printer prints 1,088 words in $4\frac{1}{4}$ minutes. About how many words does it print per minute? D

   A about 50   C about 175
   B about 100   D about 250

2. A fund-raising letter costs $0.55 to write, print, and mail. About how much will it cost to mail 7,870 letters? J

   J about $4,000   L about $6,000
   K about $5,000   M about $7,000

3. A clothing store offers a 12.5% discount off all merchandise. If a sweater's original price was $51, about how much will it cost with the discount? C

   A about $35   C about $45
   B about $40   D about $50

4. Each day from Monday through Friday, Ohmari ran 3.3 miles around a track. Estimate the total distance he ran over the 5-day period. L

   J about 5 miles   L about 15 miles
   K about 10 miles M about 20 miles

5. A recipe for 1 loaf of bread calls for $2\frac{3}{4}$ cups of flour. About how much flour would you need to bake 23 loaves? C

   A about 25 cups C about 60 cups
   B about 45 cups D about 90 cups

6. A painting frame measures $3\frac{1}{3}$ feet long by $2\frac{7}{8}$ feet high. What is the approximate area of the glass in the frame? M

   J about 6 ft^2 L about 8 ft^2
   K about 7 ft^2 M about 9 ft^2

7. A parcel of land that is 102 yards long will be divided into lots that are each $9\frac{1}{3}$ yards long. About how many lots can be made from the parcel? C

   A about 5 lots   C about 10 lots
   B about 8 lots   D about 20 lots

8. In a year-end sale at an art store, Rosario bought a box of 54 markers for $18.29. What was the approximate price of each marker? K

   J about $0.20   L about $0.70
   K about $0.40   M about $0.80

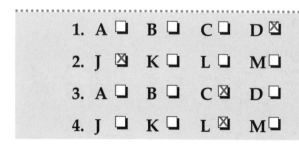

1. A☐ B☐ C☐ D☒   5. A☐ B☐ C☒ D☐
2. J☒ K☐ L☐ M☐   6. J☐ K☐ L☐ M☒
3. A☐ B☐ C☒ D☐   7. A☐ B☐ C☒ D☐
4. J☐ K☐ L☒ M☐   8. J☐ K☒ L☐ M☐

● Test-Taking Skill

Deciding What Kinds of Numbers to Use

For some problems, you'll have to rename one or more of the numbers to find the solution.

Example 1

At the fish market, swordfish costs $5.96 a pound. Sid is buying 4 lb 4 oz of swordfish. How much will the fish cost Sid?

A. **Decide what to do first.**

To find the cost of the swordfish, you must multiply the weight of the fish by its cost per pound.

Rename the weight of the fish as pounds.

THINK: There are 16 ounces in a pound, so I can rewrite 4 ounces as $\frac{4}{16}$ pound, or $\frac{1}{4}$ pound.

$4 \text{ lb } 4 \text{ oz} \rightarrow 4\frac{4}{16} \text{ lb, or } 4\frac{1}{4} \text{ lb}$

B. **For problems involving money, it is usually easier to work with decimals, so change $4\frac{1}{4}$ pounds to a decimal number.**

$4\frac{1}{4} \text{ lb} = 4.25 \text{ lb}$

C. **Solve the problem.**

$4.25 \text{ lb} \times \$5.96 \text{ per lb} = \$\underline{25.33}$

The fish will cost Sid $\underline{25.33}$.

Example 2

Angel has $16\frac{1}{2}$ ft of steel tubing. How many lengths of 2 ft 9 in. can he cut from it?

Step 1: To divide the total length by the smaller length, you need both measures to have the same units.

Rename 2 ft 9 in. as a mixed number of feet.

$2 \text{ ft } 9 \text{ in.} \rightarrow 2\frac{3}{4} \text{ ft}$

Step 2: **Solve the problem.**

$16\frac{1}{2} \div 2\frac{3}{4} \rightarrow \frac{33}{2} \div \frac{11}{4}$

$\frac{33}{2} \div \frac{11}{4} \rightarrow \frac{33}{2} \times \frac{4}{11} = 6$

So, Angel can cut 6 lengths from the pipe.

> Remember: Dividing by a fraction is the same as multiplying by the inverse of the fraction. Just turn the fraction that is the divisor upside down and multiply.

GUIDED PRACTICE

1. Ice cream costs $4.99 per gallon. How much will $3\frac{1}{2}$ gallons cost?

   Read the problem carefully. Then choose the easier plan. Circle it.

   Plan A: Rename $4.99 as a mixed number. Then multiply $4\frac{99}{100}$ by $3\frac{1}{2}$.

   Plan B: Rename $3\frac{1}{2}$ gallons as a decimal. Then multiply 4.99 by 3.5.

2. A typical marathon run is 26 miles 385 yards long. If a runner has completed $15\frac{1}{4}$ miles, how much farther does she have to go?

   Read the problem carefully. Then choose the easier plan. Circle it.

   Plan A: Rename $15\frac{1}{4}$ miles as miles and yards, and then subtract it from 26 mi 385 yd.

   Plan B: Rename both measures as decimals. Then rename their difference as a mixed number or as miles and yards.

3. Mrs. Meanly put $8\frac{3}{4}$ gallons of gasoline in her gas tank and paid $12.95. What was the gasoline's price per gallon?

   Step 1:   **Rename $8\frac{3}{4}$ as a decimal number.**

   $8\frac{3}{4}$ gallons ⟶ __8.75__ gallons

   Step 2:   **Divide the cost by the number of gallons.**

   $12.95 \div$ __8.75__ = __1.48__

   The gasoline cost $ __1.48__ per gallon.

4. This spring, Pablo planted a tree that was 4 ft 7 in. tall. By fall, the tree had grown another $1\frac{1}{4}$ ft. How tall is the tree now?

   Step 1:   In addition and subtraction problems, it's sometimes easiest to work with mixed units, such as feet and inches.

   Rename $1\frac{1}{4}$ ft as feet and inches.

   $\frac{1}{4}$ ft ⟶ $\frac{1}{4} \times$ 12 in. ⟶ __3__ in.

   $1\frac{1}{4}$ ft ⟶ __1__ ft __3__ in.

   Step 2:   **Solve.**

   4 ft 7 in. + __1 ft 3 in.__ = __5__ ft __10__ in.

   The tree is now __5 ft 10 in.__ tall.

PRACTICE

Decide what kinds of numbers to use to solve each problem. Use the conversions below if you need to.

Length		Capacity
1 foot = 12 inches 1 yard = 3 feet		1 gallon = 4 quarts
1 mile = 5,280 feet 1 mile = 1,760 yards		1 pound = 16 ounces

5. At the track meet, Aline's longest jump was 9 ft 11 in. Miriam's longest jump was $1\frac{1}{4}$ ft less than Aline's. How far did Miriam jump?

8 ft 8 in.

6. At the football game, the Booster Club served $8\frac{1}{4}$ gallons of hot chocolate. If their profit was $16.20 per gallon, how much money did the club make?

$133.65

7. Nicole bought $6\frac{1}{2}$ pounds of peaches for $0.99 a pound. How much did she pay?

$6.44

8. Janaya paid $20.25 for $4\frac{1}{2}$ pounds of chicken. What was the cost per pound?

$4.50 per pound

9. Dr. Pearce's car had $10\frac{3}{4}$ gallons of gasoline at the start of a trip. At the end of the trip, the car held 1 gallon, 2 quarts of gasoline. How much gas did she use?

$9\frac{1}{4}$ gallons

10. The first Boston Marathon was 24 miles 880 yards long. If you ran the marathon in $3\frac{1}{2}$ hours, what would your average speed in miles per hour be?

7 miles per hour

11. One year, Grayson grew 7 inches. If he was $5\frac{1}{4}$ feet at the beginning of the year, how tall was he at the end of the year?

5 feet 10 inches

12. At birth, Seth weighed 7 pounds 6 ounces. Three months later, he had gained $2\frac{1}{2}$ pounds. How much did he weigh then?

9 pounds 14 ounces

Choose the best answer for each problem. In the answer section at the bottom of the page, fill in the box of your choice.

1. House paint costs $11.50 a gallon. How much does $5\frac{1}{2}$ gallons of paint cost?

   Which of the following number sentences could you use to solve the problem? D

   A $11\frac{1}{5} \times 5\frac{1}{2} = 61.60$

   B $11\frac{50}{100} \div 5\frac{1}{2} = 2.09$

   C $11.50 + 5.5 = 17.00$

   D $11.50 \times 5.5 = 63.25$

2. The fabric store has a 25-yard length of red ribbon. If you buy 2 yards 2 feet of the ribbon, how much ribbon is left? L

   J $22\frac{1}{3}$ ft   L 22 yd 2 ft

   K 22.3 yd   M 22.5 yd

3. The Sweet Shoppe sold $6\frac{4}{5}$ gallons of ice cream in one hour. If the store receives $18 profit for each gallon sold, what was their profit for that hour? C

   A $108.00   C $122.40

   B $115.20   D $126.00

4. Neville ran $8\frac{1}{4}$ miles last week and 7.8 miles this week. How far did he run altogether? J

   J 16.05 miles   L 64.35 miles

   K 16.2 miles   M Not given

5. At the strawberry farm, Bethany picked 3 pounds 12 ounces of strawberries. If the farmer charges $0.85 a pound, how much does Bethany owe? (Round the answer to the nearest cent.) B

   A $2.65   C $4.41

   B $3.19   D $4.60

Write About It

Write a plan for solving the following problem. Then solve.

6. **Austin knows that his room is $11\frac{1}{2}$ feet wide. He measures the length and finds that the room is 14 feet 3 inches long. What is the area of Austin's room?**

   Sample answer:

   Rename 14 feet 3 inches as a mixed

   number. Then multiply the length by

   the width to find the area.

   14 ft 3 in. → $14\frac{3}{12}$ ft, or $14\frac{1}{4}$ ft;

   $11\frac{1}{2} \times 14\frac{1}{4} = 163\frac{7}{8}$ square feet

---

1. A ☐ B ☐ C ☐ D ☒

2. J ☐ K ☐ L ☒ M ☐

3. A ☐ B ☐ C ☒ D ☐

4. J ☒ K ☐ L ☐ M ☐

5. A ☐ B ☒ C ☐ D ☐

● Operations with Fractions and Decimals

Making a Diagram to Solve Multi-Step Problems

When a problem includes several steps, drawing a diagram of the problem can help you plan how to solve it.

Example

A long-distance phone company bills a fixed monthly fee, with an additional charge of $0.10 per minute for each phone call made. A customer who talked on the phone for a total of 3 hours 40 minutes received a monthly bill for $30.25. What is the fixed monthly fee?

A. **Make a simple diagram to show the problem.**

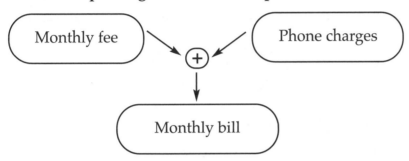

B. **Add to the diagram to fill in any steps that you'll need to do.**

THINK: The monthly fee is the solution to the problem. I already know the monthly bill. I need to find the charges for the phone calls. The charges will be the number of minutes multiplied by $0.10.

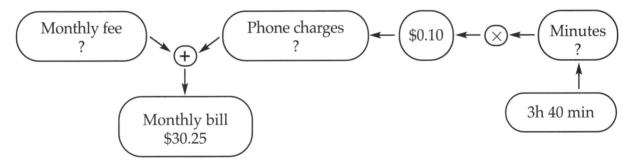

C. **Follow the steps you've diagrammed.**

Step 1: 3 h 40 min ➝ 60 + 60 + 60 + 40 min ➝ 220 min

Step 2: 220 min × $0.10 = $22.00

Step 3: $22.00 + Monthly fee = $30.25
Monthly fee = $30.25 − $22.00
= $8.25

The monthly fee is $8.25.

● Operations with Fractions, Decimals, and Whole Numbers

GUIDED PRACTICE

1. A company charges $8.00 per square foot to put in new flooring in a house. The company charges $1,056 for flooring Daud's living room. If the room is 11 feet wide, how long is it?

   Step 1: Make a simple diagram to show the problem.

   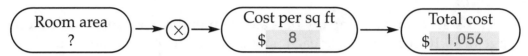

   Step 2: Add to the diagram to fill in any steps that you'll need to do.

   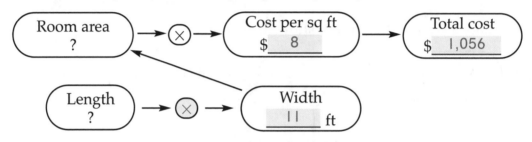

   Step 3: Follow the steps you've diagrammed.

   a. Room area × Cost per square ft = Total cost

   Room area × ___8___ = ___1,056___

   So, Room area = ___1,056___ ÷ 8 → ___132___ sq ft

   b. Length × Width = Room area

   Length × ___11___ = ___132___ so, Length = 132 ÷ ___11___ → ___12___ ft

   The length of the room is ___12___ ft.

2. A phone company bills a fixed monthly fee of $9.50, with an additional charge per minute for each phone call made. A customer's monthly bill of $22.10 included charges for 2 hours 20 minutes of calls. What is the charge per minute?

   a. Find the charges for phone calls.
   Total bill − Monthly fee = Charges for calls

   $___22.10___ − $___9.50___ = $___12.60___

   b. Find the number of minutes of phone calls.

   2 h 20 min = ___140___ min

   c. Find the charge per minute.
   Charges for calls ÷ Minutes called = Charge per minute

   $___12.60___ ÷ ___140___ = $___0.09___

   The charge is $___0.09___ per minute.

3. Camilla buys $1\frac{1}{4}$ lb of cornmeal, $2\frac{1}{2}$ lb of flour, and some sugar. Each of the items costs the same—$0.48 per pound. If she pays a total of $3.12, how much sugar does Camilla buy?

   a. **Complete the diagram.**

   b. **Follow the steps to solve.**

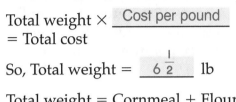

   Total weight × <u>Cost per pound</u>
   = Total cost

   So, Total weight = $\underline{6\frac{1}{2}}$ lb

   Total weight = Cornmeal + Flour
   + Sugar

   $\underline{6\frac{1}{2}}$ = $\underline{1\frac{1}{4}}$ + $\underline{1\frac{1}{2}}$ + Sugar

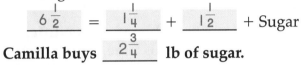

   Camilla buys $\underline{2\frac{3}{4}}$ lb of sugar.

4. Neneh bought $1\frac{1}{2}$ lb of fish for $4.20 per pound and $2\frac{1}{4}$ lb of cheese. The total price of the cheese was twice the total price of the fish. What was the cost of the cheese per pound?

   a. **Make a plan to solve the problem.**

   > Find the total cost of the fish. Multiply that amount by 2. Then divide the result by

   > the number of pounds of cheese.

   b. **Solve. What was the cost of the cheese per pound?**

   > Total cost of fish = $4.20 \times 1\frac{1}{2}$ → 6.30

   > $6.30 \times 2 = 12.60$　　　$12.60 \div 2\frac{1}{4} = 5.60$

   > The cheese cost $5.60 per pound.

Choose the best answer for each problem. In the answer section at the bottom of the page, fill in the box of your choice.

1. A tree was planted in a garden, and grew an average of $1\frac{1}{4}$ feet per year. After 5 years, the tree was 13 feet 5 inches tall. How tall was it when it was planted?

   To solve the problem, what should you find <u>first</u>? A

   A How much the tree grew in five years

   B What fraction of a foot 5 inches is

   C The number of inches in 13 feet 5 inches

   D The number of months in five years

2. An electric company charges $10.00 per month for its basic plan. Then it charges $0.08 for each kilowatt-hour (kwh) used. If a family has a bill for $32.00, how many kilowatt-hours of electricity did they use?

   To solve the problem, Mo found that $32.00 − $10.00 = $22.00. Which of the following equations should he solve <u>next</u>? M

   J $32.00 + $22.00 = $54.00

   K $32.00 − $22.00 = $10.00

   L $22.00 × $0.08 = 1.76 kwh

   M $22.00 ÷ $0.08 = 275 kwh

3. **A telephone company charges $5.25 for its basic plan, plus an additional charge per minute for each phone call. Candice spoke on the phone for 3 hours 15 minutes this month and was billed $18.90. How much is the charge per minute?** B

   A $0.04   **C** $13.65

   B $0.07   **D** Not given

Write About It

4. **Rewrite Problem 3 using different amounts. This time, let the missing information be the cost of the phone company's basic plan. Solve your problem.**

   Sample answer: A telephone company

   charges $0.10 per minute for each

   phone call. It also charges a fixed

   amount for its basic plan. Candice

   spoke on the telephone for 2 hours

   10 minutes this month and

   received a phone bill of $18.50.

   How much is the basic plan? ($5.50)

1. A ☒   B ☐   C ☐   D ☐

2. J ☐   K ☐   L ☐   M ☒

3. A ☐   B ☒   C ☐   D ☐

● Operations with Fractions, Decimals, and Whole Numbers

Estimating Products and Quotients

To estimate with fractions and mixed numbers, you can round to the nearest whole number or use compatible numbers.

Example 1

Mrs. Polovich's poppyseed cake recipe calls for $1\frac{2}{3}$ cups of canola oil. She plans to make 23 cakes for a restaurant. About how much oil does she need?

Step 1:   The problem asks "about how much oil," so you can estimate.

Round the mixed number to the nearest whole number.

$1\frac{2}{3}$ cups ⟶ ____2____ cups

THINK: I rounded one number up. This is a multiplication problem, so I'll get a better estimate if I round the other number down.

23 cakes ⟶ 20 cakes

Step 2:   **Multiply to estimate.**

____2____ × 20 = ____40____ cups

Mrs. Polovich needs about ____40____ cups of oil.

Example 2

In a drum of industrial cleaner containing $21\frac{2}{3}$ pounds, $\frac{1}{5}$ of the weight is bleach. About how many pounds of bleach are in the drum?

Step 1:   When you multiply a fraction that is less than 1, round the other number so that it's compatible with the denominator of the fraction.

Round $21\frac{2}{3}$ to a number that is compatible with 5.

THINK: What's the closest whole number that's divisible by 5?

$21\frac{2}{3}$ pounds ⟶ ____20____ pounds

Step 2:   **Multiply to estimate the weight of bleach.**

$\frac{1}{5}$ × ____20____ pounds = ____4____ pounds

There are about ____4____ pounds in the drum.

• Estimating with Fractions and Mixed Numbers

1. Mr. Ramirez is building a fence that is 43 feet long, using $4\frac{1}{4}$-foot-long planks. About how many planks will he need?

   Step 1: The problem asks "about how many," so you can estimate.

   Round the mixed number to the nearest whole number.

   $4\frac{1}{4}$ feet → ___4___ feet

   THINK: I rounded one number down. This is a division problem, so I'll get a better estimate if I round the other number down, too.

   Round the whole number.   43 feet → ___40___ feet

   Step 2: **Divide to estimate.**

   ___40___ ÷ ___4___ = ___10___

   Mr. Ramirez needs about ___10___ planks.

2. Each key ring produced by a company weighs $\frac{1}{3}$ ounce. About how many key rings could the company ship in a package that can have a maximum weight of 32 ounces?

   Step 1: **Decide what you need to do to solve.**

   You need to estimate the quotient when 32 is divided by $\frac{1}{3}$.

   THINK: $32 \div \frac{1}{3}$ is the same as 32×3. I won't need to find a number compatible with the denominator.

   Round the larger number so that it's easy to estimate.

   32 → ___30___

   Step 2: **Multiply to estimate the number of key rings.**

   ___30___ × 3 = ___90___

   The company could ship about ___90___ key rings.

3. A cupcake recipe calls for $5\frac{1}{4}$ cups flour. Janet only wants to make $\frac{2}{3}$ as many cupcakes as in the recipe. About how much flour will she need?

   Step 1: **Round the larger number to a whole number that's compatible with the denominator of the fraction $\frac{2}{3}$.**

   $5\frac{1}{4}$ cups → ___6___ cups

   Step 2: **Multiply to estimate.**

   $\frac{2}{3} \times$ ___6___ cups = ___4___ cups

   Janet needs about ___4___ cups of flour.

PRACTICE

Estimate to solve. Show your work for each problem.

4. **Each day, Zachary runs $\frac{3}{4}$ mile. About how many miles does he run in a week?**

   7 days ➝ 8 days;

   $\frac{3}{4} \times 8 = 6$ miles

   Zachary runs about 6 miles a week.

5. **Al has $2\frac{1}{4}$ times as much money as Jordan, who has \$27. About how much money does Al have?**

   $2\frac{1}{4}$ ➝ 2; \$27 ➝ \$30

   $2 \times 30 = 60$

   Al has about \$60.

6. **The fuel gauge in August's car shows that he has $\frac{1}{3}$ tank of gasoline. If the tank holds $14\frac{1}{2}$ gallons, about how much gas does August have?**

   $14\frac{1}{2}$ gallons ➝ 15 gallons

   $\frac{1}{3} \times 15 = 5$

   August has about 5 gallons of gas.

7. **A garden path is $25\frac{3}{5}$ feet long. Jacob wants to put gravel along the first $\frac{3}{8}$ of the path. About how many feet of the path will be covered with gravel?**

   $25\frac{3}{5}$ feet ➝ 24 feet

   $24 \times \frac{3}{8} = 9$ feet

   About 9 feet will be covered.

8. **A cereal box holds 19 cups. Each serving is $\frac{3}{4}$ cup. About how many servings does the box hold?**

   19 cups ➝ 18 cups

   $18 \div \frac{3}{4}$ ➝ $18 \times \frac{4}{3} = 24$

   The box holds about 24 servings.

9. **Tama's room is $12\frac{1}{2}$ feet by $14\frac{1}{2}$ feet. What is a reasonable estimate of the room's area?**

   $12\frac{1}{2}$ ft ➝ 12 ft; $14\frac{1}{2}$ ft ➝ 15 ft

   $12 \times 15 = 180$ feet^2

   The area of the room is about 180 feet^2.

10. **A recipe for herb bread calls for $1\frac{1}{8}$ teaspoons of oregano. About how much oregano would you need to make 18 loaves of bread?**

    $1\frac{1}{8}$ tsp ➝ 1 tsp; 18 ➝ 20

    $1 \times 20 = 20$

    You would need about 20 teaspoons.

11. **At the park, the red trail is 13 miles long, $3\frac{1}{2}$ times the length of the blue trail. About how long is the blue trail?**

    $3\frac{1}{2}$ ➝ 3; 13 miles ➝ 12 miles

    $12 \div 3 = 4$ miles

    The blue trail is about 4 miles long.

● Estimating with Fractions and Mixed Numbers

TEST-TAKING PRACTICE

Choose the best answer for each problem. In the answer section at the bottom of the page, fill in the box of your choice.

1. A *GoFast* bike costs $2\frac{1}{3}$ times as much as a *Speedsnail* bike, which costs $141. Which equation would give you the best estimate of the cost of a *GoFast* bike? **B**

   A $2 \times 140 = 280$
   B $2 \times 150 = 300$
   C $3 \times 140 = 420$
   D $3 \times 150 = 450$

2. Which of the following equations would give you the best estimate of the number of $7\frac{1}{2}$-ounce blocks in a 90-ounce set? **M**

   J $80 \div 8 = 10$ L $96 \div 6 = 16$
   K $91 \div 7 = 13$ M $96 \div 8 = 12$

3. Dakota owns a dog kennel. She feeds each of her dogs $2\frac{1}{3}$ cups of food each day. If she uses 76 cups of food each day, about how many dogs does she have? **C**

   A about 20   C about 35
   B about 25   D about 40

4. Jack is driving 390 miles to his uncle's. If he has already driven $\frac{5}{8}$ of the way, about how many miles has he traveled? **K**

   J about 200 mi   L about 300 mi
   K about 250 mi   M about 350 mi

5. At the park, the green trail is about $\frac{5}{6}$ the length of the yellow trail. If the yellow trail is $11\frac{3}{4}$ miles long, about how long is the green trail? **B**

   A about 5 miles   C about 12 miles
   B about 10 miles   D Not given

Write About It
Write a plan for solving the following problem. Then solve.

6. A bag of plaster weighs $7\frac{3}{4}$ pounds. If Dolores needs 151 pounds of plaster, about how many bags will she need?

   Round the mixed number to the

   closest whole number. $7\frac{3}{4}$ ➤ 8

   Then round the other number up to a

   convenient number. 151 ➤ 160

   Then divide.

   $160 \div 8 = 20$

   She will need about 20 bags.

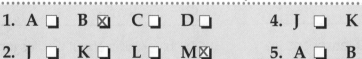

1. A ☐ B ☒ C ☐ D ☐   4. J ☐ K ☒ L ☐ M ☐
2. J ☐ K ☐ L ☐ M ☒   5. A ☐ B ☒ C ☐ D ☐
3. A ☐ B ☐ C ☒ D ☐

• Estimating with Fractions and Mixed Numbers

Estimating with Mixed Expressions

For some estimation problems, you'll find it easier if you rename one or more of the measures so that you don't have to deal with mixed units.

Example 1

Steve works at a theater supply company. He needs to ship 4 packages of theater makeup. Each package weighs 1 pound 5 ounces. If the shipping company charges $5.95 per pound, about how much will Steve have to pay?

A. Decide what you need to estimate.

To estimate Steve's shipping costs, you'll need to estimate this product:
4×1 pound 5 ounces $\times$ $5.95 per pound.

THINK: I can start by estimating the total weight of the 4 packages. Then I can estimate the total cost.

B. Carry out your plan.

Step 1: Estimate the total weight of the 4 packages. Use compatible numbers if you can.

THINK: There are 16 ounces in a pound.
1 lb 5 oz $= 1\frac{5}{16}$ lb, which is about $\rightarrow 1\frac{1}{4}$ lb

4 packages $\times 1\frac{1}{4}$ lb = __5__ lb

Step 2: Estimate the total cost.

Round $5.95/lb to the nearest dollar. $5.95 $\rightarrow$ $ __6__

Find the product of the estimated weight and the estimated cost per pound. __5__ lb $\times$ $ __6__ per lb = $ __30__

Steve will pay about $ __30__ to mail his packages.

Example 2

At the last minute, Steve finds out that there are 6 packages, instead of 4. Now what is the estimated shipping cost?

Step 1: Estimate the total weight. Use compatible numbers.
1 lb 5 oz is about $1\frac{1}{3}$ lb.

6 packages $\times 1\frac{1}{3}$ lb = __8__ lb

Step 2: Estimate the total cost.
__8__ lb $\times$ $ __6__ per lb = $ __48__

So, Steve will pay about $ __48__ to mail the packages.

● *Estimating with Fractions and Mixed Numbers*

GUIDED PRACTICE

1. An actor in a play is on stage for 17 minutes in each performance. About how many hours will she be on stage if the play is performed 34 times?

   Step 1: **Rename 17 minutes as an approximate fraction of an hour.**

   17 minutes is about 15 minutes, or $\underline{\frac{1}{4}}$ hour.

   Step 2: **Round the whole number to a number compatible with the fraction.**

   THINK: I rounded 17 minutes down, and I'm going to multiply. I should round 34 up to the next whole number compatible with the fraction. 34 → $\underline{36}$

   Step 3: **Solve.**

   $\underline{36} \times \underline{\frac{1}{4}} = \underline{9}$

   She will be on stage about $\underline{9}$ hours.

2. A set designer has a spool of 62 feet of rope. About how many lengths of 7 feet 10 inches can he cut from the spool?

   Step 1: **Round the measure with mixed units to the nearest whole number.** 7 ft 10 in. → $\underline{8}$ ft

   Step 2: **Round the whole number to a compatible number.**

   THINK: I rounded 7 ft 10 in. up, and I'm going to divide. I should round 62 up to the next whole number compatible with the smaller number. 62 → $\underline{64}$

   Step 3: **Solve.**

   $\underline{64} \div \underline{8} = \underline{8}$

   He can cut about $\underline{8}$ lengths.

3. A car's gasoline tank holds 15 gallons 3 quarts. If it costs $25.50 to fill the tank, what is the approximate cost per gallon of gasoline?

   Step 1: **Round the measure with mixed units to the nearest whole number.** 15 gal 3 qt → $\underline{16}$ gal

   Step 2: **Round the whole number to a compatible number.**

   In this case, you won't end up with a whole number after dividing. Find the nearest number that will make computing easy.

   25.50 → 24

   Step 3: **Solve.** $24 \div \underline{16} = \underline{1\frac{1}{2}}$

   Gasoline costs about $\underline{1.50}$ per gallon.

52

Estimate to solve the problem. Show your work.

4. A theater plans to pay its actors $485 a week. If the theater has $15,620 budgeted for actors, and the actors will be hired for $4\frac{1}{2}$ weeks, about how many actors can be hired?

Step 1: Estimate how much money the theater can pay per week.

$$\$15,620 \rightarrow \$15,000; 4\frac{1}{2} \rightarrow 5; \$15,000 \div 5 = \$3,000$$

Step 2: Estimate how many actors can be hired.

$$\$485 \rightarrow \$500; \$3,000 \div \$500 = 6$$

The theater can afford to hire ___6___ actors.

Estimate to solve the following problems.

5. The costume designer has a bolt of fabric $10\frac{1}{2}$ yards long. If he cuts a length of fabric that is 1 yard 20 inches long, about how much fabric will be left?

about 9 yards of fabric

6. The theater can seat 414 people. Tickets cost $18.40 each. If the theater was $\frac{3}{4}$ full on the first night, about how much money did the theater take in?

about $6,000

7. During intermission, the refreshment stand served 3 gallons 3 quarts of soda. The stand's profit was $10.42 per gallon. Estimate the total profit on the soda.

about $40.00

8. The refreshment stand also served 3 quarts 1 pint of coffee. The stand's profit was $5.89 on the first quart, and $6.70 on each quart after that. Estimate the total profit on the coffee served.

about $20

9. LaTanya paid $24.95 for 5 yards 2 feet of gold fabric. Estimate the cost per yard. Then estimate how much she would pay for $8\frac{3}{4}$ yards of the fabric.

about $5 per yard; about $45

10. A dinner-theater manager must buy 24 steaks. Each steak weighs 11 ounces. If the steaks cost $3.89 per pound, about how much will the manager pay?

about $80

Choose the best answer for each problem. In the answer section at the bottom of the page, fill in the box of your choice.

1. A pound of cheese costs $3.79. About how much would 6 pounds 5 ounces of cheese cost?

   Which of the following number sentences provides the best estimate?

   A $3.8 + 6.5 = 10.3$ C

   B $3 \times 6 = 18$

   C $4 \times 6 = 24$

   D $4 \times 7 = 28$

2. At the gas station, Mary Alice paid $9.95 for $6\frac{1}{3}$ gallons of gasoline. About how much was the gasoline per gallon?

   Which of the following number sentences provides the best estimate?

   J $10 \times 6 = 60.00$ M

   K $10 \div 5 = 2.00$

   L $9 \div 7 = 1.29$

   M $9 \div 6 = 1.50$

3. **During the track meet, Sheila jumped 9 ft 8 in. Janine jumped a distance that was $1\frac{5}{8}$ times as far as Sheila's jump. About how far did Janine jump?** C

   A About 11 ft

   B About $13\frac{1}{2}$ ft

   C About 15 ft

   D About 18 ft

4. **Craig is mailing 8 packages. Each package weighs 2 lb 7 oz. If the post office charges $3.20 per pound for mailing, about how much will it cost to mail all 8 packages?** K

   J About $40   **L** About $80

   K About $60   **M** Not given

Write About It

Write a plan for solving the following problem. Then solve.

5. **Barry bought 8 packages of mushrooms that each weighed 2 lb 3 oz. The mushrooms sell for $4.15 per pound. About how much did Barry pay?**

   Sample answer: Round the numbers to

   convenient amounts before

   multiplying, making sure you don't

   round them all the same way.

   2 lb 3 oz → 2 lb; 8 → 10;

   $4.15 → $4

   $2 \times 10 \times 4 = 80$

   Barry paid about $80.

1. A ☐ B ☐ C ☒ D ☐   3. A ☐ B ☐ C ☒ D ☐

2. J ☐ K ☐ L ☐ M ☒   4. J ☐ K ☒ L ☐ M ☐

Using Reciprocals to Solve Problems

Two fractions are **reciprocals** if their product is 1. The **reciprocal** of a fraction can be found by interchanging the numerator and denominator.

For example, the reciprocal of $\frac{4}{5}$ is $\frac{5}{4}$. $\frac{4}{5} \times \frac{5}{4} = 1$.

You can use reciprocals to "undo" multiplication.

Example 1

A sweater has been reduced to $\frac{1}{2}$ of its original price. The reduced price is $18. What was the original price?

A.   Write a word equation expressing what you know.

original price $\times \frac{1}{2}$ = new price

original price $\times \frac{1}{2} \times 2$ = new price $\times 2$

original price = new price $\times 2$

> Multiply both sides by 2, the reciprocal of $\frac{1}{2}$.

B.   Substitute values into the equation.

original price = new price $\times 2$

original price = 18×2

original price = $\underline{\ \ \$36\ \ }$

The original price was $\underline{\ \ 36\ \ }$.

Example 2

A photograph was reduced to $\frac{2}{3}$ of its original size, and now measures 4 inches wide by 6 inches high. What were the dimensions of the original photograph?

A.   Write a word equation.

THINK: The reciprocal of $\frac{2}{3}$ is $\frac{3}{2}$. I can use it to solve the problem.

original size = new size $\times \frac{3}{2}$

B.   Substitute values into the equation.

original width $= 4 \times \underline{\ \ \frac{3}{2}\ \ }$

$= \underline{\ \ 6\ \ }$

original height $= \underline{\ \ 6\ \ } \times \frac{3}{2}$

$= \underline{\ \ 9\ \ }$

The original photograph was $\underline{\ \ 6\ \ }$ inches wide and $\underline{\ \ 9\ \ }$ inches high.

● Multiplying Fractions

1. Althea multiplied each of the quantities in a cake recipe by $2\frac{1}{2}$, and used 5 tablespoons of sugar. She wants to make another cake using the original recipe, but she has lost it. How much sugar does the original recipe call for?

   Step 1: **Write a word equation using a reciprocal.**

   THINK: $2\frac{1}{2}$ is the same as $\frac{5}{2}$. The reciprocal is $\underline{\quad\frac{2}{5}\quad}$.

   original amount = increased amount $\times \underline{\quad\frac{2}{5}\quad}$

   Step 2: **Substitute values into the equation.**

   original amount = $\underline{\quad 5 \quad} \times \underline{\quad\frac{2}{5}\quad}$

   original amount = $\underline{\quad 2 \quad}$

   The original recipe calls for $\underline{\quad 2 \quad}$ tablespoons of sugar.

2. Bill sold his television for $170, which was 68% of what he had paid for it the previous year. How much had Bill paid for the television?

   Step 1: **Write a word equation using a reciprocal.**

   THINK: 68% is the same as $\frac{68}{100}$. The reciprocal is $\underline{\quad\frac{100}{68}\quad}$.

   original price = reduced price $\times \underline{\quad\frac{100}{68}\quad}$

   Step 2: **Substitute values into the equation.**

   original price = $\underline{\quad 170 \quad} \times \underline{\quad\frac{100}{68}\quad}$

   original price = $\underline{\quad 250 \quad}$

   Bill paid \$$\underline{\quad 250 \quad}$ for the television.

3. When Carla was $\frac{7}{8}$ as old as she is now, she was 28 years old. How old is Carla now?

   Step 1: **Write a word equation using a reciprocal.**

   Carla's age = previous age $\times \underline{\quad\frac{8}{7}\quad}$

   Step 2: **Substitute values into the equation.**

   Carla's age = $\underline{\quad 28 \quad} \times \underline{\quad\frac{8}{7}\quad}$

   Carla's age = $\underline{\quad 32 \quad}$

   Carla is now $\underline{\quad 32 \quad}$ years old.

PRACTICE

Use reciprocals to solve the following problems.

4. An architect's model is $\frac{1}{20}$ the size of an actual building. Write an equation you could use to find the building's actual length from the length of the model.

building length = model length × 20

5. A carpenter cut the legs of a table so that it was $\frac{4}{5}$ of its original height. If the table is now 18 inches tall, how tall was it originally?

22.5 inches

6. Hollin is exactly $\frac{3}{4}$ her older sister's height. If Hollin is 48 inches tall, how tall is her older sister?

64 inches

7. Betta spent $288—45% of her savings—on a new stereo system. How much had she saved before she bought the stereo?

$640

8. Nadine reduced a muffin recipe to $\frac{2}{3}$ of the original recipe, and used $1\frac{1}{3}$ cups of flour. How many cups of flour did the original recipe call for?

2 cups of flour

9. Chane increased a recipe to $1\frac{1}{2}$ of the original recipe, and used 6 pounds of chicken. How many pounds of chicken did the original recipe call for?

4 pounds of chicken

10. In February, calendars sell for 30% of the original price. Coral bought a calendar on sale for $2.70. What was its original price?

$9.00

11. After 2 hours, Arturo had cycled 42 miles of a bicycle race, $\frac{7}{10}$ of the total distance. How many miles long is the bicycle race?

60 miles

12. Patrick earned $2\frac{1}{5}$ times as much this week as he did last week. If he earned $418 this week, how much did he earn last week?

$190

13. A photo of a painting is $\frac{1}{10}$ the size of the actual painting. If the photo is 8.8 cm by 12.5 cm, what is the size of the painting?

88 cm by 125 cm

● Multiplying Fractions

Choose the best answer for each problem. In the answer section at the bottom of the page, fill in the box of your choice.

1. Jaime is $\frac{7}{8}$ the height of her mother. How many times as tall as Jaime is her mother? D

   A $\frac{1}{8}$ C 1

   B $\frac{7}{8}$ D $\frac{8}{7}$

2. Misako halved the quantities in a recipe, and used $1\frac{1}{2}$ teaspoons of sugar. Which equation shows s, the amount of sugar in the original recipe? M

   J $\;s = 1\frac{1}{2} \times \frac{1}{2}$

   K $\;s = 1\frac{1}{2} \div 1\frac{1}{2}$

   L $\;s = 1\frac{1}{2} \times 1\frac{1}{2}$

   M $\;s = 1\frac{1}{2} \times 2$

3. To meet a special order, a company sped up to $2\frac{1}{2}$ times its usual production. If the company is now producing 140 doohickeys per day, how many doohickeys does it usually produce per day? B

   A 35   C 210

   B 56   D 350

4. During his warm up, a pitcher threw the ball about $\frac{3}{4}$ the speed that he pitches during a game. If his warm-up pitches were 60 miles per hour, about how fast are his game pitches? L

   J 40 mph   L 80 mph

   K 75 mph   M Not given

5. Mr. Wright drove 300 miles today, covering $\frac{2}{3}$ of the distance to his destination. How many miles will he travel in all? D

   A 150 miles   C 300 miles

   B 200 miles   D 450 miles

Write About It

Write a plan for solving the following problem using a reciprocal. Then solve.

6. A model of a car is 0.24 the size of the actual car. If the model is 2.4 feet long, how long is the actual car?

Sample answer:
Write 0.24 as a fraction: $\frac{24}{100}$.
Use the reciprocal $\frac{24}{100}$ in an equation.
Actual length = model length $\times \frac{100}{24}$
Actual length = $2.4 \times \frac{100}{24} = 10$
The length of the actual car is 10 ft.

1. A ☐   B ☐   C ☐   D ☒

2. J ☐   K ☐   L ☐   M ☒

3. A ☐   B ☒   C ☐   D ☐

4. J ☐   K ☐   L ☒   M ☐

5. A ☐   B ☐   C ☐   D ☒

Making a Table to Generalize

Some problems may ask you to find an **expression**, a mathematical phrase that can be used to solve a problem for different values. Showing information in a table can help you write expressions.

Example 1

Sharif buys and sells T-shirts. If he buys the shirts for b dollars each, and sells them for s dollars each, how much profit will he earn on the sale of 2 T-shirts?

Step 1: The answer will be an expression that includes the variables b and s. To write the expression, you must decide what operation to use. It can help to substitute numbers for each variable.

Make a table using various amounts for b and s.

Buying Price	Selling Price	Profit on 1 T-shirt	Profit on 2 T-shirts
10	15	15 − 10	2 × (15 − 10)
6	9	9 − 6	2 × (9 − 6)

Step 2: Look at the table. The operations used were subtraction and multiplication.

Now substitute the variables b and s for the numbers.

THINK: The profit on 1 shirt is the selling price, s, minus the buying price, b. The expression for the profit on 1 shirt will be $s - b$.

Buying Price	Selling Price	Profit on 1 T-shirt	Profit on 2 T-shirts
10	15	15 − 10	2 × (15 − 10)
6	9	9 − 6	2 × (9 − 6)
b	s	$s - b$	2 × ($s - b$)

Sharif's profit on 2 T-shirts is ___ $2 \times (s - b)$ ___ dollars.

Example 2

Sharif bought T-shirts for $8 each and sold them for $11 each. Use the solution to Example 1 to find the profit Sharif would make on 2 T-shirts.

Substitute the buying and selling prices for the variables b and s.

$2 \times (s - b)$ ➝ $2 \times (11 - 8)$

$2 \times (11 - 8) = 2 \times$ ___ 3 ___

Sharif's profit on 2 T-shirts is $___ 6 ___.

● Order of Operations

1. a. At a restaurant, each pie is cut into 8 slices, then each slice sells for *p* dollars. How much money does the restaurant receive if it sells a total of 6 pies?

   Substitute numbers for the variable and make a table.

Price of 1 slice of pie	Price of 1 pie	Price of 6 pies
3 dollars	8 × 3	6 × (8 × 3)
2 dollars	8 × 2	6 × (8 × 2)
p dollars	8 × *p*	6 × (8 × *p*)

   The restaurant receives ___ 6 × (8 × *p*) ___ dollars.

   b. If the restaurant sells each slice of pie for $2.00, how much money does it receive from the sale of 6 pies?

   Substitute numbers for the variables in the expression you found in Problem 1a.

   $$6 \times (8 \times p) \longrightarrow 6 \times (8 \times \underline{\ 2.00\ })$$
   $$= 6 \times \underline{\ 16.00\ }$$
   $$= \underline{\ 96.00\ }$$

   The restaurant receives $___ 96.00 ___.

2. a. Ed receives *d* dollars for baby-sitting. His bus fare to the job is *s* dollars each way. How much money does Ed make?

   Substitute numbers for the variables and make a table.

   THINK: The money left will be the money Ed receives, *d*, minus the money he has to spend.

Money Ed receives	Bus fare each way	Total bus fare	Money left
20	2	2 × 2	20 − (2 × 2)
35	3	2 × 3	35 − (2 × 3)
d	*s*	2 × *s*	*d* − (2 × *s*)

   Ed makes ___ *d* − (2 × *s*) ___ dollars.

   b. If Ed receives $22.50 for baby-sitting, and his bus fare is $1.50 each way, how much money does Ed make?

   Substitute numbers for the variables in the expression you found in Problem 2a.

   $$d - (2 \times s) \longrightarrow 22.50 - (2 \times \underline{\ 1.50\ }) \longrightarrow 22.50 - \underline{\ 3.00\ }$$

   Ed makes $___ 19.50 ___.

3. a. Sally enters a walkathon and gets $12 for taking part plus $4 for each mile she walks. If she walks *m* miles, how much money will she make?

   Make a table substituting numbers for the variable. Then write an expression to solve the problem. Sample answers given.

Money for taking part	Money for miles walked	Total money made
12	4 × 10	12 + (4 × 10)
12	4 × 20	12 + (4 × 20)
12	4 × m	12 + (4 × m)

   Sally will make _____12 + (4 × m)_____ dollars.

   b. Use the expression you wrote to find how much money Sally will get if she walks 14 miles.

   Sally will get $___68___ .

SOLVE

4. **A potter makes *c* pots per hour, and gets paid *n* dollars for each pot. How much money does she make in a 7-hour workday?**

   7 × (c × n) dollars

5. **Ben runs *m* miles each day, 5 days a week. Next week, he will run an extra 2 miles a day. How many miles will he run next week?**

   5 × (m + 2) miles

6. **The cost of mailing packages is $1.23 per pound. How much would it cost Philippe to mail a package weighing *k* pounds and a package weighing *l* pounds?**

   $1.23 × (k + l)

7. **Bethania is cycling to her aunt's house, *z* miles away. After 3 hours, she is 2 miles from the house. What is her average speed for the trip so far in miles per hour?**

   (z − 2) ÷ 3 mi/h

8. **Meghan usually takes *c* hours to knit a sweater. The last 4 sweaters she knit took her, in all, 2 hours less than she expected. How long did the sweaters take Meghan?**

   (4 × c) − 2 hours

9. **The Zenco Mixer is usually priced at *g* dollars. This week, the mixer is on sale for $15 off. How much money would it cost to buy *w* mixers?**

   w × (g − 15) dollars

Choose the best answer for each problem. In the answer section at the bottom of the page, fill in the box of your choice.

1. Together, Shannon and April earn *n* dollars per hour baby-sitting. They worked for 6 hours and split their earnings equally. Which operations show April's share of the money? C
   A Add 6 to *n* and subtract 2.
   B Add 6 to *n* and divide by 2.
   C Multiply 6 by *n* and divide by 2.
   D Divide *n* by 6 and multiply by 2.

2. Kasa is $\frac{3}{8}$ of her brother's height (*b*) and her sister's height (*s*) combined. How tall is Kasa? J
   J $\frac{3}{8} \times (b + s)$ L $(b + s) \div \frac{3}{8}$
   K $\frac{3}{8} \times (b - s)$ M $\frac{3}{8} \div (b + s)$

3. Weston earned *y* dollars, then bought 3 video games at *v* dollars each. How much money does he have left? B
   A $y + (3 \times v)$ C $y \times (3 + v)$
   B $y - (3 \times v)$ D $y \div (3 \times v)$

4. Tommy's company pays him a $50 bonus for each new customer he finds. If he finds *c* customers per day, how much bonus money will he earn during a 5-day week? L
   J $50 + (5 \times c)$ dollars
   K $50 \times (5 + c)$ dollars
   L $(50 \times c) \times 5$ dollars
   M $50 \times 5 \div c$ dollars

5. For each sandwich she sells, the sandwich vendor receives $1.50 less than the price (*p*) of the sandwich. If the vendor sells 8 sandwiches, how much money will she receive? D
   A $p + 1.50$ dollars
   B $(8 \times p) + 1.50$ dollars
   C $8 \times (p + 1.50)$ dollars
   D $8 \times (p - 1.50)$ dollars

Write About It

Write a plan for solving the following problem. Then solve.

6. Riley is 3 times as old as LuAnn. LuAnn is Hannah's age, *h*, divided by 4. What is Riley's age?

   Sample answer:

   Make a table with Hannah's age in the

   first column, LuAnn's in the second,

   and Riley's in the third. Substitute

   numbers for Hannah's age (*h*) to find

   how the three ages are related.

   Riley's age is $3 \times (h \div 4)$.

1. A ☐ B ☐ C ☒ D ☐   4. J ☐ K ☐ L ☒ M ☐
2. J ☒ K ☐ L ☐ M ☐   5. A ☐ B ☐ C ☐ D ☒
3. A ☐ B ☒ C ☐ D ☐

• Order of Operations

Solving a Formula for a Desired Variable

For some problems, it helps to show the information in a formula in another way. You can rewrite the formula by solving for the variable you want to find.

Corey recorded his times and distances for each day he bicycled.

Day	Distance	Time
1	5 mi	25 min
2	6.45 mi	25.8 min
3	4.5 mi	24 min

Example 1

How fast did Corey travel on Day 1?

Step 1: **First, decide which formula to use. Use what you know.**

- You know the **distance** Corey bicycled.
- You know the **time** it took.
- You need to know how fast he bicycled (his **rate**).
- Use the formula that relates distance, time, and rate: $D = r \times t$.

Step 2: **Rewrite the formula to solve for rate. Use the numbers you know.**

$$D = r \times t \longrightarrow 5 = r \times 25$$

$$\frac{5}{25} = \frac{r \times 25}{25} \longrightarrow \frac{1}{5} = r$$

So, Corey rode $\frac{1}{5}$ mile per minute.

Example 2

On which day did Corey travel the fastest?

Step 1: **Rewrite the formula.**

THINK: I need to know several rates, so I can solve the formula for r before I substitute the distance and rate information. This way, I only have to rewrite the formula once.

$$D = r \times t \longrightarrow \frac{D}{t} = \frac{r \times t}{t} \longrightarrow r = \frac{D}{t}$$

Step 2: **Use the rewritten formula to solve the problem.**

$r = D \div t$

Day 1 rate = 5 ÷ 25 = __0.2__ miles/minute

Day 2 rate = 6.45 ÷ 25.8 = __0.25__ miles/minute

Day 3 rate = 4.5 ÷ 24 = __0.1875__ miles/minute

So, Corey traveled the fastest on __Day 2__ .

GUIDED PRACTICE

1. Each of the three triangular flags flying over a new store has an area of 12 square feet. The bases of the flags measure 3 feet, 4 feet, and 6 feet. What is the height of each flag?

   Step 1: **Decide which formula to use.**

   The formula for the area of a triangle is $A = \frac{1}{2}bh$.

   Step 2: **Rewrite the formula to solve for height.**

   $A = \frac{1}{2}bh \rightarrow 2A = bh$

   $\frac{2A}{b} = \frac{bh}{b}$ so $h = \underline{2A/b}$

   Step 3: **Use the rewritten formula to solve the problem.**

   Flag 1's height $= \quad 2 \quad \times \quad 12 \quad \div \quad 3 \quad = \underline{\quad 8 \quad}$ feet

   Flag 2's height $= \quad 2 \quad \times \underline{\quad 12 \quad} \div \underline{\quad 4 \quad} = \underline{\quad 6 \quad}$ feet

   Flag 3's height $= \underline{\quad 2 \quad} \times \underline{\quad 12 \quad} \div \underline{\quad 6 \quad} = \underline{\quad 4 \quad}$ feet

   The heights of the flags are $\underline{\quad 8 \quad}$ feet, $\underline{\quad 6 \quad}$ feet, and $\underline{\quad 4 \quad}$ feet.

2. Kitty can borrow $2,400 on a 2-year loan that will charge her $384 simple interest or a 3-year loan that will charge her $504 simple interest. On which loan is the interest rate lower? By how many percent?

   Step 1: **Decide which formula to use.**

   The formula for simple interest is $I = prt$.

   Step 2: **Rewrite the formula to solve for rate of interest (r).**

   $I = prt \rightarrow r = \underline{I/pt}$

   Step 3: **Use the rewritten formula to solve the problem.**

   2-year loan rate $= \dfrac{384}{2,400 \times 2} = \underline{\quad 0.08 \quad}$

   3-year loan rate $= \dfrac{504}{2,400 \times 3} = \underline{\quad 0.07 \quad}$

   2-year loan rate $= \underline{\quad 0.08 \quad} \times 100 = \underline{\quad 8 \quad} \%$

   3-year loan rate $= \underline{\quad 0.07 \quad} \times 100 = \underline{\quad 7 \quad} \%$

   The difference is $\underline{\quad 8 \quad} - \underline{\quad 7 \quad} = \underline{\quad 1 \quad} \%$.

   > To write a decimal as a percent, multiply by 100.

   The interest rate is lower on the $\underline{\quad 3 \quad}$-year loan, by $\underline{\quad 1 \quad} \%$.

PRACTICE

Decide what formula to use. If necessary, rewrite the formula to solve for the missing value. Then solve.

3. The area of a trapezoid is 45 square inches. If the bases of the trapezoid measure 8 inches and 10 inches, what is its height?

   a. Write the formula you need to solve the problem.

   $A = (b_1 + b_2)h/2$

   b. Rewrite the formula to solve for width.

   $h = 2A/(b_1 + b_2)$ or $h = (2 \times 45)/(8 + 10)$

   c. Solve.

   The height of the trapezoid is 5 inches.

FORMULAS

Area

Circle: $A = \pi r^2$
Triangle: $A = \frac{1}{2}bh$
Rectangle: $A = lw$
Parallelogram: $A = bh$
Trapezoid: $A = \dfrac{(b_1 + b_2)h}{2}$

Circumference

$C = \pi d \qquad C = 2\pi r$

Volume

Rectangular prism: $V = lwh$
Cylinder: $V = \pi r^2 h$

Distance

$D = rt$

Simple Interest

$I = prt$

Solve . . . .

4. The cardboard box shown at the right has a volume of 168 cubic inches. What is the width of the cardboard box?

   7 inches

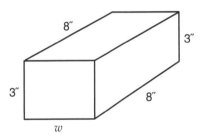

5. The circumferences of two bicycle wheels are 66 inches and 88 inches. What is the difference in the diameters of the wheels? (Use $\pi = \frac{22}{7}$.)

   The difference is 7 inches.

6. Jim completed a 10-kilometer run in 35 minutes. Sarah completed a 6-kilometer run in 20 minutes. Which runner ran at a faster rate?

   Sarah ran at a faster rate.

7. Rick will pay $4,250 in interest on a loan for $10,000. If the loan is for 5 years, what is the rate of interest?

   8.5%

8. Which takes the longer time: a train traveling 160 mi at a speed of 50 mi/h or a car traveling 120 mi at a speed of 40 mi/h?

   The train takes longer.

Choose the best answer for each problem. In the answer section at the bottom of the page, fill in the box of your choice.

1. The perimeter of a rectangular field is 220 yards. Its length is 65 yards. What is the width of the field?

   Which of the following formulas for the perimeter of a rectangle would be the best choice to solve the problem? B

   A $\ P = 2(l + w)$

   B $\ w = \frac{P}{2} - l$

   C $\ l + w = \frac{P}{2}$

   D $\ 2w = P - 2l$

2. **Which of the following describes the slowest rate?** J

   J $\ $ 100-yard dash in 16 seconds

   K $\ $ 200-yard run in 20 seconds

   L $\ $ 400-yard run in 65 seconds

   M $\ $ 800-yard run in 120 seconds

3. **Sharona will pay $1,000 interest on a loan of $5,000. If the loan is for 2 years, what is her rate of interest?** C

   A $\ $ 1% $\qquad$ C $\ $ 10%

   B $\ $ 5% $\qquad$ D $\ $ 100%

4. **A circular courtyard has a circumference of $78\frac{1}{2}$ feet. What is its radius?** M

   J $\ $ 15 feet $\qquad$ L $\ $ 314 feet

   K $\ $ 20 feet $\qquad$ M $\ $ Not given

5. **A cylindrical can has a radius of 7 centimeters and a volume of 924 cubic centimeters. What is its height? (Use $\pi = \frac{22}{7}$.)** A

   A $\ $ 6 cm $\qquad$ C $\ $ 42 cm

   B $\ $ 21 cm $\qquad$ D $\ $ 59.3 cm

Write About It

Write a plan for solving the following problem. Then solve. Sample answer given.

6. **A rectangle has an area of 45 in.² and a width of 5 in. Could it fit inside a rectangle with an area of 64 in.² and a width of 8 in.?**

   Rewrite the formula for the area of a

   rectangle to find length: $l = A / w$.

   Solve to find each length, then

   compare the dimensions of the first

   and second rectangles.

   Rectangle 1 length = 45 ÷ 5 = 9 in.

   Rectangle 2 length = 64 ÷ 8 = 8 in.

   The first rectangle cannot fit in the

   second, as its length is greater than

   either dimension of the second

   rectangle.

---

1. A ☐ B ☒ C ☐ D ☐ $\qquad$ 4. J ☐ K ☐ L ☐ M ☒

2. J ☒ K ☐ L ☐ M ☐ $\qquad$ 5. A ☒ B ☐ C ☐ D ☐

3. A ☐ B ☐ C ☒ D ☐

Using a Diagram to Write and Solve an Equation

You can find the solution to many problems by writing and solving an equation. You can use a diagram to help you write the equation.

Example

Theo ordered two CD players on the Internet. He paid a total of $166.05, which included $8.45 for shipping and handling. What was the price of one CD player?

A. Make a diagram to show the problem.

The diagram should show the information you know:
• You know the total cost—$166.05.
• You know the cost of shipping and handling—$8.45.
• You know that the remainder of the cost was the price of 2 CD players.

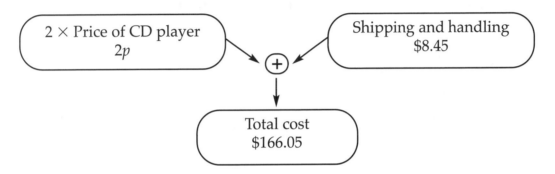

B. Use the diagram to write an equation.

$2p + 8.45 = 166.05$

C. Use the diagram to plan the solution.

THINK: I know the total cost and the shipping and handling.
First, I will use them to find the value of $2p$.
Then, I can divide by 2 to find the value of p.

D. Solve the equation.

$2p + 8.45 = 166.05$

$2p = 166.05 - 8.45$

$2p = \underline{\ 157.60\ }$

$p = \underline{\ 157.60\ } \div \underline{\ 2\ }$

$p = \underline{\ 78.80\ }$

The price of one CD player was $\underline{\ 78.80\ }$.

© 2000 Metropolitan Teaching and Learning Company

GUIDED PRACTICE

1. Sara works at an animal shelter. She has 3 bags of dog food and 1 box containing 18 pounds of dog food. When she divides the food evenly among 20 dogs, each dog gets 3 pounds. How much does each of the bags weigh?

   Step 1: **Complete the diagram to show the problem.**

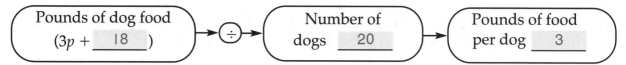

   Pounds of dog food $(3p + \underline{18})$ ÷ Number of dogs $\underline{20}$ → Pounds of food per dog $\underline{3}$

   Step 2: **Use the diagram to plan the solution.**

   First, you can use the pounds of food per dog and the number of dogs to find the $\underline{\text{pounds of dog food}}$.

   Step 3: **Use the diagram to write an equation. Then solve.**

   $$(3p + \underline{18}) ÷ \underline{20} = \underline{3}$$
   $$(3p + \underline{18}) = \underline{3} × \underline{20}$$
   $$3p + \underline{18} = \underline{60}$$
   $$3p = \underline{60} - \underline{18} = \underline{42}, \text{ so } p = \underline{14}$$

   Each bag weighs $\underline{14}$ pounds.

2. Harry's "Hungry in a Hurry" restaurant served 147 customers at breakfast and 98 at lunch. That day, the restaurant averaged 150 customers per meal. How many people ate dinner at Harry's?

   Step 1: **Complete the diagram to show the problem.**

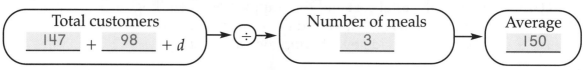

   Total customers $\underline{147} + \underline{98} + d$ ÷ Number of meals $\underline{3}$ → Average $\underline{150}$

   Step 2: **Use the diagram to plan the solution.**

   First, you can add the customers at each meal to find the $\underline{\text{total customers}}$.

   Step 3: **Use the diagram to write an equation. Then solve.**

   $$(\underline{147} + \underline{98} + d) ÷ \underline{3} = \underline{150}$$
   $$(\underline{245} + d) = \underline{150} × \underline{3}$$
   $$\underline{245} + d = \underline{450}$$
   $$d = \underline{450} - \underline{245} = \underline{205}$$

   So, $\underline{205}$ people ate dinner at Harry's.

Complete the diagram. Then write an equation to solve the problem.

3. Magda spent $90.55 when she ordered five CDs and 4 cassettes. Shipping charges were $6.25. If the CDs cost $10.50 each, how much did each cassette cost?

   a. **Complete the diagram to show the problem.**

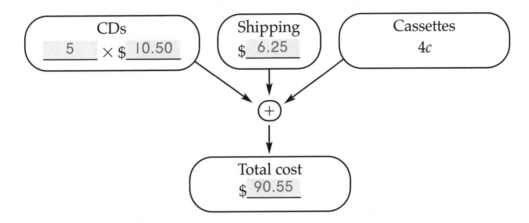

   b. **Use the diagram to plan the solution.**

   Cassettes = Total cost __−__ CDs __−__ Shipping

   c. **Write an equation and solve the problem.**

   $(5 \times 10.50) + 6.25 + 4c = 90.55$

   $58.75 + 4c = 90.55$

   $4c = 31.80 \quad c = 7.95$

   Each cassette cost $ __7.95__ .

Solve . . . .

4. Lahela is 4 times Suke's age, minus 7. If Lahela is 21, how old is Suke?
   a. **Write an equation.**

   $4s - 7 = 21$

   b. **Solve the problem.**

   Suke is 7 years old.

5. Sol bought a shirt for $29.95 and pants for $25. He received $2.30 change from $60. What tax did he pay?
   a. **Write an equation.**

   $29.95 + 25 + t = 60 - 2.30$

   b. **Solve the problem.**

   Sol paid $2.75 in tax.

Choose the best answer for each problem. In the answer section at the bottom of the page, fill in the box of your choice.

1. Mrs. Adler bought 3 hamburgers for $2.50 each, a soda for $1.15, and a chicken sandwich. She paid $11.85 in all. How much did the chicken sandwich cost?

   Which of the following equations shows the problem? A
   A $(3 \times 2.50) + 1.15 + c = 11.85$
   B $3 \times (2.50 + 1.15) + c = 11.85$
   C $11.85 - (3 \times 2.50) = c - 1.15$
   D $3 \times 11.85 = 2.50 + 1.15 + c$

2. **The highest wind speed measured in Mt. Washington, New Hampshire is 231 miles per hour. This is equal to 18.6 miles per hour plus 6 times the average wind speed. What is the average wind speed?** K
   J 18.6 mph   **L** 54 mph
   K 35.4 mph   **M** 231 mph

3. **The average age in Denny's family is 18. If the other family members are aged 2, 3, 7, 42, and 39, what is Denny's age?** C
   A 4   **C** 15
   B 8   **D** 18

4. **Trish spent three times as much money as Josh, who spent $1.00 more than Huck. If Trish spent $27.00, how much did Huck spend?** K
   J $7.00   **L** $9.00
   K $8.00   **M** $10.00

5. **Jerry wrote 3 checks, but forgot to record one in his checkbook. His checking balance started at $600 and ended at $285.79. He wrote a check for $35 and a check for $147.72. What was the amount of the missing check?** A
   A $131.49   **C** $417.28
   B $314.21   **D** Not given

Write About It
Write a plan for solving the following problem. Then solve.

6. A store is selling staplers at $3 off the regular price. Arto bought two staplers, and received $0.60 change from a $10 bill. What is the regular price of a stapler?

Sample answer given.
Write and solve an equation to find
the problem's solution.
Let s be the regular price.
$2(s - 3) = 10 - 0.60$
$(s - 3) = 9.40 \div 2$
$s = 4.70 + 3 = 7.70$
The regular price is $7.70.

1. A ☒   B ☐   C ☐   D ☐   4. J ☐   K ☒   L ☐   M ☐

2. J ☐   K ☒   L ☐   M ☐   5. A ☒   B ☐   C ☐   D ☐

3. A ☐   B ☐   C ☒   D ☐

Choosing a Strategy for Solving Problems

Choosing a strategy can help you to solve a problem. Here are some strategies you can use.

Show Information Another Way	Decide on the Kind of Answer You Need
• Make a Diagram • Decide What Kind of Numbers to Use • Make a Table to Generalize • Solve a Formula for a Desired Variable • Use Sample Data to Interpret Graphs	• Interpret Quotients • Decide Whether to Estimate • Estimate Products and Quotients • Estimate with Mixed Expressions
Find Needed Information	**Decide What to Do First**
• Read Information from a Table or Chart • Read a Graph	• Use a Diagram to Write and Solve an Equation • Use Reciprocals to Solve Problems

Example 1

A box is $2\frac{1}{2}$ feet wide, 8.2 feet long, and 10 feet high. What is the box's volume? Hint: The formula for volume of a rectangular prism is $V = lwh$.

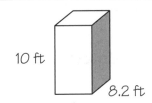

10 ft

8.2 ft

$2\frac{1}{2}$ ft

Step 1: **Strategy: Show the information another way. Rewrite the numbers as one uniform kind of numbers.**

THINK: The numbers in the problem include a mixed number and a decimal. Before using the formula, rewrite the numbers as one uniform kind of numbers. Rewrite $2\frac{1}{2}$ as a decimal.

$$2\frac{1}{2} = \underline{\quad 2.5 \quad}$$

Step 2: **Use the volume formula $V = lwh$ to solve the problem.**

$$\underline{\quad 2.5 \quad} \times 8.2 \times 10 = \underline{\quad 205 \quad}$$

So, the box's volume is $\underline{\quad 205 \text{ ft}^3 \quad}$.

Example 2

Hector is ordering pizza for 26 people. Each pizza serves 6 people. How many pizzas should he order?

Step 1: **Strategy: Decide on the kind of answer you need by interpreting the quotient.**

THINK: The problem asks how many pizzas Hector should order—so the quotient must be rounded up to a whole number.

Step 2: **Divide, rounding up to the nearest whole number.**

$$26 \div 6 \rightarrow \underline{\quad 5 \quad}$$

So, Hector should order $\underline{\quad 5 \quad}$ pizzas.

GUIDED PRACTICE

1. Cher took $80 to the mall. She bought 2 identical shirts at one store. Then she bought a pair of pants for $25 at another store. At the end of her shopping trip, she had $15.10 left. How much did each shirt cost?

   Step 1: **Choose a strategy, and describe it.**

   Sample answer: Show the information another way by drawing a diagram.

   Step 2: **Solve, using the strategy you chose.**
   Each shirt cost $19.95.

2. Dana cut a 32-foot board into 7-foot lengths. How many feet of board did she have left over?

   Step 1: **Choose a strategy, and describe it.**

   Sample answer: Decide on the kind of answer you need; you find the quotient only as

   part of the process. The remainder provides the answer.

   Step 2: **Solve, using the strategy you chose.**
   Dana will have 4 ft **of board left over.**

3. Newton's height is $\frac{3}{5}$ the height of his brother's and sister's heights combined. Newton's brother is 5 feet 4 inches tall, and his sister is 5 feet 1 inch tall. How tall is Newton?

   Step 1: **Choose a strategy, and describe it.**

   Sample answer: Show information another way by writing a formula. Let the brother's

   and sister's heights be represented by b and s.

   Step 2: **Solve, using the strategy you chose.**
   The formula to find Newton's height is $\frac{3}{5}(b + s)$.

   $$\frac{3}{5}(5 \text{ ft } 4 \text{ in.} + 5 \text{ ft } 1 \text{ in.}) \rightarrow \frac{3}{5}(10 \text{ ft } 5 \text{ in.})$$
   $$\frac{3}{5}(125)$$

   So, Newton is 6 **feet** 3 **inches tall.**

PRACTICE

Choose a strategy for each problem, and then solve.

4. The table at the right gives an estimate of the calories burned by an average 150-lb person exercising for one hour. Mike played basketball for 1 hour, while Jim biked for 2 hours. Who burned more calories? How much more?

Aerobic Activities Calories Burned Per Hour	
Basketball	510
Bicycling	340
Dancing	320
Running	540
Tennis	420
Walking	210

$(2 \times 340) - 510 = 170$; Jim burned

170 more calories than Mike burned.

5. Nora has a board that is $8\frac{1}{2}$ feet long. If she cuts a 2-foot 3-inch length from it, how long will the remaining board be?

2 ft 3 in. $= 2\frac{1}{4}$ ft; $8\frac{1}{2} - 2\frac{1}{4} = 6\frac{1}{4}$

The remaining board will $6\frac{1}{4}$ ft long.

6. Derek needs to ship 5 packages. Each package weighs 2 pounds 7 ounces. The shipping charge is $3.50 per pound. About how much will he pay?

2 lb 7 oz $\approx$ 2.5 lb; 2.5 x 5 = 12.5; 12.5

$\times$ 3.50 = 43.75; he will pay about $43.75.

7. A bread recipe calls for $\frac{7}{8}$ lb of rye flour and 20 oz of wheat flour. How much flour is that altogether?

14 + 20 = 34; 34 oz, or 2lb 2 oz

8. Casey biked 8 miles in 32 minutes. At what speed was he traveling? ($d = rt$)

$d = rt$, so r = d $\div$ t; r $= \frac{8}{32}$, or $\frac{1}{4}$

Casey was traveling at $\frac{1}{4}$ mi per min.

9. At the Seafood Place, Pearl bought 2 orders of shrimp. She also bought 1 order of fries for $2.50, and a soda for $1.50. Her order came to $21.50. How much did a single order of shrimp cost?

$2s + \$2.50 + \$1.50 = \$21.50$; s = $8.75

A single order of shrimp cost $8.75.

10. At a 3-day crafts fair, a potter took in $720 the first day and $1,255 the second day. If the potter wishes to average $1,200 per day, how much must she take in on the third day?

$(720 + 1,255 + x) \div 3 = 1,200$; $x = 1,625$;

she must take in $1,625 on the third day.

Choose the best answer for each problem. In the answer section at the bottom of the page, fill in the box of your choice.

1. A small ad in a weekly newspaper costs $15 per issue. Patti bought 2 small ads and 1 large ad. Each ad will run in 2 issues. If Patti's total cost was $110, how much does it cost to run 1 large ad in 1 issue? **A**
    A $25   C $55
    B $50   D $80

2. A sheet of paper has a surface area of 154 sq. in. If the page's width is 11 inches, what is its length? ($A = lw$) **J**
    J 14 in.   L 22 in.
    K 18 in.   M 1,694 in.

3. The dimensions of a photo have been reduced to $\frac{1}{3}$ of their original size. The reduced photo measures 2 inches by 3 inches. What were the dimensions of the original photograph? **D**

    A $\frac{2}{3}$ in. by 1 in.

    B $2\frac{1}{3}$ in. by $3\frac{1}{3}$ in.

    C 4 in. by 6 in.

    D 6 in. by 9 in.

4. An information service charges $0.45 per minute to answer questions by telephone. Mrs. Banks used the service for m minutes this month, and Mr. Banks used the service for n minutes.

    Which expression could you use to find their total cost for the service? **L**
    J $0.45m$ L $0.45(m + n)$
    K $0.45n$ M $0.45(m - n)$

5. Which of the following is a reasonable estimate of the cost of $3\frac{1}{4}$ pounds of peaches? **B**

    FRUIT STAND

    Apples........................... $0.70/lb

    Peaches......................... $0.95/lb

    Strawberries................. $2.50/pt

    A $2.00   C $4.00
    B $3.00   D $5.00

Write About It

6. Choose a problem on this page, and describe the strategy you used to solve it. Then describe a different strategy you could have used, and write about how you would use it to solve the problem.

    Answers will vary.

---

1. A ☒ B ☐ C ☐ D ☐   4. J ☐ K ☐ L ☒ M ☐

2. J ☒ K ☐ L ☐ M ☐   5. A ☐ B ☒ C ☐ D ☐

3. A ☐ B ☐ C ☐ D ☒   6. J ☐ K ☐ L ☐ M ☐

● Strategy Review

Test-Taking Skill: Writing a Plan

Some test questions will ask you how you would solve a problem. It is important to explain your thinking and show your calculations.

Example

A group of 7 people went to a movie. The 3 adults in the group paid the adult price of $7.00 each. The 4 children entered for the children's price. If the group paid a total of $35, what is the price of 1 child's ticket to the movie?

A. **Read the problem carefully. Decide what kind of answer you are looking for.**

The answer that is asked for is an amount of money—the price of one child's ticket to the movie.

B. **Make a plan. Write your plan.**

First, find the price the 3 adults paid for a ticket. Then, subtract that number from the price the group paid. Finally, divide the remaining amount by 4 to find the price of 1 child's ticket.

You could write the plan like this:

Step 1: Price 3 adults paid = 3 × Price of 1 adult ticket

Step 2: Price 4 children paid = Total price − Price 3 adults paid

Step 3: Price 1 child paid = Price 4 children paid ÷ 4

C. **Solve the problem.**

Step 1: Price 3 adults paid: $3 \times 7 =$ __21__

Step 2: Price 4 children paid = $35 -$ __21__ → __14__

Step 3: Price 1 child paid: __14__ $\div 4 =$ __3.50__

> When solving a problem, remember to show your thinking and your calculations. Feel free to change your plan if you need to.

D. **Answer the problem question.**

The price for 1 child's ticket to the movie is $ __3.50__ .

TEST-TAKING PRACTICE

Make a plan to solve the problem. Then solve. Show your work. Use the table to find the information you need.

Fair Refreshments Stand	
Popcorn	**Chips**
Small $2.50	Potato chips $2.00
Medium $4.00	Corn chips $2.00
Large $5.00	Chips and Dip ...$3.50
Juice	**Snacks**
Small $2.00	Tasty Treat $1.50
Medium $2.50	Health Bar $2.50
Large $3.00	Peanuts $2.00

1. A family bought 2 small juices, 1 medium juice, 1 large juice, and 2 bags of popcorn, spending a total of $14.50. Which size popcorn did they buy?

Sample answer: First, find the cost of

the 4 juices. Then, subtract that amount

from $14.50 to find the cost of the

popcorn. Divide that cost by 2 and

find the size of popcorn in the table.

Price of 4 juices:

2($2.00) + $2.50 + $3.00 = $9.50

Price of popcorn:

$14.50 − $9.50 = $5.00

$5.00 ÷ 2 = $2.50

They bought the small size.

2. Rey had $18.00 to buy 1 pack of corn chips, 1 small popcorn, and 5 juices. What is the largest size of juice he could buy if he bought 5 of the same size?

Sample answer: First, find the cost of a

small popcorn and a pack of corn chips.

Subtract that amount from $18 to find

how much Rey had for juices. Divide

that amount by 5 to find the greatest

amount he could spend for each juice.

$2.00 + $2.50 = $4.50

$18.00 − $4.50 = $13.50

$13.50 ÷ 5 = $2.70

Rey could buy medium juices.

● Test-Taking Skill

Drawing a Number Line

You can use a number line to help you solve problems that involve negative and positive numbers.

Example

The Lakeshore football team has the ball. In two attempts, they gain 5 yards and lose 8 yards. What is the team's total yardage for the two attempts?

> If the team loses ground, the yardage is negative.
> If the team gains ground, the yardage is positive.

Step 1: **Write the total yardage as a sum.**
You need to find the sum of 5 + ⁻8.

Draw a number line with a dot to show the starting point. Label the dot 0.

Step 2: **Show the sum on a number line.**

Draw an arrow to the right of 0 to show the team's gain of 5 yards.
Draw an arrow to the left of the new point to show the loss of 8 yards.

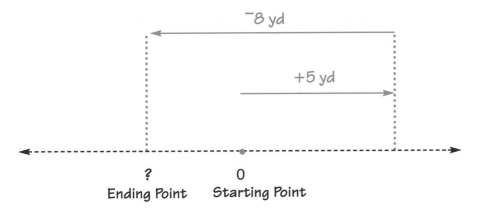

?
Ending Point   0
            Starting Point

Step 3: **Solve.**

The solution will be the overall change between the starting point and the ending point.

> The absolute value of an integer shows its magnitude, or size, but not its sign. Absolute values can be used like positive numbers.

Since the two numbers have opposite signs, you can subtract their absolute values to find the distance to the ending point.

The ending point is to the left of 0, so the solution will be negative.

8 yards − 5 yards = ___3___ yards.

The team's total yardage is ___⁻3___ yards.

1. One day, the temperature in Prospect Creek, Alaska was ⁻12°F. The temperature dropped 52 degrees during the night. What was the low temperature?

   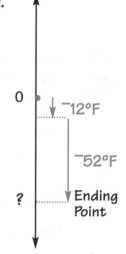

   Step 1: Draw a line with a dot to show 0°F—your starting point.

   Step 2: Draw an arrow below the starting point to show ⁻12°F.

   Draw an arrow below the new point to show the drop of 52 degrees.

   Step 3: Solve.

   THINK: The solution will be the sum of ⁻12 and ⁻52. The final point is below 0, so the result will be negative.

   Add the absolute values of the numbers.

   $12 + 52 =$ __64__

   So, the low temperature was __⁻64°__ F.

2. Marty is a running back for the football team. During the first play, he loses $3\frac{1}{2}$ yards. On the second play, he gains 10 yards. What is Marty's total yardage for the two plays?

   Step 1: Mark the line below with a dot to show the starting point.

   Step 2: Draw an arrow showing Marty's loss of $3\frac{1}{2}$ yards.

   Step 3: Draw an arrow from the new point to show the gain of 10 yards.

   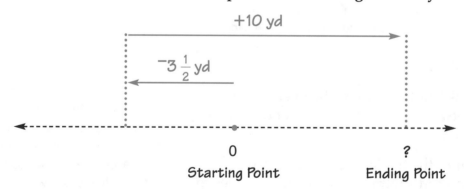

   Step 4: Solve. Use the number line to help you.

   THINK: Does the final point show a positive or negative solution?

   Find the difference using absolute values of the numbers.

   __10__ $-$ __$3\frac{1}{2}$__ $=$ __$6\frac{1}{2}$__

   Marty's total yardage is __$6\frac{1}{2}$__ yards.

PRACTICE

Mark the number lines to solve each problem.

3. In the early evening, the temperature was 15°F. By midnight, it had dropped 19 degrees. What was the temperature at midnight?

<--->

‾4°F

4. Monarch butterflies migrate long distances each year. A scientist tracked a monarch that had flown 1,200 miles to the south and then 300 miles to the north. How far was the butterfly from its starting point? In what direction?

<--->

900 miles to the south

5. Linsborough lies $\frac{1}{16}$ mile below sea level while Benton lies $\frac{1}{2}$ mile above sea level. How many miles higher is Benton than Linsborough?

<--->

$\frac{9}{16}$ mile

6. The football team lost $15\frac{1}{2}$ yards on its first play and gained 14 yards on the second attempt. What was the team's total yardage?

<--->

‾$1\frac{1}{2}$ yards

7. In May, Jeanne's stocks lost $175. In June, the stocks lost another $500. What were Jeanne's net earnings on the stocks for the two months?

<--->

‾$675

© 2000 Metropolitan Teaching and Learning Company

● Adding and Subtracting Integers

79

Choose the best answer for each problem. In the answer section at the bottom of the page, fill in the box of your choice.

1. At noon the temperature was 12°F. During the day, the temperature dropped 17 degrees. What was the temperature at the end of the day?

   Which of the following number lines could be used to solve this problem? A

   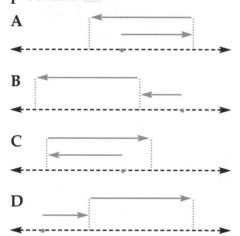

   A

   B

   C

   D

2. **The temperature at noon was ⁻14°F. By nightfall, it had risen 25 degrees. What was the new temperature?** L

   J ⁻39°F   **L** 11°F

   K ⁻11°F   **M** 39°F

3. **A submarine that was 41 feet below sea level fired a missile that rose to an altitude of 770 feet above sea level. How many feet did the missile climb?** C

   A ⁻811 ft   **C** 811 ft

   B 729 ft   **D** Not given

4. **The football team lost $2\frac{1}{2}$ yards on its first attempt, then lost another 9 yards on its second attempt. What is the team's total yardage for the two attempts?** J

   J ⁻$11\frac{1}{2}$ yd   **L** $6\frac{1}{2}$ yd

   K ⁻$6\frac{1}{2}$ yd   **M** $11\frac{1}{2}$ yd

Write About It

Write a plan for solving the following problem. Then solve.

5. **Onisha works at a large company. Today she started work on the 6th floor. Then she went up 2 floors, down 5 floors, then up 8 floors. Which floor is she on now?**

   Sample answer:

   Use a number line to diagram

   the problem. Then add and

   subtract the integers to find the

   solution.

   $6 + 2 + {}^-5 + 8 = 11$, so Onisha

   is now on the 11th floor.

1. A ⊠   B ☐   C ☐   D ☐

2. J ☐   K ☐   L ⊠   M ☐

3. A ☐   B ☐   C ⊠   D ☐

4. J ⊠   K ☐   L ☐   M ☐

● Adding and Subtracting Integers

Using Zero as a Benchmark

Using zero as a benchmark on a diagram can help you decide which numbers in a problem are positive and which are negative.

Example

Mr. Annunzio was born 276 years before the opening of the Bradford Museum. Mr. Bradford was born 100 years before Mr. Annunzio. If Mr. Bradford died on his 65th birthday, how many years before the Bradford Museum opened did he die?

A. **Draw a number line to show the information in the problem.**
Let the museum opening be the 0 point on your line.

B. **Mark the events on the number line.**

THINK: On the diagram, any date or time *before* a certain happening is *negative*. Any date or time *after* a certain happening is *positive*.

- Mr. Annunzio's birth occurred *before* the museum opening (the 0 point), so it is a negative integer.

- Mr. Bradford's birth occurred 100 years *before* Mr. Annunzio's birth, so it is also a negative integer.

- Mr. Bradford's death occurred *after* his birth, so it is a positive integer.

C. **Use the number line to write a number sentence, and solve.**

$$^-276 + {}^-100 + 65 = \underline{{}^-311}$$

THINK: A negative answer means that something happened *before* the 0 point. A positive answer means that the event happened *after* the 0 point.

Mr. Bradford died __311__ years before the museum opened.

● Adding and Subtracting Integers

1. A chemist has a sample of hydrogen chloride that is 38.2°C above its boiling point. He lowers its temperature by 51.6°C, and then raises it by 7.1°C. Should he increase or decrease the temperature of the sample to bring it to its boiling point? By how many degrees?

   Step 1: Choose a point to use as a benchmark of zero.

   Let the boiling point be 0.
   So, a positive answer will be above the boiling point, and a negative answer will be below the boiling point.

   Step 2: Mark the information on a number line.

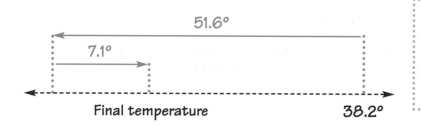

   > You can't include the boiling point on the line, as you don't know if the final temperature will be above or below the boiling point.

   Step 3: Use the number line to write a number sentence, and solve.

   $$38.2 + \underline{\quad ^-51.6 \quad} + \underline{\quad 7.1 \quad} = \underline{\quad ^-6.3 \quad}$$

   So, the chemist should __increase__ **the temperature by** __6.3__ **degrees.**

2. A spotter plane took off from the airport and flew 35 miles east. It changed direction and flew 52 miles west. The pilot then followed radio instructions to fly another 17 miles west. He then turned and flew 40 miles east, when he was asked his position. How far, and in which direction, was the plane from the airport?

   Step 1: Choose a point to use as a benchmark of zero.

   The airport is a useful point to set as 0. Miles to the east will be positive and miles to the west will be negative.

   Step 2: Write and solve a number sentence showing the plane trip.

   $$35 + {}^-52 + \underline{\quad ^-17 \quad} + \underline{\quad 40 \quad} = \underline{\quad 6 \quad}$$

   THINK: The answer is a __positive__ number,
   so the direction is __east__.

   The plane was __6__ **miles to the** __east__ **of the airport.**

PRACTICE

Decide which point to use as a benchmark of 0 for each problem. Write a number sentence to show the problem. Then solve. If you need to, draw a diagram to help.

3. **Sam took the elevator up 15 floors, then down 24 floors, then back up 3 floors. How many floors, and in which direction, must he travel to get back to the floor where he started?**

$15 + {}^-24 + 3 = {}^-6$

Sam must travel 6 floors up.

4. **Minou was born 15 years after François, and François was born 54 years before Taylor. How old was Minou when Taylor was born?**

${}^-15 + 54 = 39$

Minou was 39 years old when Taylor was born.

5. **A beaker of carbon dioxide started at 8.1°C below its freezing point. After 30 minutes, the carbon dioxide was 54.9 degrees above its freezing point. How much did its temperature change?**

$54.9 - {}^-8.1 = 63$

The temperature increased by 63°C.

6. **On Tuesday, Carlos started from his mountainside campsite and climbed 1,829 yards to the top of the mountain. Then he descended 2,486 yards and set up a new camp. The following day, he descended another 1,975 yards. How far is he from his Tuesday campsite?**

$1,829 + {}^-2,486 + {}^-1,975 = {}^-2,632$

Carlos is 2,632 yards below his Tuesday campsite.

7. **Stefan took his morning walk $1\frac{1}{2}$ hours before arriving at work. One hour before that, he ate breakfast. If Stefan got on the bus 2 hours after breakfast, how much time did the bus ride take?**

${}^-1\frac{1}{2} + {}^-1 + 2 = \frac{{}^-1}{2}$

The bus ride took $\frac{1}{2}$ hour.

Choose the best answer for each problem. In the answer section at the bottom of the page, fill in the box of your choice.

1. Wednesday's low temperature was 32°F below its high temperature. Thursday's high temperature was 65°F, which was 18°F above Wednesday's high temperature. What was Wednesday's low temperature?

   Which number sentence could be used to solve this problem? C
   A 32 + 65 + 18 = 115
   B 65 + 18 + ⁻32 = 51
   C 65 + ⁻18 + ⁻32 = 15
   D 32 + ⁻18 + ⁻65 = ⁻51

2. Jamal was born 25 years after his father and 32 years before his son. How old was Jamal's son when Jamal's father was 72?

   Which number sentence could be used to solve this problem? K
   J ⁻32 + 25 + 72 = 65
   K −32 + ⁻25 + 72 = 15
   L 32 + ⁻25 + 72 = 79
   M 25 + ⁻32 + 72 + ⁻32 = 33

3. **After a jet reaches cruising altitude, it ascends 1,200 feet. Then it descends 1,750 feet, and a few minutes later, it descends another 500 feet. How far below cruising altitude is the jet?** B
   A 500 feet   C 3,450 feet
   B 1,050 feet   D Not given

4. **Anderson is 45 km south of Burnett, and Burnett is 72 km north of Camford. Detling is 10 km north of Camford. How many kilometers, and in which direction, would you travel from Detling to Anderson?** J
   J 17 km north   L 37 km north
   K 17 km south   M 107 km south

Write About It

5. **Write a problem that might be solved using a number line and a benchmark of zero. Then show the solution to the problem. Use the following U.S. history facts:**
   1640—first book printed
   1716—first theater opened
   1825—first steam locomotive

   | Sample answer: |
   | The first locomotive was built 185 |
   | years after the first book was printed |
   | in the U.S. The first book was |
   | printed 76 years before the first |
   | theater opened. How many years after |
   | the first theater opened was the first |
   | locomotive built? |
   | ⁻76 + 185 = 109 |
   | It was built 109 years afterward. |

1. A ☐ B ☐ C ☒ D ☐   3. A ☐ B ☒ C ☐ D ☐
2. J ☐ K ☒ L ☐ M ☐   4. J ☒ K ☐ L ☐ M ☐

● Adding and Subtracting Integers

Using Unit Rates

You can use a unit rate to help you solve problems.

Example 1

Mrs. Greenspan is traveling in Saudi Arabia. When she exchanges currency, she gets 3.75 riyals per dollar. At that exchange rate, how many riyals will she receive for $400?

A. Write a word proportion to show the problem.

$$\frac{3.75 \text{ riyals}}{1 \text{ dollar}} = \frac{\text{riyals she will receive}}{\$400}$$

> The unit rate, 3.75 riyals per dollar, means
> $$\frac{3.75 \text{ riyals}}{1 \text{ dollar}}.$$

B. Replace the words with numbers and a variable, and solve.

$$\frac{3.75}{1} = \frac{r}{400}$$

$$r = 3.75 \times 400$$

So, $r = 1,500$

Mrs. Greenspan will receive 1,500 riyals for $400.

You can use the same unit rate to find out how many dollars she will receive for each riyal.

Example 2

Before Mrs. Greenspan leaves Saudi Arabia, she wants to exchange her riyals for dollars. The exchange rate is still 3.75 riyals for 1 dollar. How many dollars will she receive for 312 riyals?

A. Find the unit rate in dollars per riyals.

$$\text{dollars per riyal} = \frac{1}{3.75}$$

$$\text{dollars per riyal} = 0.267$$

So, the unit rate = 0.267 dollars per riyal.

B. Multiply by the unit rate to solve.

$$312 \times 0.267 = 83.304$$

> Note that once you know the unit rate, you can solve the problem by multiplying the amount of riyals by the unit rate.

Mrs. Greenspan will receive $83.30 for 312 riyals.

1. Suppose you're traveling in Great Britain. You find a souvenir that costs 4.5 British pounds. If the exchange rate is 0.62 pounds per dollar, how much will the souvenir cost in dollars?

> **Step 1:** **Find the unit rate in dollars per pound. Round your answer to the nearest hundredth.**
>
> Dollars per pound $= \dfrac{1}{0.62}$
>
> Unit rate = ___1.61___ dollars per pound ← To make the numbers easier to work with, round the unit rate to the nearest hundredth.
>
> **Step 2:** **Multiply by the unit rate to solve.**
>
> $4.5 \times$ ___1.61___ $=$ ___7.245___
>
> **The souvenir costs $___7.25___ .** ← Remember to round your answer to the nearest penny when working with money.

2. While traveling in Canada, Jerome puts 25 liters of gas in his car. He knows that 1 liter = 1.0567 quarts, and that there are 4 quarts in 1 gallon. How can he figure out how many gallons of gas he bought?

> **Step 1:** **Write a word proportion to show the problem.**
>
> $$\frac{1 \text{ liter}}{1.0567 \text{ quarts}} = \frac{25}{\text{quarts of gas Jerome bought}}$$
>
> **Step 2:** **Replace the words with numbers and a variable, and solve.**
>
> $$\frac{1}{1.0567} = \frac{25}{q}$$
>
> $q = 25 \times 1.0567$
>
> So, $q =$ ___26.4175___ quarts
>
> **Step 3:** **Rename the quarts as gallons.**
>
> ***THINK:*** There are 4 quarts in 1 gallon. To convert quarts to gallons, I can *divide* by 4.
>
> ___26.4175___ quarts $\div 4 =$ ___6.604375___ gallons
>
> **Round your answer to the nearest tenth of a gallon.**
>
> **Jerome bought about** ___6.6___ **gallons of gas.**

PRACTICE

Use the unit rate to solve the problems.

3. The exchange rate for Canada is 1.5 Canadian dollars for 1 U.S. dollar.

   a. How many Canadian dollars will you receive for $350?

   > 525 Canadian dollars

   b. How many U.S. dollars will you receive for 1,050 Canadian dollars?

   > $700

4. In the American system, 1 liter is equivalent to 1.0567 quarts.

   a. About how many gallons is 32 liters of gas?

   > about 8.5 gallons

   b. To the nearest hundredth liter, how many liters is 10 gallons of gas?

   > 37.85 liters

5. The scale used by an architect to build models is 2 inches for each foot.

   a. The scale model stands 22 inches tall. How tall will the actual building be?

   > 11 ft

   b. A building is 50 feet high. How tall is its model?

   > 100 inches

6. The exchange rate for Mexico is 9.35 pesos for 1 dollar.

   a. If a souvenir costs 59 pesos, how many dollars does it cost? (Round your answer to the nearest penny.)

   > $6.31

   b. How many pesos will you receive for $68?

   > 635.8 pesos

7. In the American system, 1 kilometer is equivalent to 0.625 miles.

   a. Ms. Nunez drove 370 kilometers today. How many miles did she drive?

   > 231.25 miles

   b. Mr. Latham is planning a 700-mile trip through Europe. How many kilometers is that?

   > 1,120 kilometers

8. In the American system, 1 inch is equivalent to 2.54 centimeters.

   a. How many centimeters is 1 foot?

   > 30.48 centimeters

   b. How many meters is 5 ft? (1 meter = 100 centimeters)

   > 1.52 meters

● Solving Proportions

Choose the best answer for each problem. In the answer section at the bottom of the page, fill in the box of your choice.

1. In Tibet, Kendra bought a drum that is 18 inches across. Which expression shows how wide the drum is in centimeters?
(1 inch = 2.54 centimeters) B
   A $18 \times 2.54 = 47.72$
   B $18 \times 2.54 \times 0.01 = 0.4772$
   C $18 \times 2.54 \times 100 = 4,772$
   D $18 \div 2.54 = 7.0866141$

2. Before Rosemarie leaves France, she wants to exchange her francs for dollars. The exchange rate is 6.19 francs for 1 dollar. How many dollars will she receive for 180 francs? L
   J $6.00   L $29.08
   K $24.19   M $1,114.20

3. Duane drove 60 miles today. How many kilometers did he drive?
(1 mile = 1.6 kilometers) D
   A 37.5 miles
   B 90 miles
   C 37.5 kilometers
   D 96 kilometers

4. Marta bought 42 liters of gas. How many gallons was that?
(1 liter = 1.0567 quarts) K
   J 9.9 gallons   L 39.75 gallons
   K 11.1 gallons   M 44.38 gallons

5. Most European countries share a currency called the euro. The exchange rate is 0.94 euros for 1 dollar. If you buy a souvenir for 39 euros, how many dollars did you spend? B
   A $35.72   C $39.00
   B $36.66   D $41.49

6. The scale used by a theater designer to build models is 3 inches for each yard. A stage is 16 yards wide. How wide is the model? J
   J 48 inches   L 16 feet
   K 480 inches   M 5.3 yards

Write About It

Write a plan for solving the following problem. Then solve.

7. In Kenya, Marco bought a 6-meter length of handwoven cloth. About how long was the cloth in feet?
(1 foot = 30.48 centimeters)

Sample answer: Convert meters to
centimeters. Then use the unit
rate to find the length in feet.
6 m = 600 cm
Unit rate: $\frac{1}{30.48} = 0.0328$ ft/cm
$600 \times 0.0328 = 19.68$
The cloth was about 20 feet long.

1. A ☐ B ☒ C ☐ D ☐   4. J ☐ K ☒ L ☐ M ☐
2. J ☐ K ☐ L ☒ M ☐   5. A ☐ B ☒ C ☐ D ☐
3. A ☐ B ☐ C ☐ D ☒   6. J ☒ K ☐ L ☐ M ☐

● Solving Proportions

Calculating Unit Rates

Some rate problems are easier to solve if you calculate the unit rate first.

Example 1

Jacy's car will travel 341 miles on a full tank of gasoline. The tank holds $15\frac{1}{2}$ gallons. How far can the car travel on $6\frac{1}{2}$ gallons of gas? On $13\frac{1}{2}$ gallons of gas?

A. Find the unit rate in miles per gallon.

THINK: The calculation will be easier if I rename the fractions as decimals.

miles per gallon $= \dfrac{341}{15.5}$

unit rate $= 22$ miles per gallon

B. Multiply by the unit rate to solve.

$6.5 \times 22 = 143$

$13.5 \times 22 = 297$

Jacy's car can travel 143 miles on $6\frac{1}{2}$ gallons of gas. It can travel 297 miles on $13\frac{1}{2}$ gallons.

Example 2

Jacy paid \$8.58 for $6\frac{1}{2}$ gallons of gasoline. How much would he pay for $15\frac{1}{2}$ gallons? How many gallons could he buy for \$6.60?

Step 1: Find the unit rate in dollars per gallon.

dollars per gallon $= \dfrac{8.58}{6.5}$

unit rate $= \$1.32$ per gallon, or 1.32 dollars/gallon

Step 2: Use the unit rate to solve.

THINK: The unit rate is in dollars per gallon.
The first answer will be in dollars—*multiply* gallons by the unit rate.
The second answer will be in gallons—*divide* dollars by the unit rate.

15.5 gallons $\times$ 1.32 dollars/gallon = 20.46 dollars

6.60 dollars $\div$ 1.32 dollars/gallon = 5 gallons

Jacy would pay \$20.46 for $15\frac{1}{2}$ gallons. He could buy 5 gallons for \$6.60.

● Solving Proportions

1. Last week, Janet worked for 32 hours and earned $216. This week, she is going to work for 28 hours. How much will she earn?

   Step 1:   **Find the unit rate in dollars per hour.**

   $$\frac{\text{dollars}}{\text{hours}} = \frac{216}{32}$$

   So, dollars per hour = 6.75

   Step 2:   **Multiply by the unit rate to solve.**

   28 hours $\times$ 6.75 dollars/hour = ___189___ dollars

   So, Janet will earn $___189___ this week.

2. A grocery store sold a customer 24 pounds of apples for $14.40. A second customer bought $10\frac{1}{2}$ pounds of apples, and a third customer bought 3 pounds of apples. How much did the second customer pay? How much did the third customer pay?

   Step 1:   **Find the unit rate in dollars per pound.**

   $$\text{dollars per pound} = \frac{14.40}{24}$$

   unit rate = $___0.60___ per pound

   Step 2:   **Multiply by the unit rate to solve.**

   $10\frac{1}{2} \times$ ___0.60___ = ___6.30___

   $3 \times$ ___0.60___ = ___1.80___

   The second customer paid $___6.30___ and the third customer paid $___1.80___.

3. Kora heard the sound of thunder 12 seconds after she saw the lightning flash. The lightning was 2.4 miles away. The next flash of lightning was 0.8 miles away. After she saw the the flash, how long did it take the sound to reach Kora?

   Step 1:   **Find the unit rate in miles per second.**

   $$\frac{\text{miles}}{\text{seconds}} = \frac{2.4}{12}$$

   So, miles per second = 0.2

   Step 2:   **Use the unit rate to solve.**

   THINK: The answer will be in seconds—I must divide by the unit rate.

   0.8 miles $\div$ 0.2 miles/sec = ___4___ seconds

   So, the sound took ___4___ seconds to reach Kora.

Find the unit rate and solve.

4. Chane paid $11.60 for 8 gallons of gasoline. It takes 10 gallons to fill his car's tank. How much would it cost to fill the tank?

Unit rate: $1.45 per gallon

It would cost $14.50.

5. Chane can drive his car 265 miles on a full tank of gas. How many miles could he drive on 6 gallons?

Unit rate: 26.5 miles per gallon

He could drive 159 miles.

6. When Ralph visited Japan, one U.S. dollar was worth 102 Japanese yen. How many dollars would a souvenir priced at 3,825 yen cost?

Unit rate: 102 yen per dollar,

or $\frac{1}{102}$ dollars per yen

It would cost $37.50.

7. On Wednesday, Carly got paid $20 for picking 25 pounds of blueberries. On Thursday, she got paid $24 for picking blueberries. How many pounds did she pick on Thursday?

Unit rate: 0.80 dollars/pound

She picked 30 pounds.

8. It took a machine in a factory $2\frac{1}{2}$ hours to cap 350 bottles. How many bottles could the machine cap in an 8-hour day?

Unit rate: 140 bottles per hour

It could cap 1,120 bottles.

9. Rosa bought 7.2 kilograms of rice, and spent $32. How many kilograms of rice could she buy for $12?

Unit rate: 0.225 kilos per dollar

She could buy 2.7 kilos.

10. A printer ships copies of a new book to various bookstores. A package of 14 books weighs 21 pounds. A second package weighs 27 pounds. How many books are in the second package?

Unit rate: 1.5 pounds/book

There are 18 books in the package.

11. Geraldo spent $17.00 on gasoline when he made a 306-mile trip in his car. How much could he expect to spend on gas for a trip of 360 miles?

Unit rate: 18 miles per dollar

He could expect to spend $20.00.

● Solving Proportions

Choose the best answer for each problem. In the answer section at the bottom of the page, fill in the box of your choice.

1. A river flows 5 miles in 36 minutes. Which expression shows how many minutes it will take the river to flow 20 miles? D

   A $5 \times \frac{36}{20}$

   B $5 \times 36 \times 20$

   C $36 \times \frac{20}{5}$

   D $20 \times \frac{36}{5}$

2. Nicole paid $9.38 for 7 gallons of diesel fuel. What is the unit rate in dollars per gallon? K

   J 0.75 gallons per dollar

   K $1.34 per gallon

   L $9.38 per gallon

   M $13.40 per gallon

3. Nat earns $273 for working a 35-hour week. How much money would he earn for a week in which he only worked 31 hours? B

   A $101.40   C $304.00

   B $241.80   D $308.23

4. A team of bricklayers takes 48 minutes to increase the height of a wall by 0.8 meters. By how many meters could they increase the height of the wall in 1 hour? K

   J 0.64 m   L 5 m

   K 1 m   M Not given

5. The Goopy-Soup labeling machine puts labels on 64 soup cans every 4 minutes. How many cans does the machine label per hour? C

   A 4 cans   C 960 cans

   B 640 cans   D 15,360 cans

Write About It

Write a plan for solving the following problem. Then solve.

6. A writer takes a 14-page story to a copy center. It costs $0.84 to make one copy of the entire story. At that rate, how much will it cost to copy a 305-page novel?

   Sample answer:

   Find the unit rate in dollars per

   page. Multiply the unit rate by

   the number of pages in the novel.

   Unit rate: $\frac{0.84}{14}$ = $0.06 per page

   $0.06 \times 305 = 18.30$

   It will cost $18.30.

1. A ☐ B ☐ C ☐ D ☒

2. J ☐ K ☒ L ☐ M ☐

3. A ☐ B ☒ C ☐ D ☐

4. J ☐ K ☒ L ☐ M ☐

5. A ☐ B ☐ C ☒ D ☐

● Solving Proportions

Renaming Measures That Are Rates

You can rename one rate as another, equivalent rate.

Example 1

Anne is driving 45 miles per hour. How fast is she traveling per minute?

Step 1: **Decide what conversion you need to rename the measure.**

1 hour = 60 minutes

Step 2: **Write the conversion as a rate.**

$$\frac{1\ h}{60\ min} \quad \text{or} \quad \frac{60\ min}{1\ h}$$

THINK: Since 1 h = 60 min, each rate is the same as 1.

Step 3: **Multiply by the rate to solve.**

You want to find miles/minute, so use the form of the rate that has minutes in the denominator.

this is the same as 45 miles per hour

$$\frac{45\ mi}{1\ h} \times \frac{1\ h}{60\ min}$$

Cancel like units to check that the rate is correct.

$$\frac{45\ mi}{1\ \cancel{h}} \times \frac{1\ \cancel{h}}{60\ min} \rightarrow 0.75\ mi/min$$

Anne is traveling 0.75 miles per minute.

Example 2

How many feet per second is a rate of 15 miles per hour?

Step 1: **Decide what conversions you need.**

1 mi = 5,280 ft   1 h = 60 min   1 min = 60 sec

Step 2: **Write the conversions as rates.**

THINK: You want to find feet/seconds, so you'll need to use rates with feet in the numerator and seconds in the denominator.

$$\frac{5,280\ ft}{1\ mi} \qquad \frac{1\ h}{60\ min} \qquad \frac{1\ min}{60\ sec}$$

Step 3: **Multiply by the rates to solve, canceling like units.**

$$\frac{15\ \cancel{mi}}{1\ \cancel{h}} \times \frac{5,280\ ft}{1\ \cancel{mi}} \times \frac{1\ \cancel{h}}{60\ \cancel{min}} \times \frac{1\ \cancel{min}}{60\ sec} \rightarrow \underline{\quad 22 \quad}\ ft/sec$$

So, 15 miles per hour is $\underline{\quad 22 \quad}$ **feet per second.**

● Multiplying Rates

GUIDED PRACTICE

1. Light travels at a speed of about 186,000 miles per second. What is the speed of light in miles per hour?

   Step 1: **Decide what conversions you need.**

   1 min = ___60___ sec   1 h = ___60___ min

   Step 2: **Write the conversions as rates.**

   THINK: You want to find miles/hour, so you'll need to use a rate with hours in the denominator.

   $$\frac{60 \text{ sec}}{1 \text{ min}} \qquad \frac{60 \text{ min}}{1 \text{ h}}$$

   Step 3: **Multiply by the rates to solve, canceling like units.**

   $$\frac{186,000 \text{ mi}}{1 \text{ sec}} \times \frac{60 \text{ sec}}{1 \text{ min}} \times \frac{60 \text{ min}}{1 \text{ h}} \longrightarrow \underline{\quad 669,600,000 \quad} \text{ mi/h}$$

   Light travels at a speed of ___669,600,000___ miles per hour.

2. The grocery store sells cashews for $4.48 a pound. What is the price of cashews per ounce?

   Step 1: **Decide what conversion you need.**

   1 lb = ___16___ oz

   Step 2: **Write the conversion as a rate.**

   THINK: You want to find dollars/ounce, so you'll need to use the rate with ounces in the denominator.

   $$\frac{1 \text{ lb}}{16 \text{ oz}}$$

   Step 3: **Multiply by the rate to solve, canceling like units.**

   $$\frac{4.48 \text{ dollars}}{1 \text{ lb}} \times \frac{1 \text{ lb}}{16 \text{ oz}} \longrightarrow \$ \underline{\quad 0.28 \quad} / \text{oz}$$

   The price of cashews is $___0.28___ per ounce.

PRACTICE

Solve, renaming as an equivalent rate. Show your work.

3. **Mr. Castillo is driving at 36 miles per hour. How fast is the car traveling in feet per second?**

$$\frac{36 \text{ mi}}{1 \text{ h}} \times \frac{5{,}280 \text{ ft}}{1 \text{ mi}} \times \frac{1 \text{ h}}{60 \text{ min}} \times \frac{1 \text{ min}}{60 \text{ sec}} = 52.8 \text{ ft/sec}$$

4. **The speed of sound traveling through air is about 1,088 feet per second. What is the speed of sound, to the nearest mile, in miles per hour?**

$$\frac{1{,}088 \text{ ft}}{1 \text{ sec}} \times \frac{1 \text{ mi}}{5{,}280 \text{ ft}} \times \frac{60 \text{ sec}}{1 \text{ min}} \times \frac{60 \text{ min}}{1 \text{ h}} = 742 \text{ mi/h}$$

5. **Each foot length of copper pipe weighs $1\frac{1}{2}$ pounds. What is the weight of copper pipe in ounces per inch?**

$$\frac{1.5 \text{ lb}}{1 \text{ ft}} \times \frac{1 \text{ ft}}{12 \text{ in.}} \times \frac{16 \text{ oz}}{1 \text{ lb}} = 2 \text{ oz/in.}$$

6. **The grocery store sells peanuts for $3.52 a pound. How much do the peanuts cost per ounce?**

$$\frac{\$3.52}{1 \text{ lb}} \times \frac{1 \text{ lb}}{16 \text{ oz}} = \$0.22/\text{oz}$$

7. **The food co-op sells tea for $0.25 an oz. How much does the tea cost per pound?**

$$\frac{\$0.25}{1 \text{ oz}} \times \frac{16 \text{ oz}}{1 \text{ lb}} = \$4.00/\text{lb}$$

8. **Gasoline costs $1.45 a gallon. How much, to the nearest penny, does gasoline cost per fluid ounce?**
(1 gallon = 4 quarts; 1 quart = 32 fluid ounces)

$$\frac{1.45}{1 \text{ gal}} \times \frac{1 \text{ gal}}{4 \text{ qt}} \times \frac{1 \text{ qt}}{32 \text{ fl. oz}} = \$0.01/\text{fl. oz}$$

9. **The first liquid-fuel rocket, launched by Robert Goddard in 1926, traveled 96 kilometers per hour. How many meters per minute did it travel?**

$$\frac{96 \text{ km}}{1 \text{ h}} \times \frac{1{,}000 \text{ m}}{1 \text{ km}} \times \frac{1 \text{ h}}{60 \text{ min}} = 1{,}600 \text{ m/min}$$

10. **Tandy earns $15 an hour. How much money does she earn per minute?**

$$\frac{\$15.00}{1 \text{ h}} \times \frac{1 \text{ h}}{60 \text{ min}} = \$0.25/\text{min}$$

Choose the best answer for each problem. In the answer section at the bottom of the page, fill in the box of your choice.

1. Mr. Pollard can type 55 words per minute. Which of the following expressions could you use to find his typing speed in words per second? A

   A $\dfrac{55 \text{ words}}{1 \text{ min}} \times \dfrac{1 \text{ min}}{60 \text{ sec}}$

   B $\dfrac{55 \text{ words}}{1 \text{ min}} \times \dfrac{60 \text{ sec}}{1 \text{ min}}$

   C $\dfrac{1 \text{ min}}{55 \text{ words}} \times \dfrac{60 \text{ sec}}{1 \text{ min}}$

   D $\dfrac{1 \text{ min}}{55 \text{ words}} \times \dfrac{1 \text{ min}}{60 \text{ sec}}$

2. Miriam is bicycling at a rate of 10 miles per hour. How many feet per minute is she traveling? (1 mile = 5,280 feet) L

   J 1.467 ft/min   L 880 ft/min
   K 14.67 ft/sec   M 52,800 ft/h

3. Water weighs 8.33 pounds per gallon. How much does it weigh in ounces per pint? B

   A 4.165 oz/pt   C 133.28 oz/pt
   B 16.66 oz/pt   D 1,066.24 oz/pt

4. Fishburn and Wottledink handmade soaps sell for $0.75 an ounce. What do they cost per pound? M

   J $0.05/lb   L $7.50/lb
   K $0.75/lb   M $12.00/lb

5. The space shuttle orbits Earth at a speed of 30,000 kilometers per hour. What is its speed in kilometers per second? A

   A 8.33 km/sec   C 44,000 km/sec
   B 500 km/sec   D 1,800,000 km/sec

6. In 1997, the world speed record on land was set at just over 763 miles per hour. How many miles per second is that record? J

   J 0.21 mi/sec   L 45,780 mi/sec
   K 12.72 mi/sec   M Not given

Write About It

Write a plan for solving the following problem. Then solve.

7. The Green Grocery Store has grapes for $1.92 a pound. The Blue Grocery Store has grapes for $0.10 an ounce. Which is the better deal?

   Sample answer:

   Change the Green Grocery's price of

   dollars per pound to dollars per

   ounce and compare the answer to

   the Blue Grocery's price.

   $\dfrac{\$1.92}{1 \text{ lb}} \times \dfrac{1 \text{ lb}}{16 \text{ oz}} = \$0.12$

   $0.12 > $0.10, so the Blue Grocery

   Store has the better deal.

1. A ☒ B ☐ C ☐ D ☐   4. J ☐ K ☐ L ☐ M ☒
2. J ☐ K ☐ L ☒ M ☐   5. A ☒ B ☐ C ☐ D ☐
3. A ☐ B ☒ C ☐ D ☐   6. J ☒ K ☐ L ☐ M ☐

Test-Taking Skill: **Try Out Choices**

Sometimes it is difficult to find the correct answer to a multiple-choice question. Trying out the answer choices can help you.

Example

If two of the numbers shown below are switched with each other, each of the three equations will have the same answer. Which two numbers should be switched?

$$72 \div 6 = \square$$

$$54 \div 9 = \square$$

$$36 \div 12 = \square$$

A 72 and 54   **C** 9 and 12
B 6 and 12   **D** 54 and 36

Step 1: Read the question again. Then try Choice A. Switch 72 and 54.

$$54 \div 6 = 9$$

$$72 \div 9 = 8$$

$$36 \div 12 = 3$$

THINK: The three equations do not equal the same number.

Choice A is *not* the correct choice.

Step 2: Try Choice B. Switch 6 and 12.

$$72 \div 12 = 6$$

$$54 \div 9 = 6$$

$$36 \div 6 = 6$$

THINK: All the equations equal the same number, 6.
I don't need to try any other choices.

Choice B is the correct choice.

Choose the best answer for each problem. In the answer section at the bottom of this page, fill in the box of your choice.

1. **Which two numbers below should be switched so that all the equations have the same answer?** C

    $3 \times 12 = ❑$

    $10 \times 6 = ❑$

    $5 \times 20 = ❑$

    A 3 and 10   **C** 3 and 5

    B 12 and 6   **D** 6 and 20

2. **What is the missing number in the set {60, 63, 59, ?} if the set has a mean (average) of 62?** L

    J 60   **L** 66

    K 62   **M** 68

3. **Which number must be changed to its opposite (a negative number) in order to make the equation correct?** C

    $(7 \times 2) + 3 = 11$

    A 7   **C** 3

    B 2   **D** 11

4. **Which set of five numbers has a mean (average) of 10?** J

    J 2, 12, 10, 20, 6

    L 6, 17, 20, 25, 18

    K 5, 8, 11, 9, 10

    M 8, 9, 15, 11, 19

5. **Which two numbers below should be switched so that all the equations have the same answer?** B

    $39 \div 6 = ❑$

    $78 \div 3 = ❑$

    $52 \div 4 = ❑$

    A 39 and 4   **C** 78 and 52

    B 6 and 3   **D** 3 and 4

6. **Which two numbers below can be switched so that the fractions are equivalent fractions?** J

    $$\frac{16}{3} = \frac{2}{24}$$

    J 16 and 2   **L** 3 and 2

    K 16 and 3   **M** 2 and 24

7. **Which numbers could you switch so that each inequality could be correct for x?** B

    $72 > x$ $x < 36$

    $54 < x$ $x > 49$

    A 72 and 36   **C** 72 and 54

    B 36 and 54   **D** 54 and 49

8. **Which three numbers have a sum of 6.2?** M

    J $1.2 + 3.0 + 3.0$

    K $2.1 + 1.3 + 3.1$

    L $0.8 + 1.2 + 3.2$

    M $1.0 + 3.1 + 2.1$

1. A ☐ B ☐ C ☒ D ☐   5. A ☐ B ☒ C ☐ D ☐

2. J ☐ K ☐ L ☒ M ☐   6. J ☒ K ☐ L ☐ M ☐

3. A ☐ B ☐ C ☒ D ☐   7. A ☐ B ☒ C ☐ D ☐

4. J ☒ K ☐ L ☐ M ☐   8. J ☐ K ☐ L ☐ M ☒

Using Rates to Write Measures in a Different System

In some problems, you'll have to convert between customary and metric units. You can use rates to help you solve these problems.

CUSTOMARY–METRIC CONVERSIONS

1 inch (in.) = 2.54 centimeters (cm)	1 ounce (oz) = 28.35 grams (g)
1 mile (mi) = 1.6 kilometers (km)	1 pound (lb) = 0.45 kilograms (kg)

Example 1

A jeweler needs a 5-inch length of chain. The chain is sold by the centimeter. How many centimeters of chain does the jeweler need?

A. Use the chart to find the conversion you need.

1 inch (in.) = 2.54 centimeters (cm)

B. Write the conversion as a rate.

The rate can be written in two ways:

$$\frac{2.54 \text{ cm}}{1 \text{ in.}} \quad \text{or} \quad \frac{1 \text{ in.}}{2.54 \text{ cm}}$$

THINK: Since 1 in. = 2.54 cm, each rate is the same as 1.

C. Multiply by the rate to solve the problem.

Use the rate in which the numerator is given in the units you want.

$$5 \text{ in.} \times \frac{2.54 \text{ cm}}{1 \text{ in.}} = 12.7 \text{ cm}$$

The jeweler needs 12.7 cm of chain.

> Cancel similar units on the top and bottom of the expression to make sure that you are using the correct form of the rate.

Example 2

Maureen is going to run an 8-kilometer race. How many miles will she run?

Step 1: Find the conversion you need.

1 mile (mi) = 1.6 kilometers (km)

Step 2: Write the conversion as a rate.

$$\frac{1.6 \text{ km}}{1 \text{ mi}} \quad \text{or} \quad \frac{1 \text{ mi}}{1.6 \text{ km}}$$

THINK: I'll need the rate that has *miles* in the numerator.

Step 3: Multiply by the rate to solve the problem.

$$8 \text{ km} \times \frac{1 \text{ mi}}{1.6 \text{ km}} = \underline{\quad 5 \quad} \text{ mi}$$

Maureen will run __5__ miles.

1. An apple weighs 4 ounces. What is its weight in grams?

  a. **Write the conversion you need.**

    1 ounce = __28.35__ grams

  b. **Rewrite as a rate with the correct numerator.**

$$\frac{28.35}{1} \frac{g}{oz}$$

  c. **Multiply to solve the problem.**

$$4 \ \cancel{oz} \times \frac{28.35}{1} \frac{g}{\cancel{oz}} = \underline{113.4} \ g$$

  The apple weighs __113.4__ grams.

2. Pat needs 18 pounds of plaster to make a mold of a statue. If the plaster is sold in kilograms, how much should he buy?

  a. **Write the conversion as a rate with the correct numerator.**

$$\frac{0.45 \ kg}{1 \ lb}$$

  b. **Multiply to find the weight in kilograms.**

$$18 \ \cancel{lb} \times \frac{0.45 \ kg}{1 \ \cancel{lb}} = \underline{8.1} \ kg$$

  Pat should buy __8.1__ kilograms of plaster.

3. A sign on a highway in France states that the distance to Paris is 56 kilometers. How many miles is the sign from Paris?

  a. **Write the conversion as a rate with the correct numerator.**

$$\frac{1 \ mi}{1.6 \ km}$$

  b. **Multiply to find the distance in miles.**

$$56 \ km \times \frac{1 \ mi}{1.6 \ km} = \underline{35} \ mi$$

  The sign is __35__ miles from Paris.

PRACTICE

Decide which conversion to use. Rewrite the conversion as a rate. Then solve.
Round any decimal answers to the nearest hundredth.

4. **A car's gas tank holds 15 gallons. What is its capacity in liters?**

    a. Write the conversion you need.

    I gallon = 3.78 liters

    b. Rewrite the conversion as a rate.

    3.78 L
    ──────
    I gal

    c. Solve.

    The tank's capacity is 56.7 liters.

CUSTOMARY–METRIC CONVERSIONS

1 inch (in.) = 2.54 centimeters (cm)
1 mile (mi) = 1.6 kilometers (km)
1 ounce (oz) = 28.35 grams (g)
1 pound (lb) = 0.45 kilograms (kg)
1 gallon (gal) = 3.78 liters (L)

5. **A plant grows 28 centimeters per year. What is its growth in inches per year?**

    11.02 inches per year

6. **Paul ran a 26-mile marathon race and a 40-kilometer race. Which race was longer?**

    the 26-mile race

7. **The speed of light is 186,000 miles per second. What is the speed of light in kilometers per second?**

    297,600 km per sec

8. **A delivery service has a weight limit of 50 lb. Will the company deliver a package weighing 22 kg?**

    yes

9. **How many liters of water could a 55-gallon drum contain?**

    207.9 liters

10. **How many ounces of pepper are there in a 150-gram package?**

    5.29 oz

11. **How many centimeters are there in a foot?**

    30.48 cm

12. **How many miles will a racer drive in a 1,000-kilometer car race?**

    625 miles

● Multiplying Decimals

TEST-TAKING PRACTICE

Choose the best answer for each problem. In the answer section at the bottom of the page, fill in the box of your choice.

CUSTOMARY–METRIC CONVERSIONS

1 inch (in.) = 2.54 centimeters (cm)	1 ounce (oz) = 28.35 grams (g)
1 mile (mi) = 1.6 kilometers (km)	1 pound (lb) = 0.45 kilograms (kg)
1 gallon (gal) = 3.78 liters (L)	

1. **While traveling in France, Leandra bought 20 liters of gasoline. How many gallons did she buy?**

   Which expression could you use to solve the problem? A

   A $20 \text{ liters} \times \dfrac{1 \text{ gallon}}{3.78 \text{ liters}}$

   B $20 \text{ liters} \times \dfrac{3.78 \text{ liters}}{1 \text{ gallon}}$

   C $20 \text{ liters} \div \dfrac{1 \text{ gallon}}{3.78 \text{ liters}}$

   D $1 \text{ gallon} \times \dfrac{3.78 \text{ liters}}{20 \text{ liters}}$

2. **The weight limit on an elevator is 360 kilograms. How many pounds can the elevator carry?** M

   J 162 lb   **L** 720 lb
   K 360 lb   **M** 800 lb

3. **The speed limit is 55 miles per hour. What is the speed limit in kilometers per hour?** C

   A 34.375 km/h   **C** 88 km/h
   B 56.6 km/h   **D** 139.7 km/h

4. **How many ounces of rice are there in a 500-gram package?** J

   J 17.64 oz   **L** 14,175 oz
   K 225 oz   **M** Not given

5. **A meter rule is 100 cm long. How many inches long is the rule?** B

   A 25.4 in.   **C** 254 cm
   B 39.37 in.   **D** 650 cm

6. **How many kilograms can you mail if the weight limit for a package is 60 pounds?** K

   J 22.2 kg   **L** 60 kg
   K 27 kg   **M** 133.3 kg

Write About It
Write a plan for solving the following problem. Then solve.

7. **In a European country, a liter of gasoline costs $0.95. How much does the gas cost per gallon?**

   Use the conversion 1 gallon = 3.78

   liters.

   Multiply the price by the conversion

   rate.

   $0.95 \times \dfrac{3.78}{gal} = 3.59$

   The gas costs $3.59 per gallon.

---

1. A ☒ B ☐ C ☐ D ☐		4. J ☒ K ☐ L ☐ M ☐	
2. J ☐ K ☐ L ☐ M ☒		5. A ☐ B ☒ C ☐ D ☐	
3. A ☐ B ☐ C ☒ D ☐		6. J ☐ K ☒ L ☐ M ☐	

© 2000 Metropolitan Teaching and Learning Company

● Multiplying Decimals

Using Proportions to Solve Scale Models

You can use a word proportion to solve problems that involve similar figures such as scale models.

Example 1

A scale model of the Empire State Building was built for a movie set. The model stands 50 feet tall. If the scale used to build the model is 1:25, how tall is the actual building?

> A scale gives the ratio of the size of a model to the size of the object it represents. A scale of 1:25 means that 1 unit on the model represents 25 units on the actual object.

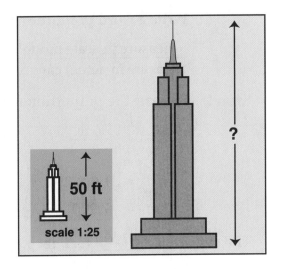

50 ft

scale 1:25

A. Write a word proportion to show the problem.

$$\frac{\text{measure in scale model}}{\text{measure in actual building}} = \frac{\text{height of scale model}}{\text{height of Empire State Building}}$$

B. Rewrite the proportion using numbers from the problem, and solve.

$$\frac{1}{25} = \frac{50}{h}$$

$1 \times h = 25 \times 50$, so $h = 1{,}250$

THINK: The units of h, the height of the building, will be the same as the units of the scale model—feet.

The Empire State Building is 1,250 feet tall.

Example 2

On an architect's drawing, a parking lot is 10 inches long. The real parking lot is 200 feet long. The same drawing shows the parking lot's width as 8 inches. What is its actual width?

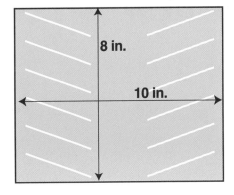

8 in.

10 in.

A. Write a word proportion to show the problem.

$$\frac{\text{length in scale drawing}}{\text{length of parking lot}} = \frac{\text{width in scale drawing}}{\text{width of parking lot}}$$

B. Rewrite the proportion using numbers from the problem, and solve.

$$\frac{10 \text{ in.}}{200 \text{ ft}} = \frac{8 \text{ in.}}{w}$$

$10 \times w = 200 \times 8$, so $w = \boxed{160}$

THINK: The units of w, the width of the lot, will be feet so that the sides of the proportion match.

● Ratios

1. The deepest gorge in the United States is found on the Snake River along the Oregon/Idaho border. On a model built to a scale of 1 inch : 250 feet, the canyon is 31.6 inches deep. How deep is the actual canyon?

   Step 1: **Write a word proportion to show the problem.**

   $$\frac{\text{measure in scale model}}{\text{measure in actual canyon}} = \frac{\text{depth of scale model}}{\text{depth of canyon}}$$

   Step 2: **Rewrite the proportion using numbers from the problem, and solve.**

   $$\frac{1 \text{ in.}}{250 \text{ ft}} = \frac{31.6 \text{ in.}}{d}$$

   $$1 \times d = 31.6 \times 250$$

   $$d = \boxed{7,900}$$

   THINK: The units of d, the depth of the canyon, will be feet so that the sides of the proportion match.

   The canyon is __7,900__ feet deep.

2. In a photograph of a man standing next to a flagpole, the man is 3 inches tall and the flagpole is 9 inches tall. If the man is actually 6 feet tall, how tall is the flagpole?

   a. **Circle the proportion you could use to solve the problem.**

   $$\frac{\text{height of man in photo}}{\text{height of flagpole in photo}} = \frac{\text{actual height of flagpole}}{\text{actual height of man}}$$

   $$\boxed{\frac{\text{height of man in photo}}{\text{actual height of man}} = \frac{\text{height of flagpole in photo}}{\text{actual height of flagpole}}}$$

   b. **Rewrite the proportion using numbers from the problem, and solve.**

   $$\frac{3 \text{ in.}}{6 \text{ ft}} = \frac{9 \text{ in.}}{h}$$

   $$h \times \boxed{3} = \boxed{6} \times \boxed{9} \text{, so } h = \boxed{18}$$

   The flagpole is __18__ feet tall.

3. A scale model of a car is 2 feet long. The actual car is 12 feet long. What is the scale of the model?

   Write and solve a proportion showing the problem.

   $$\frac{\text{measure in scale model}}{\text{measure in actual car}} = \frac{\text{length of scale model}}{\text{length of car}} = \frac{2 \text{ ft}}{12 \text{ ft}} = \frac{1}{6}$$

   The scale of the model is __1__ : __6__ .

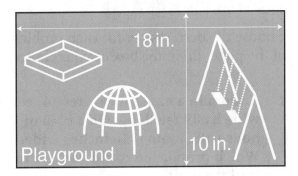

18 in.

10 in.

Playground

4. On a blueprint of a new playground, the playground is 18 inches long and 10 inches wide. The actual playground will be 90 feet long. How wide will it be?

a. Write a word proportion to show the problem.

$$\frac{\text{length in blueprint}}{\text{actual length}} = \frac{\text{width in blueprint}}{\text{actual width}}$$

b. Rewrite the proportion with numbers from the problem, and solve.

$$\frac{18}{90} = \frac{10}{w}; \quad w = 50$$

The playground will be __50 ft__ wide.

Write a proportion and solve.

5. A scale model of a bridge in a train set is $1\frac{1}{4}$ feet long. If the scale used to build the bridge is 1:60, how long is the actual bridge?

$$\frac{1}{60} = \frac{1.25}{l}$$

The bridge is 75 feet long.

6. A planned hotel will be 140 feet tall and 105 feet wide. A scale model of the hotel is 2 feet high. How wide is the model?

$$\frac{2}{140} = \frac{w}{105}$$

The model is 1.5 ft wide.

7. A reproduction of a painting is 8 inches wide. The actual painting is 6 feet wide and 9 feet high. What is the height of the reproduction?

$$\frac{8}{6} = \frac{h}{9}$$

The reproduction is 12 inches high.

8. On a model ship, 1 centimeter represents 2.5 meters. How tall is the mast of the ship if the mast on the model is 6 cm tall?

$$\frac{1}{2.5} = \frac{6}{t}$$

The mast is 15 meters tall.

9. On a map, the distance between two towns is 5 inches. The actual distance is 45 miles. What is the scale of the map?

$$\frac{1 \text{ in.}}{s \text{ mi}} = \frac{5}{45}$$

The scale is 1 in.:9 mi.

10. A statue of Gertie's brother is $3\frac{1}{2}$ feet tall. If the statue is built to a scale of 1:1.5, how tall is Gertie's brother in real life?

$$\frac{1}{1.5} = \frac{3.5}{t}$$

Gertie's brother is $5\frac{1}{4}$ feet tall.

● Ratios

Choose the best answer for each problem. In the answer section at the bottom of the page, fill in the box of your choice.

1. A room in a house measures 14 feet wide by 19 feet long. On a plan of the house, the room is 10 inches wide. Which proportion could you use to find the width of the room on the plan? C

A $\dfrac{\text{width on plan}}{\text{actual length}} = \dfrac{\text{actual width}}{\text{length on plan}}$

B $\dfrac{\text{width on plan}}{\text{length on plan}} = \dfrac{\text{actual length}}{\text{actual width}}$

C $\dfrac{\text{width on plan}}{\text{actual width}} = \dfrac{\text{width on plan}}{\text{actual length}}$

D $\dfrac{\text{actual width}}{\text{actual length}} = \dfrac{\text{length on plan}}{\text{width on plan}}$

2. A model train is 9 inches long and 2 inches wide. The actual train is 27 feet long. Which proportion could you use to find the actual width of the train? J

J $\dfrac{9}{27} = \dfrac{2}{w}$ L $\dfrac{2}{27} = \dfrac{9}{w}$

K $\dfrac{2}{9} = \dfrac{27}{w}$ M $\dfrac{9}{27} = \dfrac{w}{2}$

3. A scale model of a house is 6 inches tall. The scale used to build the house was 1:60. Which proportion could you use to find the actual height of the house? D

A $\dfrac{1}{60} = \dfrac{h}{6}$ C $\dfrac{1}{6} = \dfrac{h}{60}$

B $\dfrac{1}{h} = \dfrac{60}{6}$ D $\dfrac{1}{60} = \dfrac{6}{h}$

4. In a photo of a man in a doorway, the man is 3 inches tall and the doorway is 4 inches tall. If the man is really 6 feet tall, how tall is the doorway?
J 2 ft   L 8 ft   L
K $4\tfrac{1}{2}$ ft   M 10 ft

Write About It

5. An architect builds a model of a building that is 60 ft high, 20 ft wide, and 30 ft long. The model is 15 in. high. What is the scale of the model? Use the scale to find the width and length of the model. Sample answer given.

To find the scale, write and solve a

ratio comparing the tower's

actual height to the model's height:

$\dfrac{15 \text{ in.}}{60 \text{ ft}}$ → 1 in. : 4 ft

Use the scale to write proportions to

find the model's other dimensions.

Width: $\dfrac{1}{4} = \dfrac{w}{20}$; $w = 5$

Length: $\dfrac{1}{4} = \dfrac{l}{30}$; $l = 7.5$

The width of the model is 5 in.

The length of the model is 7.5 in.

1. A ☐ B ☐ C ☒ D ☐   3. A ☐ B ☐ C ☐ D ☒

2. J ☒ K ☐ L ☐ M ☐   4. J ☐ K ☐ L ☒ M ☐

● Ratios

Writing Word Proportions for Similar Figures

Some problems involve figures whose similarity isn't immediately obvious. You can use word proportions to solve these problems.

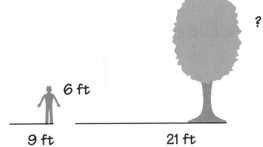

Example

Hugh is 6 feet tall. He casts a shadow that is 9 feet long. At the same time, the tree that Hugh is standing next to casts a shadow that is 21 feet long. How tall is the tree?

Step 1: **Draw triangles to show the information given.**

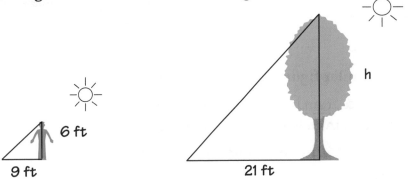

THINK: The sunlight hits the tree and the person at the same angle.
The tree and the person both form right angles with the ground.
The triangles have two congruent angles, so they must be similar.

Step 2: **Write a word proportion for the similar figures.**

$$\frac{\text{height of person}}{\text{height of tree}} = \frac{\text{length of person's shadow}}{\text{length of tree's shadow}}$$

Step 3: **Rewrite the proportion with numbers, and solve.**

$$\frac{6}{h} = \frac{9}{21}$$

$$6 \times 21 = 9 \times h$$

$$126 = 9 \times h$$

$$\underline{\quad 14 \quad} = h$$

So, the tree is $\underline{\quad 14 \quad}$ feet tall.

GUIDED PRACTICE

1. A rope attached to the top of a flagpole is fastened to the ground with a hook 16 feet from the base of the pole. At a point 4 feet from the hook, the height from the ground to the rope is 11 feet. What is the height of the flagpole?

    a. Draw a diagram showing the information.

    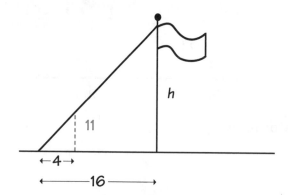

    > The two triangles share a common angle where the rope meets the ground. Each vertical side makes a right angle with the ground. So, the two triangles are similar.

    b. If there are similar figures, write a word proportion.

    $$\frac{\text{shorter distance from hook}}{\text{longer distance from hook}} = \frac{\text{shorter height}}{\text{longer height}}$$

    c. Rewrite the proportion with numbers, and solve.

    $$\frac{4}{16} = \frac{11}{h}$$

    $4 \times h = \underline{} \times \underline{}$, so $h = \underline{}$

    ($4 \times h = \underline{11} \times \underline{16}$, so $h = \underline{44}$)

    The height of the flagpole is __44__ feet.

2. A child standing next to his mother casts a 3-foot shadow. His mother casts a $3\frac{3}{4}$-foot shadow. If the child is 4 feet tall, how tall is his mother?

    a. Circle the proportion you could use to solve the problem.

    $$\boxed{\frac{\text{height of mother}}{\text{height of child}} = \frac{\text{length of mother's shadow}}{\text{length of child's shadow}}}$$

    $$\frac{\text{height of mother}}{\text{height of child}} = \frac{\text{length of child's shadow}}{\text{length of mother's shadow}}$$

    b. Solve, letting h stand for the mother's height.

    $$\frac{h}{4} = \frac{3\frac{3}{4}}{3}$$

    $h \times \underline{3} = \underline{3\frac{3}{4}} \times \underline{4}$

    $h = \underline{5}$

    The mother is __5__ feet tall.

3. An archaeologist wants to know the height above ground level of a pyramid. He measures the length along one face as 40 meters from the base to the peak. A point 15 m from the base is 12 m above ground level. What is the height of the pyramid?

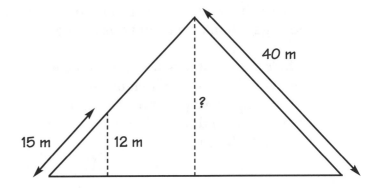

a. Write a word proportion.

$$\frac{\text{height at 15 m}}{\text{height at top}} = \frac{\text{length from base at 15 m}}{\text{length from base at top}}$$

b. Use the word proportion to solve the problem.

$\frac{12}{h} = \frac{15}{40}$; $h = 32$ The height of the pyramid is 32 meters.

4. Two ladders are leaning at the same angle against a wall. The first ladder is 8 feet tall, and its base is 2 feet from the wall. The base of the second ladder is 2.5 feet from the wall. How tall is the second ladder?

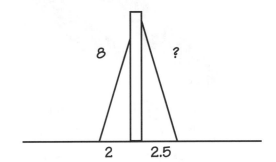

a. Write a word proportion.

$$\frac{\text{L-1 height}}{\text{L-2 height}} = \frac{\text{L-1 distance from wall}}{\text{L-2 distance from wall}}$$

b. Solve the problem.

$\frac{8}{h} = \frac{2}{2.5}$; $h = 10$ The second ladder is 10 feet tall.

5. The bank and the theater are neighboring buildings. The bank is 26 feet tall and casts a 60-foot shadow. The theater casts a 90-foot shadow. Write a word proportion and find the height of the theater.

$$\frac{\text{bank's height}}{\text{theater's height}} = \frac{\text{bank's shadow}}{\text{theater's shadow}}$$

$\frac{26}{h} = \frac{60}{90}$; $h = 39$ The height of the theater is 39 feet.

● Solving Proportions

Choose the best answer for each problem. In the answer section at the bottom of the page, fill in the box of your choice.

1. **The diagram shows the shadows cast by two buildings. Which of the following word proportions could you use to find the height of Building B?** D

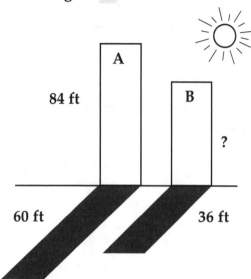

84 ft

60 ft   36 ft

A $\dfrac{\text{A's height}}{\text{B's height}} = \dfrac{\text{B's shadow}}{\text{A's shadow}}$

B $\dfrac{\text{A's height}}{\text{A's shadow}} = \dfrac{\text{B's shadow}}{\text{B's height}}$

C $\dfrac{\text{A's shadow}}{\text{B's shadow}} = \dfrac{\text{B's height}}{\text{A's height}}$

D $\dfrac{\text{A's height}}{\text{B's height}} = \dfrac{\text{A's shadow}}{\text{B's shadow}}$

2. **Two poles are leaning at the same angle against a wall. The first pole is 10 feet long, and is 3 feet from the wall. The second pole is 5.4 feet from the wall. How long is the second pole?** L

   J 12 ft   L 18 ft
   K 15 ft   M 54 ft

3. **A ski lift going up a mountain is 1.8 km long. After traveling 0.3 km on the ski lift, passengers are 0.1 km above their starting point. How far above the starting point will they be at the end of the ski lift?** B

   A 0.17 km   C 5.4 km
   B 0.6 km   D Not given

Write About It

4. **How could you use yourself and a yardstick to find the height of a tall tree on a sunny day? (Note: You are not allowed to climb the tree or use a ladder to measure its height.)**

   Sample answer: First, use the

   yardstick to measure your height.

   Then, measure the length of your

   shadow and the length of the tree's

   shadow. Write a word proportion, and

   then solve it for the tree's height using

   the measures you have taken.

1. A ☐ B ☐ C ☐ D ☒

2. J ☐ K ☐ L ☒ M ☐

3. A ☐ B ☒ C ☐ D ☐

● Solving Proportions

Choosing a Strategy for Solving Problems

To solve a problem, you have to choose a strategy. Here are some strategies you can use.

Show Information Another Way • Make a Diagram • Decide What Kind of Numbers to Use • Make a Table to Generalize • Solve a Formula for a Desired Variable • Draw a Number Line	**Decide on the Kind of Answer You Need** • Interpret Quotients • Decide Whether to Estimate • Estimate Products and Quotients • Estimate with Mixed Expressions • Use Rates to Write Measures in a Different System
Find Needed Information • Read Information from a Table or Chart • Read a Graph	**Decide What to Do First** • Use a Diagram to Write and Solve an Equation • Write a Word Equation • Write a Proportion or a Unit Rate

Example

The school cafeteria has fruit salad in different-sized cans. Of the cans, 45 are 2-pound cans, and 32 are 5-pound cans. The head chef wants to divide the fruit salad evenly among 500 students. How much fruit salad will each student receive?

A. Decide what to do first.

> *THINK:* To decide what to do first, I can make a diagram or write a word equation. The two methods are shown below. The first step in each method is shown in red.

Strategy A: Make a diagram.

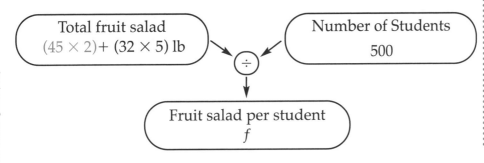

> If you can use either method to solve part of the problem, the answer may help you solve the rest of the problem.

Strategy B: Write a word equation.

> Fruit salad per student $= (45 \text{ cans} \times 2 \text{ lb}) + (32 \text{ cans} \times 5 \text{ lb}) \div 500 \text{ students}$

B. Use the diagram or the word equation to write an equation. Then solve.

$$f = \frac{(45 \times 2) + (32 \times 5)}{500}$$

$$f = \frac{1}{2}$$

So, each student will receive $\frac{1}{2}$ pound of fruit salad.

1. At noon, the temperature was 15°F. During the day, the temperature dropped 20 degrees. What was the temperature at the end of the day?

   Step 1: **Choose a strategy, and describe it.**

   Sample answer: Show information another way by drawing a number line.

   Step 2: **Solve, using the strategy you chose.**

   At the end of the day, the temperature was ⁻5°F.

2. At The Lunch Place, Mr. Arimoto spent $3.20 on a sandwich and $2.00 on a drink before tax. He paid with a $10 bill and received $4.49 in change. How much tax did he pay?

   Step 1: **Choose a strategy. Write your strategy below.**

   Sample answer: Decide what to do first by using a diagram or a word equation.

   Step 2: **Solve, using the strategy you chose.**

   Mr. Arimoto paid a tax of $0.31.

3. A paperback book weighs 9 ounces. What is the book's mass in grams?

   Step 1: **Choose a strategy and describe it.**

   CUSTOMARY-METRIC CONVERSIONS
   1 inch (in.) = 2.54 centimeters (cm)
   1 mile (mi) = 1.6 kilometers (km)
   1 ounce (oz) = 28.35 grams (g)
   1 pound (lb) = 0.45 kilograms (kg)

   Find needed information by finding the necessary conversion in the chart.

   Then multiply to find the book's mass in grams.

   Step 2: **Solve, using the strategy you chose.**

   The book's mass in grams is 255.15 **grams.**

PRACTICE

Choose a strategy for each problem. Then solve.

4. **Suppose the car in the graph averages 20 miles per gallon of gas. About how many miles did the car travel during the first $3\frac{1}{2}$ hours?**

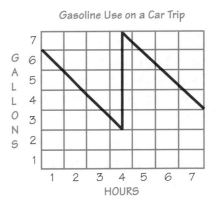

Gasoline Use on a Car Trip

6 – 2 = 4 gallons used;

4 x 20 = 80 gallons;

the driver traveled about 80 miles.

5. **Jen drove 53.7 miles to Ashtabula, 37 miles to Burton, and then finished her trip in Chardon. If she traveled a total of 97.1 miles, what is the distance between Burton and Chardon?**

53.7 + 37 + m = 97.1; m = 6.4

The distance between Burton and Chardon is 6.4 miles.

6. **During the first down, a football team gains $4\frac{1}{2}$ yards. On the second down, the team loses 8 yards. How many yards has the team gained or lost so far?**

Use a number line to show a gain of $4\frac{1}{2}$ and a loss of 8, or write a number sentence:

$4\frac{1}{2} - 8 = {}^-3\frac{1}{2}$. The team has lost $3\frac{1}{2}$ yards.

7. **Christina paid \$8.10 for taxi fare from her home to a restaurant, including a \$1 tip. The taxi company charges \$2.10 for the first mile, plus \$1.00 for each additional mile. How many miles is Christina's home from the restaurant?**

Subtract tip: \$8.10 – \$1 = \$7.10; Subtract cost of first mile: \$7.10 – \$2.10 = \$5.00;

Divide by \$1 to find the additional miles: \$5.00 ÷ \$1.00 = 5; add 5 miles to the first mile to

find total miles traveled: 5 miles + 1 mile = 6 miles; Christina's home is 6 miles from the

restaurant.

Choose the best answer for each problem. In the answer section at the bottom of the page, fill in the box of your choice.

1. A teacher has 6 boxes of pencils with 12 pencils each and 8 boxes of pencils with 24 pencils each. He wants to divide the pencils evenly among 60 students.

   Which equation could be used to determine the number of pencils each student will receive? A

   A $p = \dfrac{(6 \times 12) + (8 \times 24)}{60}$

   B $p = (6 \times 12) + (8 \times 24) + 60$

   C $p = \dfrac{(6 \times 12 \times 8 \times 24)}{60}$

   D $p = 60 \times (6 \times 12) + (8 \times 24)$

2. At the market, ground beef costs $2.95 a pound.

   Which of the following choices is a reasonable estimate of the cost of 2 pounds 2 ounces of ground beef? M

   J $3   L $5
   K $4   M $6

3. In the first 51 weeks of the year, Danielle earned $3,162. She wants to average $63 per week for the year. How much does she need to earn during the last (52nd) week? C

   A $50   C $114
   B $63   D $163

4. **Chelsea pays $39.95 for cable television each month, plus an additional fee for each pay-for-view movie she watches. This month she watched 3 movies and received a bill for $47.45. What is the charge to watch one movie?** K

   J $2.00   L $5.00
   K $2.50   M $7.50

5. **A pattern shows 2 circles and 3 triangles. Each triangle has at least one circle between it and another triangle. What does the pattern look like?** C

   A ●▼▼▼●   C ▼●▼●▼
   B ●▼●▼▼   D ▼●▼●●

Write About It

6. **Choose a problem on this page, and describe the strategy you used to solve it. Then describe a different strategy you could have used, and write about how you would use it to solve the problem.**

Answers will vary.

---

1. A ☒ B ☐ C ☐ D ☐   4. J ☐ K ☒ L ☐ M ☐

2. J ☐ K ☐ L ☐ M ☒   5. A ☐ B ☐ C ☒ D ☐

3. A ☐ B ☐ C ☒ D ☐

● Strategy Review

Using Part-Part-Whole Percent Diagrams

Using diagrams can help you set up proportions to solve percent problems.

Example 1

Lucille saved $60 when she bought a chair that was on sale for 25% off the original price. What was the chair's original price?

Step 1: Draw diagrams to show what you know and what you need to find.

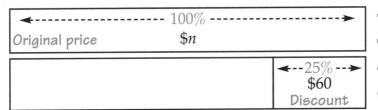

This shows 100%—the original price of the chair.

This shows the discount—25% of the original price.

Step 2: Use the diagrams to write a proportion, and solve.

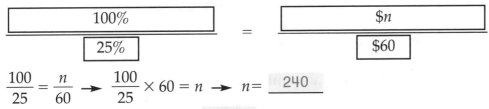

$$\frac{100}{25} = \frac{n}{60} \rightarrow \frac{100}{25} \times 60 = n \rightarrow n = \underline{\quad 240 \quad}$$

The chair's original price was $__240__.

Example 2

A television that was on sale for 20% off the original price sold for $180. What was the amount it was discounted?

Step 1: Draw diagrams to show what you know and what you need to find.

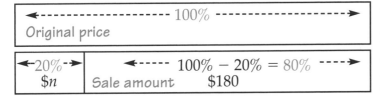

This shows 100%—the original price of the chair.

This shows the discount—20%. It also shows the sale amount.

Step 2: **Use the diagrams to write a proportion, and solve.**

$$\frac{20}{80} = \frac{n}{180} \rightarrow \frac{20}{80} \times 180 = n \rightarrow n = \underline{\quad 45 \quad}$$

The amount the television was discounted was $__45__.

● Solving Proportions

GUIDED PRACTICE

1. Bert keeps 20% of his money in his savings account and 80% in his checking account. If Bert has $60 in his savings account, how much does he have in his checking account?

Step 1: Draw a diagram to show what you know and what you need to find.

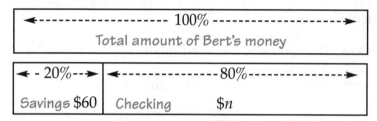

Step 2: Use the diagram to write a proportion, and solve.

$$\frac{80\%}{20\%} = \frac{\$n}{\$60}$$

$$\frac{80}{20} = \frac{n}{60} \quad \longrightarrow \quad \frac{80}{20} \times \underline{\ 60\ } = n$$

Bert has $ __240__ in his checking account.

2. Fannie bought a book that was on sale for 35% off the original price. She paid $26. How much did she save?

Step 1: Draw a diagram to show what you know and what you need to find.

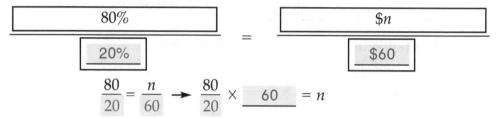

Step 2: Use the diagram to write a proportion, and solve.

$$\frac{35\%}{65\%} = \frac{\$n}{\$26}$$

$$\frac{35}{65} = \frac{n}{26} \quad \longrightarrow \quad \frac{35}{65} \times \underline{\ 26\ } = n$$

$$n = \underline{\ 14\ }$$

Fannie saved $ __14__ on the book.

PRACTICE

Mark each diagram to show the problem. Then write a proportion and solve.

3. Kane paid $161.50 for a bicycle that was on sale for 15% off the original price. What was the bicycle's original price?

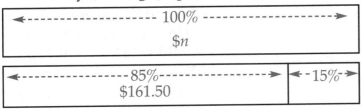

$\frac{100}{85} = \frac{n}{161.50}$ The original price was $190.

4. Bo saved $33 when she bought a pair of skates on sale for 30% off the original price. How much did she pay for the skates?

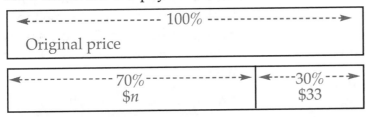

$\frac{70}{30} = \frac{n}{33}$ She paid $77.

5. Marge's company deducts 12% of her earnings for a savings plan. Last year, Marge was paid $22,000 after the deduction was taken out of her earnings. How much did Marge save last year?

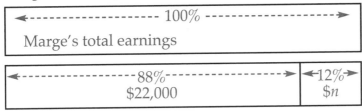

$\frac{12}{88} = \frac{n}{22,000}$ Marge saved $3,000.

6. Josh paid $78 for a winter coat that was on sale for 35% off the original price. What was the original price of the coat?

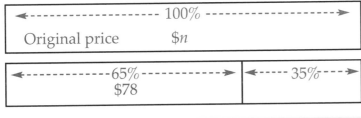

$\frac{100}{65} = \frac{n}{78}$ The original price was $120.

• Solving Proportions

Choose the best answer for each problem. In the answer section at the bottom of the page, fill in the box of your choice.

1. When the price of a sweater was reduced by 20%, the sale price was $38.

   Which proportion could you use to find the original price of the sweater? B

   A $\frac{n}{38} = \frac{20}{100}$

   B $\frac{n}{38} = \frac{100}{80}$

   C $\frac{n}{100} = \frac{20}{38}$

   D $\frac{n}{80} = \frac{100}{38}$

2. **Delaney keeps 25% of her money in a savings account and 75% in a checking account. If she has $200 in her savings account, how much money does she have in all?** M

   J $50   L $600

   K $66.67   M $800

3. **Conor bought a skateboard at 40% off the original price, saving $54. How much did he pay for the skateboard?**

   C

   A $21.60   C $81

   B $36   D $135

4. **Emily received a 20% discount off her health club membership. If she saved $85, what was the original cost?** K

   J $340   L $510

   K $425   M Not given

5. **Of those surveyed, 26%—156 people—said they would vote for Frank. How many people didn't say they would vote for Frank?** C

   A 210 people   C 444 people

   B 288 people   D 600 people

Write About It

Write a plan for solving the following problem. Then solve. Sample answer given.

5. **Nuru keeps 60% of his money in his checking account and the rest in savings. If he has $75 in his savings account, how much does he have in checking?**

   Draw a diagram showing that 60%

   of the money is in checking, and

   40%, $75, is in savings.

   Write a proportion:

   $\frac{60}{40} = \frac{n}{75}$

   $n = 112.50$

   Nuru has $112.50 in checking.

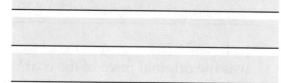

1. A ☐ B ☒ C ☐ D ☐   4. J ☐ K ☒ L ☐ M ☐

2. J ☐ K ☐ L ☐ M ☒   5. A ☐ B ☐ C ☒ D ☐

3. A ☐ B ☐ C ☒ D ☐

Using Percents Greater than 100

You can use proportions to solve problems that involve percents greater than 100. Drawing diagrams can help you set up the proportions.

Example 1

Carlos paid $15.37, including sales tax of 6%, for a book. What was the marked price of the book?

Step 1:   **Draw diagrams to show what you know and what you need to find.**

THINK: I should let 100% be the marked price of the book. The price with tax will be 100% + 6%.

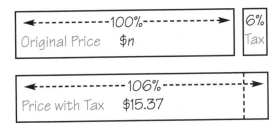

Step 2:   **Use the diagrams to write a proportion, and solve.**

$$\frac{100\%}{106\%} = \frac{\$n}{\$15.37}$$

$$\frac{100}{106} = \frac{n}{15.37} \rightarrow \frac{100}{106} \times 15.37 = n \rightarrow n = \$\ \underline{14.50}$$

The book's marked price was $ 14.50 .

Example 2

Jackie's stocks in the Cooperation Corporation increased in value from $350 to $420 last year. What was the percent increase of the value of Jackie's stocks?

Step 1:   **Draw diagrams to show what you know and what you need to find.**

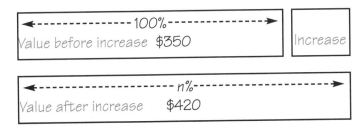

Step 2:   **Use the diagrams to write a proportion, and solve.**

$$\frac{n\%}{100\%} = \frac{\$420}{\$350}$$

$$\frac{n}{100} = \frac{420}{350} \rightarrow n = \frac{420}{350} \times 100 \rightarrow n = \underline{120}$$

The percent increase is $n - 100$, or ___20___ %.

The percent increase was ___20___ %.

GUIDED PRACTICE

1. Chuck was given a 15% tip on a meal he had served. The total amount he was paid was $36.80. How much was Chuck's tip?

   a. Draw diagrams to show what you know and what you need to find.

   THINK: The total amount Chuck was paid is 100% of the bill plus 15% of the bill.

   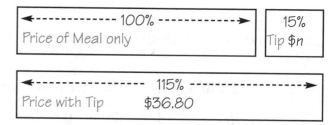

   b. Use the diagrams to write a proportion, and solve.

   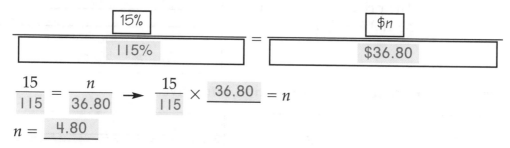

   $$\frac{15}{115} = \frac{n}{36.80} \rightarrow \frac{15}{115} \times \underline{36.80} = n$$

   $n = \underline{4.80}$

   Chuck's tip was $ _4.80_ .

2. An antiques dealer sold a painting for 40% more than he had paid for it, earning a profit of $620. How much did the dealer sell the painting for?

   a. Draw diagrams to show what you know and what you need to find.

   THINK: The dealer sold the painting for 100% of what he had paid plus his profit, 40% of what he had paid.

   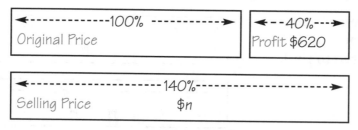

   b. Use the diagrams to write a proportion, and solve.

   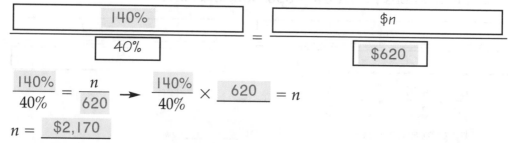

   $$\frac{140\%}{40\%} = \frac{n}{620} \rightarrow \frac{140\%}{40\%} \times \underline{620} = n$$

   $n = \underline{\$2{,}170}$

   He sold the painting for $ _$2,170_ .

PRACTICE

Write and solve proportions for each problem.

3. **Mr. Castille paid 7% sales tax when he bought a lawn mower. The total cost was $267.50. What was the marked price of the lawn mower?**

$\frac{100}{107} = \frac{n}{267.50}$ The marked price was $250.

4. **Lisa paid a 15% tip—$2.40—when she ate dinner at a restaurant. How much did Lisa pay in all?**

$\frac{115}{15} = \frac{n}{2.40}$ She paid $18.40 in all.

5. **Ms. Lazarus bought her house for $96,000 and sold it four years later for $120,000. What was the percent increase in the value of Ms. Lazarus's house?**

$\frac{120,000}{96,000} = \frac{n}{100}$ $n - 100 = 125$ The percent increase was 25%.

6. **Nell bought a compact disc player. After paying a 5% sales tax, her total cost was $94.50. What was the cost of the compact disc player before sales tax?**

$\frac{100}{105} = \frac{n}{94.50}$ The cost was $90.

7. **Miguel made $16, a profit of 40%, on the sale of a baseball card he bought and sold last week. How much did he sell the card for?**

$\frac{140}{40} = \frac{n}{16}$ He sold the card for $56.

8. **Didier paid shipping charges of $18.50 for merchandise he bought through a catalog. If the shipping charges were 8% of the cost of the merchandise, what was the cost of the merchandise?**

$\frac{100}{8} = \frac{n}{18.5}$ The cost was $231.25.

Choose the best answer for each problem. In the answer section at the bottom of the page, fill in the box of your choice.

1. Charles gave his waiter a $10 tip— 18% of the bill.

   Which of the following proportions could you use to find the total amount Charles paid? D

   A $\frac{100}{18} = \frac{n}{10}$ **C** $\frac{n}{18} = \frac{100}{118}$

   B $\frac{n}{18} = \frac{10}{100}$ **D** $\frac{118}{18} = \frac{n}{10}$

2. Sue paid 6% sales tax on a television. She paid $21 in tax.

   Which of the following proportions could you use to find the marked price of the television? J

   J $\frac{100}{6} = \frac{n}{21}$

   K $\frac{106}{6} = \frac{n}{21}$

   L $\frac{100}{21} = \frac{n}{6}$

   M $\frac{6}{106} = \frac{n}{21}$

3. **Victor sold his house for $165,000, making a profit of 20%. How much had he paid for the house?** C

   A $33,000   **C** $137,500

   B $123,750   **D** $198,000

4. **Kirstie paid the cab driver $15.00 on a ride that cost $12.00. What percent tip did she give?** M

   J 8%   **L** 20%

   K 15%   **M** 25%

5. **Tral paid a total of $288.90, including 7% sales tax, for a new bicycle. What was the cost of the bicycle before tax?** B

   A $202.23   **C** $309.12

   B $270.00   **D** $310.65

Write About It

6. **Dan said he'd rather have 25% of $180, while Sheila said she'd rather have 180% of $25. Jet said she had no preference. Who do you agree with? Why?**

   Jet is correct, in that 25% of $180 is

   the same as 180% of $25.

   This can be shown by writing the

   expressions:

   $\frac{25}{100} \times 180 = \frac{180}{100} \times 25$

---

1. A ☐ B ☐ C ☐ D ☒

2. J ☒ K ☐ L ☐ M ☐

3. A ☐ B ☐ C ☒ D ☐

4. J ☐ K ☐ L ☐ M ☒

5. A ☐ B ☒ C ☐ D ☐

● Percent of a Number

Solving Percent Problems Involving Measures

You can set up a proportion to solve a percent problem inolving measures.
It's often easiest to use 100% to represent the given, or original, measure.

Example 1

Ezra has a print that is 13 cm x 8 cm.
He uses a copier to enlarge the
dimensions of the print by 40%.
What are the dimensions of the
enlargement?

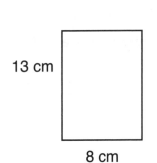 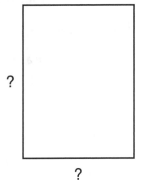

13 cm   ?

8 cm   ?

**A. Write proportions to find the
length and the width. Use 100% for the original measures.**

Length	Width

$$\frac{100\% + 40\%}{100\%} = \frac{l}{13 \text{ cm}}$$ ← enlargement → $$\frac{100\% + 40\%}{100\%} = \frac{w}{8 \text{ cm}}$$
← original →

B. Use cross products to solve.

Length

$$\frac{140\%}{100\%} = \frac{l}{13 \text{ cm}}$$

$$13 \times 140 = 100 \times l$$
$$1{,}820 = 100l \quad 18.2 = l$$

Width

$$\frac{140\%}{100\%} = \frac{w}{8 \text{ cm}}$$

$$8 \times 140 = 100 \times w$$
$$1{,}120 = 100w \quad 11.2 = w$$

So, the enlargement measures 18.2 centimeters by 11.2 centimeters.

Example 2

Marie designed an iron-on patch with a diameter of 7 inches.
Then she reduced the dimensions of the design by 40% before
transferring it to the patch. What is the diameter of the reduced design?

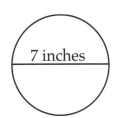

7 inches

Write and solve a proportion.

$$\frac{100\% - 40\%}{100\%} = \frac{d}{7 \text{ in.}}$$ ← reduction
← original

$$7 \times 60 = 100 \times d$$

$$\underline{420} = 100d$$

$$\underline{4.2} = d$$

So, the diameter is ____4.2____ inches.

● Proportions

GUIDED PRACTICE

1. A cereal box label states: "Crispy Wheats! Now with 20% more cereal!" If each old box of Crispy Wheats held 18 ounces of cereal, how much cereal will a new box hold?

   a. The original measure is the number on which the percent change is based.

   What is the original measure? 18 ounces

   b. **Use the original measure to write and solve a proportion.**

   $$\frac{120\%}{100\%} = \frac{c}{18 \text{ ounces}} \quad \leftarrow \text{increased measure} \\ \leftarrow \text{original measure}$$

   $$\underline{18} \times \underline{120} = 100 \times c$$

   $$\underline{2,160} = 100c$$

   $$\underline{21.6} = c$$

   So, a new box of Crispy Wheats will hold __21.6__ ounces of cereal.

2. Rufus came in second in the 100-meter dash with a time of 12 seconds. The winner took 15% less time to complete the race. What was the winner's time?

   a. **What is the original measure?** 12 seconds

   b. **Use the original measure to write and solve a proportion.**

   $$\frac{100\% - 15\%}{100\%} = \frac{t}{12 \text{ seconds}} \quad \leftarrow \text{reduced measure} \\ \leftarrow \text{original measure}$$

   $$\underline{85} \times \underline{12} = \underline{100} \times t$$

   $$\underline{10.2} = t$$

   So, the winner's time was __10.2__ seconds.

3. The height of a building is increased by 12% when a television antenna is added. The building was originally 250 feet tall. How tall is the building now?

   a. **What is the original measure?** 250 feet

   b. **Use the original measure to write and solve a proportion.**

   $$\frac{112\%}{100\%} = \frac{h}{250 \text{ feet}} \quad \leftarrow \text{increased measure} \\ \leftarrow \text{original measure}$$

   $$\underline{112} \times \underline{250} = \underline{100} \times h$$

   $$\underline{28,000} = \underline{100} \, h$$

   $$\underline{280} = h$$

   So, the building is __280__ feet tall.

PRACTICE

Decide what number is the original measure. Then use it to write and solve a proportion.

4. Gordon took two days to drive to Florida. On Tuesday, he drove 400 miles. On Wednesday, he drove 25% farther. How many miles did he drive on Wednesday?

   a. Write the original measure. __400__

   b. Write and solve a proportion.

   $$\frac{125\%}{100\%} = \frac{m}{400 \text{ miles}}$$

   $$400 \times 125 = 100m$$
   $$50{,}000 = 100m$$
   $$500 = m$$

   c. How many miles did Gordon drive on Wednesday? __500__

Solve . . . .

5. A model of a chair weighs 80% less than the actual chair. If the chair weighs 25 lb, how much does the model weigh?

   5 lb

6. Sandra received a 5% raise. She currently makes $6.00 per hour. How much money will she make after the raise?

   $6.30

7. Nora uses a copier to enlarge the dimensions of a print that is 4 inches by 6 inches by 30%. What is the size of the enlarged print?

   5.2 in. by 7.8 in.

8. Emilio's junk sculpture stands 70 centimeters tall. If he reduces its height by 40%, how tall will the sculpture be?

   42 cm

9. During one year, Jimmy Unusual grew 20% taller. If he started the year measuring 1.5 meters in height, how tall was he at the end of the year?

   1.8 meters

10. Jimmy Unusual's friend Strange Steve actually shrunk 5% during the year. He started at a height of 2 meters. How tall was he at the end of the year?

    1.9 meters

Choose the best answer for each problem. In the answer section at the bottom of the page, fill in the box of your choice.

1. A building is 150 feet tall. A second building is planned that will be 20% shorter. How tall will the new building be?

   Which proportion could you use to solve the problem? A

   A $\dfrac{80\%}{100\%} = \dfrac{x}{150 \text{ feet}}$

   B $\dfrac{80\%}{120\%} = \dfrac{x}{150 \text{ feet}}$

   C $\dfrac{100\%}{120\%} = \dfrac{x}{150 \text{ feet}}$

   D $\dfrac{120\%}{100\%} = \dfrac{x}{150 \text{ feet}}$

2. This year, Ronnie increased his running distance over last year by 15%. If he ran 2 miles a day last year, how far does he run each day this year?

   Which proportion could you use to solve the problem? K

   J $\dfrac{85\%}{100\%} = \dfrac{x}{2 \text{ miles}}$

   K $\dfrac{115\%}{100\%} = \dfrac{x}{2 \text{ miles}}$

   L $\dfrac{115\%}{100\%} = \dfrac{2 \text{ miles}}{x}$

   M $\dfrac{115\%}{200\%} = \dfrac{x}{2 \text{ miles}}$

3. **Deva worked 30% fewer hours this week than last week. If she worked 30 hours last week, how many hours did she work this week?** A

   A 21 hours   **C** 33 hours

   B 27 hours   **D** 35 hours

4. **At his new job, Ralph received a 20% increase in pay. If he was paid $12 an hour at his former job, how much is he paid at his new job?** L

   J $2.40   **L** $14.40

   K $9.60   **M** Not given

Write About It

Write a plan for solving the following problem. Then solve.

5. **A photo whose dimensions were reduced by 20% now measures 10 inches by 16 inches. What were the photo's original dimensions?**

   Sample answer: Use proportions to

   show the reduction in size compared

   to the original, using 100% for the

   original measures. Then use

   cross products to solve for the

   dimensions.

   $\dfrac{80\%}{100\%} = \dfrac{10}{w}$; w = 12.5

   $\dfrac{80\%}{100\%} = \dfrac{16}{l}$; l = 20

   The original photo measured 12.5

   inches by 20 inches.

1. A ☒   B ☐   C ☐   D ☐
2. J ☐   K ☒   L ☐   M ☐
3. A ☒   B ☐   C ☐   D ☐
4. J ☐   K ☐   L ☒   M ☐

Using a Diagram to Solve Multi-Step Percent Problems

You can use a diagram to plan a solution to a percent problem with two or more steps.

Example

Louise bought a set of tools that were discounted to 75% of the original price. She also used a coupon for an additional 10% off the sale price. If the final price was $32.40, what was the original price of the tool set?

Step 1: **Make a diagram to show the problem.**

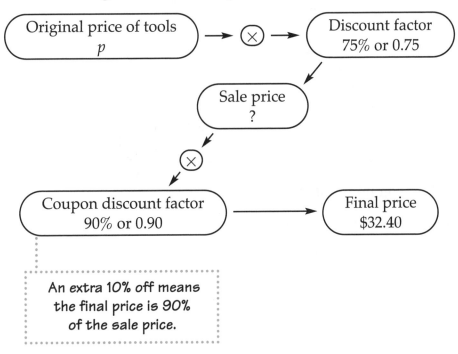

An extra 10% off means the final price is 90% of the sale price.

Step 2: **Use the diagram to solve the problem.**

a. **Find the sale price of the tool set.**

Sale price × 0.90 = 32.40

Sale price = 32.40 ÷ 0.90

Sale price = 36

b. **Find the original price of the tool set.**

$p \times 0.75 = 36$

$p = 36 \div 0.75$

$p = \underline{\quad 48 \quad}$

The original price of the tool set was $ \underline{\quad 48 \quad}.

GUIDED PRACTICE

1. William bought a grill that was on sale for 40% off. He also bought a chef's hat for $8.50. If he spent a total of $98.50, what was the original price of the grill?

   Step 1: **Complete the diagram to show the problem.**

   THINK: 40% off means that you pay 100% − 40%, or 60%, of the original price.

   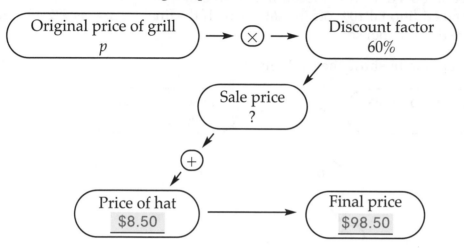

   Step 2: **Use the diagram to solve the problem.**

   a. **Find the sale price of the grill.**

   Sale price + Price of hat = Final price

   Sale price = Final price − Price of hat

   Sale price = __98.50__ − __8.50__ = __90.00__

   b. **Use the sale price to find *p*, the original price of the grill.**

   Original price × Discount factor = Sale price

   Original price = Sale price ÷ Discount factor

   $p =$ __90.00__ ÷ __0.60__ = __150.00__

   The grill's original price was $__150.00__.

2. Kuri bought a computer for 25% off the original price. If the sale price was $900, what was the original price?

   Decide what discount factor to multiply by.

   Since the computer was 25% off, multiply by __0.75__.

   $p \times$ __0.75__ $= 900$, so $p =$ __1,200__

   The original price was $__1,200__.

Draw a diagram on a separate piece of paper to plan your solution.
Write down the equations you use, and solve.

3. **Ashley bought a coat that was marked 30% off the original price. She also used a coupon for an additional 10% off the sale price. If the final price was $28.35, what was the coat's original price?**

Sale price × 0.90 = 28.35; Sale price = $31.50

Original price × 0.70 = 31.50; Original price = $45

The coat's original price was $45.

4. **Savion bought a video for 75% of the original price. If he paid $13.50, how much money did he save from the original price?**

Original price × 0.75 = 13.50; Original price = $18

Amount saved = 18 − 13.50 = 4.50

Savion saved $4.50 off the original price.

5. **Antonio bought a drum set that was on sale for 50% off. He also bought drum sticks for $12.95. If he spent a total of $210.45, what was the original price of the drum set?**

Sale price = 210.45 − 12.95 = 197.50; Sale price = $197.50

Original price × 0.50 = 197.50; Original price = $395

The drum set originally cost $395.

6. **A television was on sale for $45 off the original price. The price was then reduced by 15%. If a customer paid a final price of $340, what was the original price of the television?**

Sale price = 340 ÷ 0.85; Sale price = $400

Original price − 45 = 400; Original price = $445

The original price was $445.

Choose the best answer for each problem. In the answer section at the bottom of the page, fill in the box of your choice.

1. In a theater, 78% of the audience are students. Of the students, 45% are female. If there are 50 female students, how many people are in the audience?

   Which of the following equations could *not* be used to help solve the problem? C

   A Students × 0.45 = Female students
   B 50 ÷ 0.45 = Number of students
   C Female students ÷ 0.78 = a
   D Number of students ÷ 0.78 = a

2. A newspaper advertisement states that a computer is on sale for 80% of the original price. If the sale price is $720, how much money will a buyer save? L
   J $20   L $180
   K $140   M $720

3. Of 500 students, 72% take the bus to school. Another 60 students walk to school, and the rest are driven by a family member. How many students are driven by a family member to school? A
   A 80   C 368
   B 140   D Not given

4. Amir bought a trumpet on sale for 25% off. He also bought a music book for $9.95. If he spent a total of $159.95, what was the original price of the trumpet? M
   J $25.00   L $150.00
   K $100.95   M $200.00

Write About It

5. An item costs $100. Which is the better deal: a discount on the item of 35%, or a discount of 25% and then an additional 10% off the sale price? Explain.

   The discount of 35% is the better

   deal.

   If you get a 35% discount on a $100

   item, you pay $65 for the item.

   If you get a 25% discount on a $100

   item, the cost will be $75. The

   additional discount of 10% brings the

   final cost to $67.50.

   $65 < $67.50, so the first discount is

   the better deal.

1. A ☐ B ☐ C ☒ D ☐
2. J ☐ K ☐ L ☒ M ☐
3. A ☒ B ☐ C ☐ D ☐
4. J ☐ K ☐ L ☐ M ☒

● Operations with Percents

Using a Repeated Factor to Find Interest

Some problems ask you to use a percent as a repeated factor to find how an amount changes after a period of time. You can use diagrams to help you show the problem and to find a solution.

Example

Sheryl paid $100 for a rare stamp. Each year, the value of the stamp increased by 50%. How much money was the stamp worth after 3 years?

Step 1: Draw diagrams to show the information in the problem.

After 0 years

$100

After 1 year

$100	50% of $100

◄------- $100 × 150% = $150 -------►

THINK: $100 + (50% of $100) is the same as 150% of $100. After 1 year the value is 150% of $100.

After 2 years

$150	50% of $150

◄----------------$150 × 150% = $225----------------►

After 3 years

$225	50% of $225

◄--------------------- $225 × 150% = $337.50 ---------------------►

Step 2: Use the last diagram to solve the problem.

The stamp was worth $ __337.50__ after 3 years.

GUIDED PRACTICE

1. Lyman's stock account gained 10% per year. If he started with $300 in the account, how much was the account worth after 3 years?

   a. Use diagrams to show the problem.

   After 0 years

$300

   After 1 year

$300	10% of $300

   ◄-- $300 × 110% = $330 --►

   After 2 years

$330	10% of $330

   ◄----$330 × 110% = $ __363__ ----►

   After 3 years

$ __363__	10% of $ __363__

   ◄----- $ __363__ × __110__ % = __399.30__ -----►

   b. Solve.

   After three years, the account was worth $__399.30__.

2. LaShonda planted a tree that was 1 meter tall. Each year, its height increased by 20%. To the nearest tenth of a meter, how tall was the tree after 4 years?

   a. Show the problem.

   Height after 0 years: 1 m

   Height after 1 year: 1 × 120% = __1.2__ m

   Height after 2 years: __1.2__ × __120__ % = __1.44__ m

   Height after 3 years: __1.44__ × __120__ % = __1.728__ m

   Height after 4 years: __1.728__ × __120__ % = __2.0736__ m

   b. Solve.

   After four years, the tree was __2.1__ meters tall.

PRACTICE

Solve, using diagrams if you need them.

3. **Pearl's bank pays 5% interest on her account each year. If she starts with $400 at the beginning of 2000, how much money will she have at the beginning of 2003?**

   Show the problem.

   After 0 years: $ __400__

   After 1 year: $ __420__

   After 2 years: $ __441__

   After 3 years: $ __463.05__

   Pearl will have $ __463.05__ .

4. **Ms. Torres is starting an exercise program. Each day, she intends to run 20% further than the previous day. She runs 1,000 yards the first day. How far, to the nearest 100 yards, will she run on the fifth day?**

   Show the problem.

   Day 1: 1,000 yd

   Day 2: __1,200__ yd

   Day 3: __1,440__ yd

   Day 4: __1,728__ yd

   Day 5: __2,073.60__ yd

   She will run __2,100__ yd.

5. **Every hour, the number of a certain kind of bacteria doubles. If an experiment begins with 4 bacteria, how many will there be after 5 hours?**

   There will be 128 bacteria.

6. **The stock of Plink, Inc. has decreased by 10% each year for the last three years. If Earl had Plink stock that was worth $200 three years ago, how much is it now worth?**

   Show the problem.

   After 0 years: $ __200__

   After 1 year: $ __180__

   After 2 years: $ __162__

   After 3 years: $ __145.80__

   The stock is now worth $ __145.80__ .

7. **Mr. Evans started an investment account of $500 for his daughter on the day that she was born. The account increased by 25% each year. How much money was in the account when she turned two years old?**

   There was $781.25.

8. **The weight of a superchicken increases by 50% each year. The average weight of a one-year-old superchicken is 16 lb. What is the average weight of a four-year-old superchicken?**

   The average weight is 54 lb.

9. **A bamboo plant in a greenhouse increased in height 60% each month. If its height was 80 cm when it was planted, how tall, to the nearest cm, was it after three months?**

   It was 328 cm tall.

Choose the best answer for each problem. In the answer section at the bottom of the page, fill in the box of your choice.

1. Joe starts a savings account with $100. The account pays 7% interest each year.

   Which expression shows what the account will be worth after 2 years? B
   A $100 \times 7\% \times 7\%$
   B $100 \times 1.07 \times 1.07$
   C $100 \times 1.07 \times 1.07 \times 1.07$
   D $107\% \times 107\%$

2. **The number of Internet customers for Zoomers increased by 40% each month. The company started out with 500 customers. How many customers did it have after 3 months?** M
   J 620   L 1,100
   K 980   M 1,372

3. **A stock increased by 20% each year. If it starts out costing $30 per share, how much will it cost after 3 years?** B
   A $30.20   C $62.21
   B $51.84   D $90.00

4. **After a record year in which a company earned $400,000 profit, the profits decreased by 25% each year. How much profit did the company earn two years after their record year?** K
   J $200,000   L $300,000
   K $225,000   M $350,000

5. **On a hiking trip, Tanya plans to walk 25% further each day. If she walks 16 km the first day, how far will she walk on the fourth day?** C
   A 25 km   C 31.25 km
   B 28 km   D Not given

Write About It
Write a plan for solving the following problem. Then solve.

6. **Mao has $200 to invest for two years. He can invest in a plan that offers 20% interest for the two years, or a plan that gives 10% interest each year. Which plan should he choose?**

   The first plan will give Mao interest

   of $200 × 0.20, or $40. His total

   amount will be $240.

   The second plan will give Mao a

   total of 200 × 1.10 × 1.10, or $242.

   Mao should choose the second plan.

© 2000 Metropolitan Teaching and Learning Company

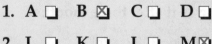

1. A ☐ B ☒ C ☐ D ☐   4. J ☐ K ☒ L ☐ M ☐

2. J ☐ K ☐ L ☐ M ☒   5. A ☐ B ☐ C ☒ D ☐

3. A ☐ B ☒ C ☐ D ☐

Estimating Percents

You can solve some percent problems by estimating. Estimating is also a good way to check that your answers to percent problems are reasonable.

Example 1

Mr. Chapman's bill at a restaurant is $28.72. He wants to leave a tip that is about 20%. About how much should he leave as a tip?

Step 1: **Decide what you need to find.**

THINK: I need to find 20% of $28.72.

Step 2: **You don't need an exact answer, so estimate.**
Find a useful equivalent to 20%.

20% is the same as $2 \times \frac{1}{10}$, or $\frac{1}{5}$.

$28.72 is almost $30. You can find the product of $30 \times \frac{1}{5}$.

$30 \times \frac{1}{5} = \underline{ 6 }$

Mr. Chapman should leave a tip of about $\underline{ 6 }$.

Example 2

A ticket to Willow Grove Amusement Park was $18.95 in 1980. By 2000, it had increased by 162%. About how much did a ticket cost in 2000?

Step 1: **Decide what you need to find.**

The price increased by 162%. So, the new price will be 100% of the old price plus 162% of the old price. You need to find $18.95 × 262%.

Step 2: **You don't need an exact answer, so estimate.**
Find a useful equivalent to 262%.

262% is about 250%, or 2.5.

THINK: I rounded one number down. This is a multiplication problem, so I'll get a better estimate if I round the other number up.

$18.95 is almost $20. You can find the product of $20 × 2.5$.

$20 \times 2.5 = \underline{ 50 }$

In 2000, a ticket to Willow Grove cost about $\underline{ 50 }$.

GUIDED PRACTICE

Use the table of equivalents to help you estimate.

Percents	0	12.5%	25%	$33\frac{1}{3}$%	37.5%	50%	62.5%	$66\frac{2}{3}$%	75%	87.5%	100%
Fractions	0	$\frac{1}{8}$	$\frac{1}{4}$	$\frac{1}{3}$	$\frac{3}{8}$	$\frac{1}{2}$	$\frac{5}{8}$	$\frac{2}{3}$	$\frac{3}{4}$	$\frac{7}{8}$	1

1. Clara bought a motorcycle that was marked down 15% from an original price of $3,120. About how much did she save?

   a. **Decide what you need to find.** You need to find 15% × $ _3,120_ .

   b. **You don't need an exact answer, so estimate.**

   Find a useful equivalent to 15%. 15% is a little more than 12.5%, or $\frac{1}{8}$.

   3,120 is a little less than 3,200, which is easily divisible by 8.

   Find the product of _3,120_ × _$\frac{1}{8}$_ .

   Clara saved about $_400_ on the motorcycle.

2. After the first of the year, the price of a bicycle increased by 30%. If the bicycle used to cost $128, about how much did its price increase?

   a. **Decide what you need to find.** You need to find _30_ % × $_128_ .

   b. **You don't need an exact answer, so estimate.**

   Find a useful equivalent to 30%. 30% is a little less than 33.3%, or _$\frac{1}{3}$_ .

   128 is a little more than _120_ , which is easily divisible by 3.

   Find the product of _120_ × _$\frac{1}{3}$_ .

   The bicycle's price increased by about $_40_ .

3. The population of Hart was 58,200 in 1955. Forty years later, it had increased by 315%. About how many people lived in Hart in 1995?

   a. **Decide what you need to find.**

   THINK: The population increased by 315%, so the 1995 population was 415% of the 1955 population. I need to find 415% of 58,200.

   b. **You don't need an exact answer, so estimate.**

   Find a useful equivalent to 415%. 415% is a little more than _400% or 4_ .

   58,200 is a little less than _60,000_ .

   Find _60,000_ × _4_ .

   In 1995, about _240,000_ people lived in Hart.

PRACTICE

Estimate to solve. Use the table of equivalents, and show the equations you use.

Percents	0	12.5%	25%	$33\frac{1}{3}$%	37.5%	50%	62.5%	$66\frac{2}{3}$%	75%	87.5%	100%
Fractions	0	$\frac{1}{8}$	$\frac{1}{4}$	$\frac{1}{3}$	$\frac{3}{8}$	$\frac{1}{2}$	$\frac{5}{8}$	$\frac{2}{3}$	$\frac{3}{4}$	$\frac{7}{8}$	1

4. A department store buys a shirt for $15.60 and sells it for 82% more than it paid. Estimate the store's profit on the sale of a shirt.

   $16 \times \frac{3}{4} = 12$

   The store's profit is about $12.

5. The population of Green Town started at 89 people and increased by 265%. About how many people live in Green Town now?

   $100 \times 3.5 = 350$

   About 350 people live in Green Town.

6. Chucha's bill at a restaurant is $41.87. She wants to leave a little more than 20% as a tip. About how much should Chucha tip?

   $40 \times \frac{1}{4} = 10$

   Chucha should tip about $10.

7. Nita bought a compact disc that was marked down 22%. About how much did she save if the original price of the disc was $14.35?

   $15 \times \frac{1}{5} = 3$

   She saved about $3.

8. Carson bought a used car for $1,100 and fixed it up. He sold it for 95% more than he paid. About how much did he sell the car for?

   $1,000 \times 2 = 2,000$

   He sold the car for about $2,000.

9. Khaleel charged $370 for catering a party. His client wanted to give Khaleel a tip of about 35%. About how much should she tip?

   $400 \times \frac{3}{8} = 150$

   She should tip about $150.

10. MathGifts' monthly profit was $25,780. After introducing Attila's Percent Attack, its profit increased by 288%. About how much was MathGifts' monthly profit after it introduced the game?

    $25,000 \times 4 = 100,000$

    Its profit was about $100,000.

11. An architect increased the dimensions of a floor plan by 69% on a copying machine. The length of the original floor plan was 28.5 cm. About how long was the copy of the floor plan?

    $30 \times 1\frac{2}{3} = 50$

    The copy was about 50 cm long.

● Multiplying Fractions and Decimals

Choose the best answer for each problem. In the answer section at the bottom of the page, fill in the box of your choice.

1. A department store buys one suit for $189. The store marks the suit up 55% before selling it to a customer. Which expression could you use to estimate the suit's cost to the customer? D

   A $150 \times \frac{1}{2}$ C 190×55

   B $180 \times \frac{5}{8}$ D $200 \times 1\frac{1}{2}$

2. During a sale, the price of a computer decreased by 18%. The computer originally sold for $713.50. Which expression would give the best estimate of the savings on the computer? K

   J $700 \times \frac{1}{8}$ L $700 \times \frac{3}{8}$

   K $700 \times \frac{1}{5}$ M $700 \times 1\frac{1}{5}$

3. The Suttley family bill at a restaurant came to $88.95. About how much should they leave as a tip if they want it to be about 15% of the bill? C

   A About $1.20   C About $15
   B About $9   D About $20

4. Sid paid $48 for a rare duck's toothbrush. On New Year's Eve, he was offered 520% more than he paid for the toothbrush. About how much was Sid offered? L

   J About $200   L About $300
   K About $250   M About $500

5. Nuna sells wreaths made from dried flowers. It costs her $29 to make each wreath. If she sells them for 105% more than her costs, about how much does she receive for each wreath? D

   A About $35   C About $50
   B About $40   D About $60

6. Of the 2,489 people who live in New Town, 31% have lived there less than one year. About how many people have lived in New Town for less than one year? M

   J About 80   L About 400
   K About 200   M Not given

Write About It

7. A stock that sold for $59 decreased to 35% of its value. A week later, the price increased by 28%. How could you estimate the final value of the stock?

Sample answer:
Find a useful equivalent for 35% and
multiply it by approximately $59.
Multiply the product by about 128%.
$60 \times \frac{1}{3} = 20;$ $20 \times 1\frac{1}{4} = 25$
The final value was about $25.

1. A ☐ B ☐ C ☐ D ☒   4. J ☐ K ☐ L ☒ M ☐

2. J ☐ K ☒ L ☐ M ☐   5. A ☐ B ☐ C ☐ D ☒

3. A ☐ B ☐ C ☒ D ☐   6. J ☐ K ☐ L ☐ M ☒

• Multiplying Fractions and Decimals

Test-Taking Skill: Writing a Plan

Some test questions will ask you how you would solve a problem. It is important to explain your thinking and show your calculations.

Example

Beth took three days to drive to California, a trip of 1,490 miles. On the second day she drove 20% further than she did on the first day. On the third day she drove 50 miles more than she did on the first day. If she drove 500 miles on the third day, how many miles did Beth drive on the second day?

A. **Read the problem carefully. You can write word equations to show the information in the problem.**

The first day's miles multiplied by 120 percent equals the second day's miles.

The first day's miles plus 50 equals the third day's miles.

B. **Substitute information that you already know into one equation.**

THINK: I know Beth drove 500 miles on the third day.

The first day's miles plus 50 equals the third day's miles.

So, the first day's miles + 50 = 500.

The first day's miles = ___450___.

C. **Substitute the amount you have found into the other equation.**

The first day's miles multiplied by 120 percent equals the second day's miles.

So, ___450___ miles × 120% = the second day's miles.

THINK: 120% is the same as 1.2.

So, ___450___ miles × 1.2 = the second day's miles.

Beth drove ___540___ miles on the second day.

> Note that you don't need Beth's total mileage to solve the problem. However, you can use that figure to check your answer.

$$450 + 540 + 500 = 1,490$$

TEST-TAKING PRACTICE

Make a plan to solve the problem. Then solve. Show your work.

1. **What is the value of x?**

Input	9	4.5	120	x
Output	6	3	80	10

Sample answer: Use guess-and-check to find the relationship between any

pairs of inputs and outputs. Then test the relationship with all the other pairs

of inputs and outputs. If it is correct, use the relationship to write and solve

an equation for x.

$9 \div 6 = 1.5$; $4.5 \div 3 = 1.5$; $120 \div 80 = 1.5$.

So, $x \div 10 = 1.5$; $x = 10 \times 1.5$; $x = 15$

The value of x is 15.

2. **The _Whatwasthat_ can travel at 60 miles an hour, and the _Nowyouseeit_ can travel at 0.1 mile per second. Which vehicle can travel at the faster speed?**

Sample answer: Use rates to rename the units of the speed of the

Whatwasthat so that they are in miles per second. Then compare the result

to the speed of the _Nowyouseeit_.

$$\frac{60 \text{ mi}}{\text{h}} \times \frac{1 \text{ h}}{60 \text{ min}} \longrightarrow \frac{1 \text{ mi}}{\text{min}}$$

$$\frac{1 \text{ mi}}{\text{min}} \times \frac{1 \text{ min}}{60 \text{ sec}} \longrightarrow \frac{0.0166 \text{ mi}}{\text{sec}}$$

$$\frac{0.0166 \text{ mi}}{\text{sec}} < \frac{0.1 \text{ mi}}{\text{sec}}$$

The _Nowyouseeit_ can travel at the faster speed.

© 2000 Metropolitan Teaching and Learning Company

● Test-Taking Skill

Comparing Perimeters, Areas, and Volumes of Similar Figures

You can use your knowledge of similar figures and ratios to help you solve problems involving perimeter, area, and volume.

Example

Rectangles A and B are similar. The ratio of sides of rectangle B to sides of rectangle A is 1:2, or $\frac{1}{2}$.

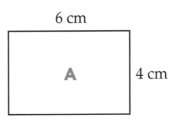

6 cm

A   4 cm

B

a. What is the perimeter of rectangle B?

Step 1: **Find the perimeter of rectangle A.**

Perimeter = $(2 \times l) + (2 \times w)$ ➔ $(2 \times 6) + (2 \times 4)$

Perimeter = ___12___ + ___8___

The perimeter of rectangle A is ___20___ cm.

Step 2: **Find the perimeter of rectangle B.**

THINK: Units of perimeter are the same as units of length or width. The ratio of sides of B:sides of A is $\frac{1}{2}$, so the perimeter of rectangle B will be $\frac{1}{2}$ the perimeter of rectangle A.

Perimeter rectangle B = $\frac{1}{2} \times$ Perimeter rectangle A

Perimeter rectangle B = $\frac{1}{2} \times$ ___20___

The perimeter of rectangle B is ___10___ cm.

> **Check that it works:**
>
> Length of B = $\frac{1}{2} \times 6 = 3$
>
> Width of B = $\frac{1}{2} \times 4 = 2$
>
> Perimeter of B =
> $2 \times 3 + 2 \times 4 = 10$

b. What is the area of rectangle B?

Step 1: **Find the area of rectangle A.**

Area = $l \times w$ ➔ ___6___ $\times$ ___4___

The area of rectangle A is ___24___ cm².

Step 2: **Find the area of rectangle B.**

THINK: Units of area are units of length <u>squared</u>. So, the ratio Area of B:Area of A is $(\frac{1}{2})^2$, or $\frac{1}{4}$. The area of rectangle B will be $\frac{1}{2}$ <u>squared</u>, or $\frac{1}{4}$, the area of rectangle A.

Area of rectangle B = $\frac{1}{4}$ Area of rectangle A

Area of rectangle B = $\frac{1}{4} \times$ ___24___

The area of rectangle B is ___6___ cm².

> **Check that it works:**
>
> Length of B = $\frac{1}{2} \times 6 = 3$
>
> Width of B = $\frac{1}{2} \times 4 = 2$
>
> Area of B = $2 \times 3 = 6$

● Ratios

1. Triangles C and D are similar. The ratio of sides of triangle C to sides of triangle D is 1:4. The perimeter of triangle C is 12 cm, and its area is 6 cm². What are the perimeter and area of triangle D?

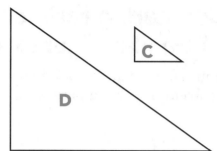

   a. Find the perimeter of triangle D.

   The ratio of C:D is 1:4, so the perimeter of triangle D will be 4 times the perimeter of triangle C.

   Perimeter of triangle D = ___12___ × 4 = ___48___ cm

   b. Find the area of triangle D.

   Units of area are units of length <u>squared</u>. The area of triangle D will be 4 <u>squared</u>, or 16, times the area of triangle C.

   Area of triangle D = 16 × ___6___ = ___96___ cm²

2. Cubes P and Q are similar. The ratio of edges of cube P to edges of cube Q is 1:3. What is the volume of cube Q?

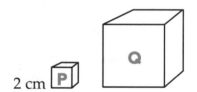
2 cm

   a. Find the volume of cube P.

   Volume of cube P = s^3 → 2 × 2 × 2 → ___8___ cm³

   b. Find the volume of cube Q.

   THINK: Units of volume are units of length <u>cubed</u>. The volume of cube Q will be 3 <u>cubed</u>, or 27, times the volume of cube P.

   Volume of cube Q = ___8___ × 27 = ___216___ cm³

   The volume of cube Q is ___216___ cm³.

   ```
   Check that it works:
   Edges of cube Q = 3 × 2 = 6
   Volume of cube Q = 6 × 6 × 6 = 216
   ```

3. Figures M and N are similar rectangular prisms. The ratio of prism M to prism N is 2:1. What is the volume of prism N?

   THINK: The volume of prism N will be $\frac{1}{2}$ <u>cubed</u>, or $\frac{1}{8}$, times the volume of prism M.

   Volume of prism N = $\frac{1}{8}$ × ___48___

   The volume of prism N is ___6___ cubic inches.

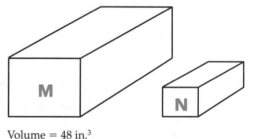
Volume = 48 in.³

4. **All squares are similar figures. The ratio of sides of square J to sides of square K is 5:1. What is the perimeter and area of square K?**

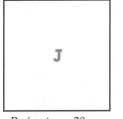

Perimeter = 20 cm
Area = 25 cm²

Perimeter = $20 \times \frac{1}{5}$ = 4 cm

Area = $25 \times \frac{1}{25}$ = 1 cm²

5. **The rectangular prisms shown at right are similar. The ratio of edges of prism C to edges of prism D is 1:3. What is the volume of prism D?**

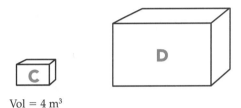

Vol = 4 m³

Volume of prism D = $4 \times 3^3 = 4 \times 27$

Volume of prism D = 108 m³

6. **Triangles L and M are similar. The ratio of sides of triangle L to triangle M is 4:1. What are the perimeter and the area of triangle M?**
[area of a triangle = $\frac{1}{2} (b \times h)$]

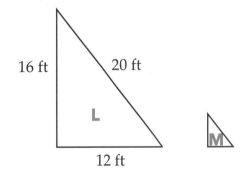

16 ft   20 ft

L

12 ft

M

Perimeter = $48 \times \frac{1}{4}$ = 12 ft

Area = $96 \times \frac{1}{16}$ = 6 ft²

7. **The ratio of edges of two cubes is 1:10. The smaller cube has edges measuring 1 meter. How long are the edges of the larger cube? What is the volume of the larger cube?**

Side = 10 m

Volume = $1 \times 10^3 = 1,000$ m³

8. **The ratio of sides of two similar rectangles is 6:1. The area of the larger rectangle is 72 square inches. What is the area of the smaller rectangle?**

Area = $72 \times \frac{1}{(6 \times 6)} = 72 \times \frac{1}{36}$

The area is 2 square inches.

Choose the best answer for each problem. In the answer section at the bottom
of the page, fill in the box of your choice.

1. Triangles G and H are similar. The
    ratio of sides of triangle G to sides of
    triangle H is 1:2. Which expression
    shows the area of triangle H? D

    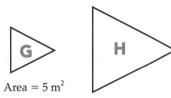

    Area = 5 m²

    A 5×2 **C** $5 \times \frac{1}{2} \times \frac{1}{2}$

    B $5^2 \times 2$ **D** 5×2^2

2. Rectangles C and D are similar. The
    ratio of rectangle C to rectangle D is
    3:1. Which expression shows the
    perimeter of rectangle D? J

    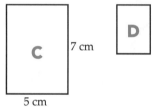

    7 cm

    5 cm

    J $2(5+7) \times \frac{1}{3}$ **L** $2(5+7) \times 3$

    K $(5+7) \times 3$ **M** $5 \times 7 \times \frac{1}{3}$

3. The ratio of cube M to cube N is 1:3.
    The volume of cube M is 2 ft³. What
    is the volume of cube N? D

    A 6 ft^3 **C** 24 ft^3

    B 18 ft^3 **D** 54 ft^3

4. Rectangles E and F are similar. The
    ratio of rectangle E to rectangle F is
    1:6. If the perimeter of rectangle E
    measures 3 m, what is the perimeter
    of rectangle F? L

    J 0.5 m   **L** 18 m

    K 2 m   **M** 54 m

5. The ratio of two similar cylinders is
    4:1. If the volume of the smaller
    cylinder is 2 m³, what is the volume
    of the larger cylinder? C

    A 8 m^3 **C** 128 m^3

    B 32 m^3 **D** Not given

Write About It

6. The area of triangle A is 25 times the
    area of triangle B. What is the ratio
    of triangle A to triangle B? Explain
    your answer.

    Sample answer:

    The ratio of the areas of two figures is

    the ratio of the two figures squared.

    25 is the same as 5 squared. So, the

    ratio of triangle A to triangle B is 5:1.

---

1. A ☐ B ☐ C ☐ D ☒   4. J ☐ K ☐ L ☒ M ☐

2. J ☒ K ☐ L ☐ M ☐   5. A ☐ B ☐ C ☒ D ☐

3. A ☐ B ☐ C ☐ D ☒

● Ratios

Using a Diagram to Solve Multi-Step Problems

Sometimes it takes several steps to solve a problem involving area or volume. It may help to draw a diagram of the problem, then use the diagram to decide what steps to follow to solve the problem.

Example

The new park shown on the right will have grass in the •shaded region only. What area will the grass cover?

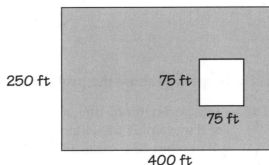

250 ft   75 ft

75 ft

400 ft

Step 1: **Make a diagram to show the problem.**

     THINK: To solve the problem, I need to find the area of the shaded region only.

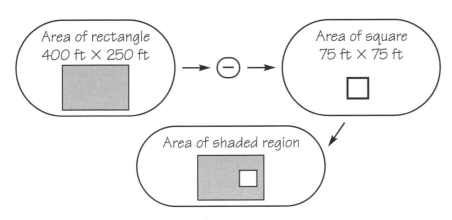

Step 2: **Follow the plan in your diagram to solve.**

     Area of rectangle − Area of square = Area of shaded region

     Area of rectangle: 400 ft × 250 ft = 100,000 ft^2

     Area of square: 75 ft × 75 ft = 5,625 ft^2

     Area of rectangle − Area of square = Area of shaded region

     100,000   −   5,625   =   94,375

So, the grass will cover an area of 94,375 **ft^2.**

GUIDED PRACTICE

1. A landscaper is going to fence the perimeter of the yard shown on the right. What length of fencing will she need? (Use $\pi = \frac{22}{7}$.)

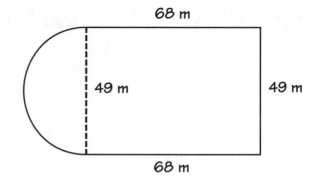

68 m

49 m   49 m

68 m

Step 1: **Make a diagram to show the problem.**

THINK: The perimeter of the yard will be the three open sides of the rectangle plus the circumference of the half circle. The diameter is the same as the width of the rectangle.

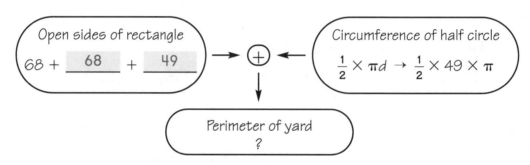

Open sides of rectangle

$68 + \underline{ 68 } + \underline{ 49 }$

$\oplus$

Circumference of half circle

$\frac{1}{2} \times \pi d \rightarrow \frac{1}{2} \times 49 \times \pi$

Perimeter of yard
?

Step 2: **Follow the plan in your diagram to solve.**

Open sides of rectangle: $\underline{ 68 } + \underline{ 68 } + \underline{ 49 } = \underline{ 185 }$

Circumference of half circle: $\frac{1}{2} \times 49 \times \frac{22}{7} = \underline{ 77 }$

Perimeter of yard: $\underline{ 185 } + \underline{ 77 } = \underline{ 262 }$

The landscaper will need $\underline{ 262 }$ **meters of fencing.**

2. An architect wishes to find the area of the entire figure shown on the right. Circle the word sentence that shows the calculations she must make.

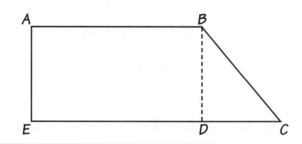

A   B

E   D   C

$\boxed{\text{a. Area of rectangle } ABDE + \text{ Area of triangle } BCD = \text{ Area of figure}}$

b. Area of rectangle $ABDE -$ Area of triangle $BCD =$ Area of figure

3. **Complete each step to find the area of the figure shown on the right.**

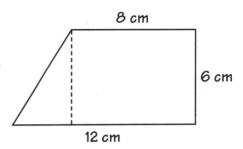

8 cm

6 cm

12 cm

Area = Area of rectangle ___+___ Area of triangle

Area of rectangle: __8__ × __6__ = __48__

Height of triangle: __6__

Base of triangle: __12__ – __8__ = __4__

Area of triangle: $\frac{1}{2}$ × __4__ × __6__ = __12__

Area of figure: __48 + 12__ = __60__ cm²

4. **Ms. Marillo wants to find the perimeter of her yard so that she can buy fencing. Complete each step to find the perimeter.**

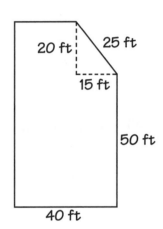

20 ft   25 ft

15 ft

50 ft

40 ft

Height of rectangle: __50__ + __20__ = __70__

Length at top: __40__ – __15__ = __25__

Perimeter of yard: __210__ ft

5. **The shaded area of the garden shown in the diagram on the right is going to be planted with grass seed. Complete each step to find the area that will be planted. (Area of a circle = πr^2.)**

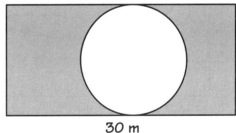

14 m

30 m

Area = Area of rectangle ___–___ Area of circle

Area of rectangle: __14__ × __30__ = __420__

Radius of circle: __14__ ÷ 2 = __7__

Area of circle: $\frac{22}{7}$ × __7__ × __7__ = __154__

Shaded area: __420 – 154__ = __266__ m²

Choose the best answer for each problem. In the answer section at the bottom of the page, fill in the box of your choice.

1. **A painter needs to find the area of the painting shown below. Which expression shows the total area?** C

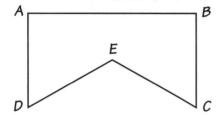

   A   Area of *ABCD*
   B   Area of *ABCD* + Area of *CED*
   C   Area of *ABCD* − Area of *CED*
   D   Area of *CED* − Area of *ABCD*

2. **What is the perimeter of the figure shown below?** M

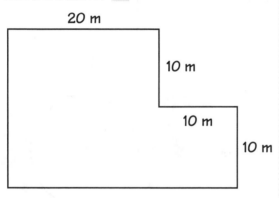

   J   50 m   L   80 m
   K   70 m   M   100 m

3. **What is the area of the figure shown in Problem 2?** B
   A   100 m^2 C   600 m^2
   B   500 m^2 D   700 m^2

4. **What is the perimeter of the figure shown below? Use 3.14 for π.** J

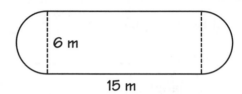

   J   48.84 m   L   90 m
   K   60.84 m   M   108.84 m

Write About It

Write a plan for solving the following problem. Then solve.

5. **What is the area of the figure shown in Problem 4?**

Sample answer:
Treat the two half circles as a single
circle with a radius of 6 ÷ 2, or 3 m.
The area of the circle is π × 3^2 = 28.26.
Then find the area of the rectangle:
6 × 15 = 90
Add the area of the circle and the
rectangle: 28.26 + 90 = 118.26
The area is 118.26 m^2.

1. A ☐   B ☐   C ☒   D ☐   3. A ☐   B ☒   C ☐   D ☐

2. J ☐   K ☐   L ☐   M ☒   4. J ☒   K ☐   L ☐   M ☐

● Area and Perimeter

Breaking a Figure into Parts

To solve problems that involve three-dimensional figures, it may help to break the figure into parts.

Example

The cube shown on the right is made up of 27 small blocks. The outside of the cube is painted red. How many of the blocks have exactly 2 red faces?

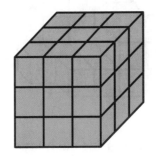

THINK: I can break the cube into three layers, and count the number of cubes with 2 red faces in each layer.

Step 1: **Visualize each layer of the cube.**

The blocks with two red faces are marked with an *X*.
Note that some of the faces are hidden—you have to visualize the hidden faces to determine whether they are red or not.

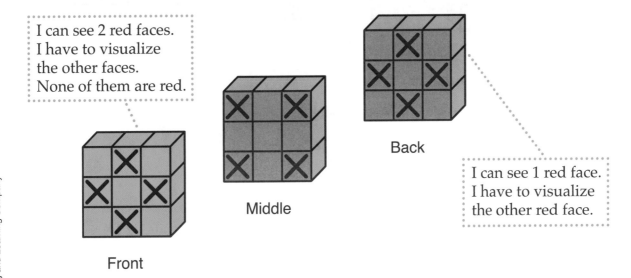

I can see 2 red faces.
I have to visualize the other faces.
None of them are red.

Front

Middle

Back

I can see 1 red face.
I have to visualize the other red face.

Step 2: **Find the sum of the blocks with two red faces.**

Front layer + Middle layer + Back layer

<u> 4 </u> + <u> 4 </u> + <u> 4 </u> = <u> 12 </u>

There are <u> 12 </u> blocks with exactly two red faces.

● Visualizing Solid Figures

GUIDED PRACTICE

1. The figure below is formed of cubes. How many cubes are there in the figure?

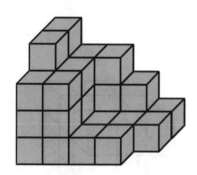

Step 1: **Visualize each layer of the figure.**

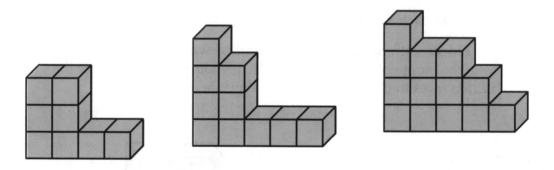

Step 2: **Count the number of cubes.**

Front layer + Middle layer + Back layer = Total cubes

$$\underline{\quad 8 \quad} + \underline{\quad 10 \quad} + \underline{\quad 13 \quad} = \underline{\quad 31 \quad}$$

There are $\underline{\quad 31 \quad}$ **cubes in the figure.**

2. The figures on the right show two views of the same square pyramid. What letter is on the face opposite the A?

Visualize the two faces of the pyramid behind the A and B faces.

Which letter is next to the B? $\underline{\quad F \quad}$

Which letter is opposite the A? $\underline{\quad F \quad}$

So, the $\underline{\quad F \quad}$ **is on the face opposite the A.**

3. **The cube on the right is made up of 64 blocks. The surface of the entire cube has been painted red. How many blocks are there in the cube that have exactly one red face each? (Hint: Break the cube into its faces.)**

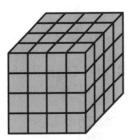

There are 24 blocks with one red face.

4. **The cube on the right is made up of 125 blocks. The surface of the entire cube has been painted red.**

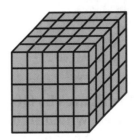

a. **How many blocks are there in the cube that have three red faces each?**

There are 8 blocks with three red

faces.

b. **If the cube was made up of nine times as many blocks, how many blocks would have three red faces?**

8 blocks (the corner blocks)

5. **How many blocks are there in the figure shown on the right?**

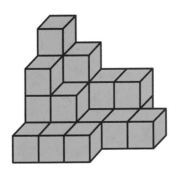

Front layer: ___3___ blocks

Middle layer: ___8___ blocks

Back layer: ___11___ blocks

There are a total of ___22___ blocks.

6. **The figures on the right are three views of the same cube. What design is on the face opposite the face that has the red circle?**

the white circle

● Visualizing Solid Figures

Choose the best answer for each problem. In the answer section at the bottom of the page, fill in the box of your choice.

Use figures A, B, and C for Problems 1–4.

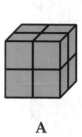

A

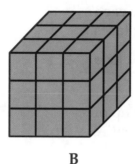

B

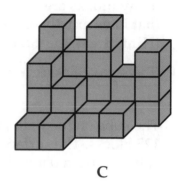

C

1. If each of the figures has its entire surface painted, which figure will have a block that has no paint on it? B
   - **A** Figure A
   - **C** Figure C
   - **B** Figure B
   - **D** Not given

2. If each of the figures has its entire surface painted, in which figure will all of the blocks have the same number of painted faces? J
   - **J** Figure A
   - **L** Figure C
   - **K** Figure B
   - **M** Not given

3. If the entire surface of Figure C is painted, how many blocks will have 5 painted surfaces? C
   - **A** 0
   - **C** 3
   - **B** 2
   - **D** 7

4. What is the total number of blocks in Figure C? M
   - **J** 16
   - **L** 23
   - **K** 21
   - **M** 25

Write About It

5. Eight small cube blocks are placed together to form a square ring that has sides of three blocks each. The entire surface of the square ring is then painted. What can you say about each of the blocks in the ring? How did you find out?

   Each of the blocks has the same

   number of painted faces.

   Students may visualize the

   arrangement of blocks, draw a

   diagram, or use models.

1. A ☐ B ☒ C ☐ D ☐   3. A ☐ B ☐ C ☒ D ☐

2. J ☒ K ☐ L ☐ M ☐   4. J ☐ K ☐ L ☐ M ☒

● Visualizing Solid Figures

Choosing a Strategy for Solving Problems

To solve a problem, you have to choose a strategy. Here are some strategies you can use.

Show Information Another Way	Decide on the Kind of Answer You Need
• Make a Diagram • Decide What Kind of Numbers to Use • Make a Table to Generalize • Solve a Formula for a Desired Variable • Draw a Number Line	• Interpret Quotients • Decide Whether to Estimate • Estimate Products, Quotients, and Mixed Expressions • Estimate Percents • Use Rates to Write Measures in a Different System
Find Needed Information	**Decide What to Do First**
• Read Information from a Table or Chart • Read a Graph • Compare Perimeters, Areas, and Volumes of Similar Figures • Read Information from a Diagram	• Use a Diagram to Solve Multi-Step Problems • Write a Word Equation • Write a Proportion, a Unit Rate, or a Ratio • Break a Figure into Parts

Example

The rectangles shown at the right are similar figures. What is the perimeter of rectangle B?

2 cm ⬚ A ⬚   8 cm ⬚ B ⬚
5.5 cm

A.   Strategy: Find needed information in a diagram.

THINK: The information I need is in the diagram of the two rectangles.

Rectangle A has a length of ___5.5 centimeters___ **and a width of**
___2 centimeters___ **. Rectangle B has a width of** ___8 centimeters___ .

Because the rectangles are similar, a proportion can be used:

$$\frac{2}{8} = \frac{5.5}{x} \longrightarrow \frac{1}{4} = \frac{5.5}{x}$$

$$x = \underline{22}$$

Check: $\dfrac{5.5}{22} = \dfrac{1}{4}$

B. Solve.

Perimeter of Rectangle A: $2(5.5 + 2) = \underline{15}$

Perimeter of Rectangle B: ___2(8 + 22)___ = ___60___

So, the perimeter of Rectangle B is ___60 centimeters___ .

• Strategy Review

153

GUIDED PRACTICE

1. Jorge is buying a bicycle. The bike he wants was originally $189 but is now on sale for 20% off the original price. What is the bike's sale price?

   Step 1: Choose a strategy, and describe it.

   Sample answer: Draw a part-part-whole diagram to help you visualize the

   problem and decide what to do first.

   Step 2: Solve, using the strategy you chose.

   $100\% - 20\% = 80\%$; $80\% \times \$189 = \$151.20$. The sale price is $151.20.

2. A wallpaper border is 4 inches high and 15 ft long. What is its area in square feet?

   Step 1: Choose a strategy, and describe it.

   Sample answer: Decide on the kind of answer you need. Then rename units to

   match those in the answer.

   Step 2: Solve, using the strategy you chose.

   4 inches $= \frac{1}{3}$ ft; $\frac{1}{3} \times 15 = 5$; the border's area is 5 ft².

3. Frank, Gabe, Hillary, and Ian are standing in a line. Ian is ahead of Gabe, and Frank is at the end of the line. Hillary is farthest from Frank. What is their order from first to last?

   Step 1: Choose a strategy, and describe it.

   Sample answer: Show the information another way by drawing a diagram or

   a number line to show each person's position.

   Step 2: Solve, using the strategy you chose.

   Order from first to last: Hillary, Ian, Gabe, Frank

Practice

Choose a strategy for each problem. Then solve.

4. The table at the right shows the percentage of her savings that Ms. Chang has in each stock fund. If she has a total of $10,000 in the five funds, how much money does she have in the Growth Equity Fund?

MS. CHANG'S STOCK FUNDS	
Small Company Fund	30%
Growth Equity Fund	20%
Utility Income Fund	20%
Real Estate Fund	15%
Overseas Fund	15%

$20\% \times 10{,}000 = 2{,}000$

Ms. Chang has $2,000 in the fund.

5. Paul flew 652 miles west and then 829 miles east. How far is he from his starting point, and is he east or west of it?

$^{-}652 + 829 = 177$

Paul is 177 mi east of his starting point.

6. Joan cut a 6-foot length of string into 8 pieces, each of which was 7 inches long. How long was the leftover piece of string?

6 ft = 72 inches; $72 - (8 \times 7) = 16$

The leftover piece was 16 inches long.

7. A one-story house has an area of 2,000 square feet. If the house's length is 50 feet, what is the perimeter of the house?

$A = lw, w = A/l; w = 2{,}000/50; w = 40$

The perimeter of the house is 180 feet.

8. A car is 15 feet long and 5 feet high. A scale model of the car is 9 inches long. What is the model car's height?

5 ft / 15 ft = x in. / 9 in.; $x = 3$ in.; the

model car's height is 3 in.

9. Silverton bought a table at 25% off the original price. He also used a coupon for an additional 15% off the sale price. If his final price was $127.50, what was the original price of the table?

Sale price: $127.50 \div 0.85 = \$150$

Original price: $150 \div 0.75 = \$200$

10. The bus company charges n dollars to travel from Philadelphia to New York, and $15 to travel from New York to Westport. The Marins paid $78 for 2 tickets from Philadelphia to Westport. What is the cost of 1 ticket from Philadelphia to New York (n)?

$2(n + 15) = 78; n = 24$

One ticket to New York costs $24.

Choose the best answer for each problem. In the answer section at the bottom of this page, fill in the box of your choice.

1. A store owner buys a couch for $500 and sells it for 75% more than its original cost. Which of the following equations could be used to find the couch's price? D

   A $500 \times 75\% = p$
   B $75\% \times p = 500$
   C $500 \div 75\% = p$
   D $500 \times 175\% = p$

2. The graph shows Ron's mileage during a 6-hour hike. During which one-hour period was he most likely eating lunch? L

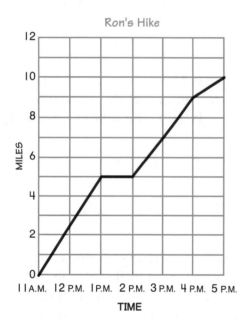

Ron's Hike

   J   Between 11 A.M. and 12 P.M.
   K   Between 12 P.M. and 1 P.M.
   L   Between 1 P.M. and 2 P.M.
   M   Between 2 P.M. and 3 P.M.

3. Bria earned $57 by selling wreaths and $21 from sales of cards and wrapping paper. She had spent $72 on supplies. What were her net earnings? C

   A   ⁻$2   C $6
   B   ⁻$6   D   Not given

4. A closet door is 90 centimeters wide and 2 meters high. What is its area in square meters? L

   J   0.45 m²   L   1.8 m²
   K   0.9 m²   M   180 m²

Write About It

5. Choose a problem on this page, and describe the strategy you used to solve it. Then describe a different strategy you could have used, and write about how you would use it to solve the problem.

   Answers will vary.

---

1. A ☐   B ☐   C ☐   D ☒   3. A ☐   B ☐   C ☒   D ☐
2. J ☐   K ☐   L ☒   M ☐   4. J ☐   K ☐   L ☒   M ☐

● Strategy Review

Using a Tree Diagram to Compute Probabilities

You can use a tree diagram to find probabilities for both independent and dependent events.

Example

A bowl contains five cards. The cards are lettered *A*, *B*, *C*, *D*, and *E*. If you draw two cards at random, what is the probability of drawing at least one vowel?

A. Compute the probabilities for the first draw, and show them on a tree diagram.

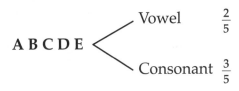

> 2 of the 5 letters are vowels, so the probability of drawing a vowel is $\frac{2}{5}$.
> 3 of the 5 letters are consonants, so the probability of drawing a consonant is $\frac{3}{5}$.

B. Compute the probabilities for the second draw, and show them on a tree diagram.

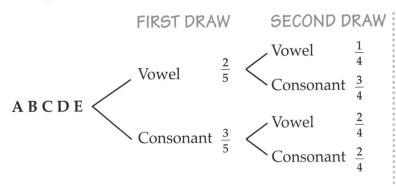

> If a vowel was already drawn, 1 of the remaining letters is a vowel. The probability of drawing a vowel is $\frac{1}{4}$.
> If a consonant was already drawn, 2 of the letters are vowels. The probability of drawing a vowel is $\frac{2}{4}$.

C. Compute the probabilities for each of the four cases and solve.

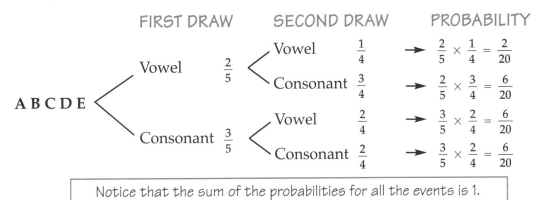

> Notice that the sum of the probabilities for all the events is 1.

Add the probabilities of the cases in which a vowel is drawn.

$$\frac{2}{20} + \frac{6}{20} + \frac{6}{20} = \underline{\frac{14}{20} \text{ or } \frac{7}{10}}$$

The probability of drawing at least one vowel is $\underline{\frac{14}{20} \text{ or } \frac{7}{10}}$.

GUIDED PRACTICE

1. A box contains 4 marbles: a red marble, a green marble, and 2 blue marbles. If you take 2 marbles from the box at random, what is the probability that at least 1 of the marbles is blue?

   Step 1: **Compute the probabilities to complete the tree diagram.**

   THINK: The first draw is from 4 marbles, the second is from 3 marbles.

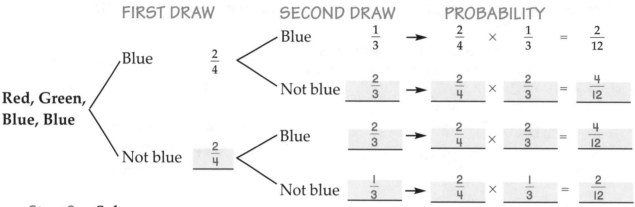

   Step 2: **Solve.**

   $$\frac{2}{12} + \frac{4}{12} + \frac{4}{12} = \frac{10}{12}$$

   The probability of drawing at least 1 blue marble is $\frac{10}{12}$ **or** $\frac{5}{6}$.

2. A box contains 2 green cards and 3 red cards. Suppose you draw a card, replace it, and then draw a second card. What is the probability that you will draw at least one red card?

   Step 1: **Compute the probabilities to complete the tree diagram.**

   THINK: There will be 2 green and 3 red cards for each draw.

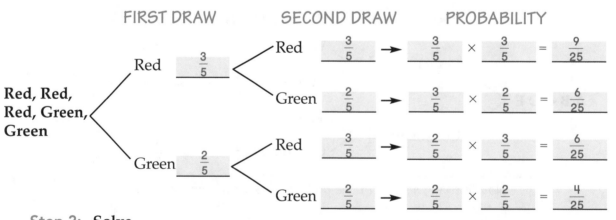

   Step 2: **Solve.**

   $$\frac{9}{25} + \frac{6}{25} + \frac{6}{25} = \frac{21}{25}$$

   The probability of drawing at least 1 red card is $\frac{21}{25}$.

PRACTICE

A box contains 4 red and 2 blue marbles. Suppose you draw 2 marbles at random.

3. **Complete the tree diagram to find the probability of each case.**

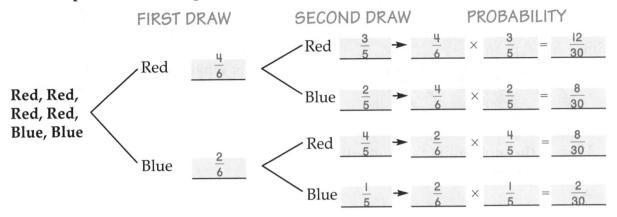

Use the tree diagram to find each probability.

4. **What is the probability of drawing at least 1 blue marble?**

$$\frac{8}{30} + \frac{8}{30} + \frac{2}{30} = \frac{18}{30}, \text{ or } \frac{9}{15}$$

5. **What is the probability of drawing exactly 1 red and 1 blue marble?**

$$\frac{8}{30} + \frac{8}{30} = \frac{16}{30}, \text{ or } \frac{8}{15}$$

A box contains 3 red marbles and 1 green marble. Suppose you draw a marble, replace it, and then draw a marble again.

6. **Complete the tree diagram to find the probability of each case.**

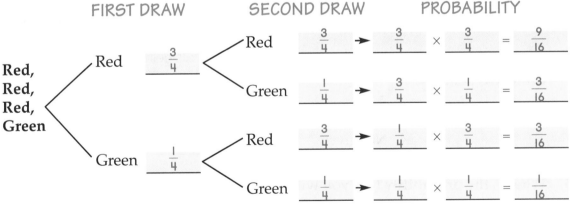

Use the tree diagram to find each probability.

7. **What is the probability of drawing 1 marble of each color?**

$$\frac{3}{16} + \frac{3}{16} = \frac{6}{16}, \text{ or } \frac{3}{8}$$

8. **What is the probability of drawing at least 1 red marble?**

$$\frac{9}{16} + \frac{3}{16} + \frac{3}{16} = \frac{15}{16}$$

Choose the best answer for each problem. In the answer section at the bottom of the page, fill in the box of your choice.

For Problems 1–5, suppose you draw 2 coins at random from a box containing 3 dimes and 2 pennies.

1. **What is the probability that you will draw a dime on the first draw?** C

   A $\frac{1}{5}$ C $\frac{3}{5}$

   B $\frac{2}{5}$ D $\frac{4}{5}$

2. **Which of the following is the sum of the probabilities of the four cases?** M

   J 0   L $\frac{3}{5}$

   K $\frac{2}{5}$ M 1

3. **What is the probability that you will draw at least one penny?** D

   A $\frac{1}{10}$ C $\frac{1}{2}$

   B $\frac{3}{10}$ D $\frac{7}{10}$

4. **What is the probability that you will draw two pennies?** J

   J $\frac{1}{10}$ L $\frac{7}{10}$

   K $\frac{2}{5}$ M Not given

5. **What is the probability that you will draw a dime and a penny?** B

   A $\frac{3}{10}$ C $\frac{9}{10}$

   B $\frac{3}{5}$ D 1

6. **A bag contains a \$1 bill and four \$5 bills. Suppose you draw a bill at random, replace it, and draw a bill again. What is the probability that you'll pick the \$1 bill both times?** K

   J 0   L $\frac{4}{25}$

   K $\frac{1}{25}$ M $\frac{16}{25}$

Write About It

Write a plan for solving the following problem. Then solve.

7. **A bag contains two \$20 bills and three \$1 bills. If you pick three bills at random, what is the probability of getting \$3?**

Sample answer:

Make a tree diagram to show the

probabilities for three events.

There are 8 possible outcomes.

Only 1 outcome results in three

\$1 bills being picked. The probability is

$\frac{3}{5} \times \frac{2}{4} \times \frac{1}{3}$, or $\frac{1}{10}$.

---

1. A ☐ B ☐ C ☒ D ☐   4. J ☒ K ☐ L ☐ M ☐

2. J ☐ K ☐ L ☐ M ☒   5. A ☐ B ☒ C ☐ D ☐

3. A ☐ B ☐ C ☐ D ☒   6. J ☐ K ☒ L ☐ M ☐

● Probability

Using Venn Diagrams

You can use a Venn diagram to show the possible outcomes in a probability problem.

Example

A card is drawn at random from a set of 20 cards that are numbered 1 through 20. What is the probability that the drawn card shows:

a. a multiple of 2 and a multiple of 3?
b. a multiple of 2 or a multiple of 3?

c. neither a multiple of 2 nor a multiple of 3?

A. Draw a Venn diagram to show the possible outcomes.

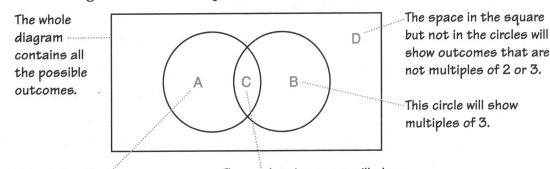

The whole diagram contains all the possible outcomes.

The space in the square but not in the circles will show outcomes that are not multiples of 2 or 3.

This circle will show multiples of 3.

This circle will show multiples of 2.

The overlapping space will show multiples of both 2 and 3.

B. Complete the Venn diagram to show the whole sample space.

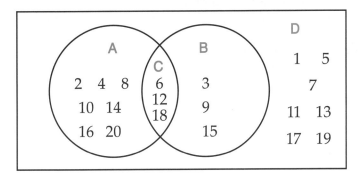

C. Use the diagram to solve the problem.

a. P(multiple of 2 and 3) = $\dfrac{\text{outcomes in C}}{\text{possible outcomes}}$ → $\dfrac{3}{20}$

b. P(multiple of 2 or 3) = $\dfrac{\text{outcomes in A + B − C}}{}$

→ $\dfrac{10 + 6 − 3}{20}$ → $\dfrac{13}{20}$

Be sure that you subtract the number in C so that you don't count it twice.

c. P(neither a multiple of 2 nor of 3) = $\dfrac{\text{outcomes in D}}{\text{possible outcomes}}$ → $\dfrac{7}{20}$

● Probability

GUIDED PRACTICE

1. A card is drawn at random from a set of 20 cards that are numbered 1 through 20. What is the probability that the drawn card shows:

   a. a multiple of 2?

   b. a multiple of 5?

   c. a multiple of 2 *and* a multiple of 5?

   d. a multiple of 2 *or* a multiple of 5?

   e. neither a multiple of 2 nor a multiple of 5?

   A. **Complete the Venn diagram to show the problem.**

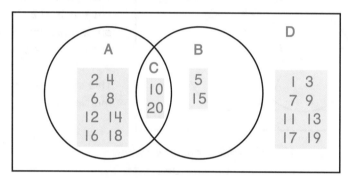

   Let A show multiples of 2.

   Let B show multiples of 5.

   C will show multiples of 2 and 5.

   D will show numbers that are neither multiples of 2 nor 5.

   B. **Use the Venn diagram to solve the problem.**

   a. P(multiple of 2) is the same as P(A).
   Count the outcomes in A in the diagram. $P(A) = \dfrac{10}{20}$ or $\dfrac{1}{2}$

   b. P(multiple of 5) is the same as P(B).
   Count the outcomes in B in the diagram. $P(B) = \dfrac{4}{20}$ or $\dfrac{1}{5}$

   c. P(multiple of 2 *and* of 5) is the same as P(C).
   Count the outcomes in C in the diagram. $P(C) = \dfrac{2}{20}$ or $\dfrac{1}{10}$

   d. P(multiple of 2 *or* of 5) is the same as P(A or B).

   $P(A \text{ or } B) = \dfrac{12}{20}$ or $\dfrac{3}{5}$

   > Note that P(A or B) equals P(A) + P(B) − P(C).
   > $$\frac{12}{20} = \frac{10}{20} + \frac{4}{20} - \frac{2}{20}$$

   e. P(neither multiple of 2 nor of 5) is the same as P(D).

   $P(D) = \dfrac{8}{20}$ or $\dfrac{2}{5}$

   > Note that P(D) is the same thing as P(neither A nor B).
   > P(neither A nor B) equals 1 − P(A or B).
   > $$\frac{8}{20} = \frac{20}{20} - \frac{12}{20}$$

PRACTICE

A card is drawn at random from a set of 16 cards marked 1 through 16. The problems on this page deal with probabilities of drawing cards that show multiples of 3 and of 4.

2. **Complete the Venn diagram to show the problem.**

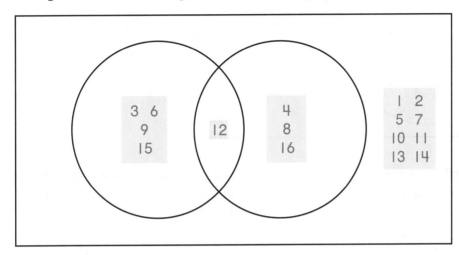

3 6
9
15

12

4
8
16

1 2
5 7
10 11
13 14

Sample answer: Students may switch the entries in the two circles.

3. **How many possible outcomes are there when a single card is drawn at random?**

16

4. **What is the probability that a card drawn at random will show a multiple of 3?**

$\frac{5}{16}$

5. **What is the probability that a card drawn at random will show a multiple of 4?**

$\frac{4}{16}$, or $\frac{1}{4}$

6. **What is the probability that a card drawn at random will be a multiple of both 3 and of 4?**

$\frac{1}{16}$

7. **What is the probability that a card drawn at random will show either a multiple of 3 or a multiple of 4?**

$\frac{8}{16}$, or $\frac{1}{2}$

8. **What is the probability that a card drawn at random will show neither a multiple of 3 nor of 4?**

$\frac{8}{16}$, or $\frac{1}{2}$

9. **What is the probability that a card drawn at random will show a multiple of 3 that is not also a multiple of 4?**

$\frac{3}{16}$

10. **What is the probability that a card drawn at random will show a number that is not a multiple of 4?**

$\frac{12}{16}$, or $\frac{3}{4}$

The Venn diagram shows the outcomes of drawing a single card from a set of 15 cards numbered 1 through 15. Use the diagram to choose the best answer for each problem. In the answer section at the bottom of the page, fill in the box of your choice.

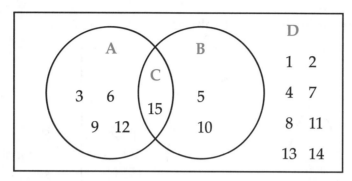

1. **How many possible outcomes does the Venn diagram show?** D
   A 4   C 8
   B 6   D 15

2. **What do the numbers in region D represent?** L
   J numbers from 1 through 14
   K multiples of 3
   L neither multiples of 3 nor of 5
   M multiples of 3 and of 5

3. **What is the probability of drawing a card that shows a multiple of 3 and of 5?** A
   A $\frac{1}{15}$ C $\frac{1}{3}$
   B $\frac{1}{5}$ D $\frac{8}{15}$

4. **What is the probability of drawing a card that shows neither a multiple of 3 nor a multiple of 5?** L
   J $\frac{1}{15}$ L $\frac{8}{15}$
   K $\frac{7}{15}$ M Not given

5. **What is the probability of drawing a card that shows a multiple of 3 or of 5?** C
   A $\frac{1}{15}$ C $\frac{7}{15}$
   B $\frac{1}{5}$ D $\frac{8}{15}$

Write About It

6. **How could you change the Venn diagram to find the probability of drawing a card that shows a multiple of both 3 and of 5 from a set of 20 cards numbered 1 through 20? What is the probability?**

   Sample answer: Add the numbers 16

   through 20 in the appropriate regions

   of the Venn diagram. Then count the

   numbers in region C to find how many

   outcomes are multiples of both 3 and

   5, and divide by the total number of

   outcomes. The probability is $\frac{1}{20}$.

---

1. A ☐ B ☐ C ☐ D ☒   4. J ☐ K ☐ L ☒ M ☐

2. J ☐ K ☐ L ☒ M ☐   5. A ☐ B ☐ C ☒ D ☐

3. A ☒ B ☐ C ☐ D ☐

● Probability

Using Venn Diagrams to Show Probabilities

Venn diagrams can be used not only for showing outcomes, but also for showing probabilities without listing all the outcomes.

Example

Consider the set of all counting numbers.
What is the probability of a number being neither a multiple of 2 nor a multiple of 3?

Step 1: **Draw and label a Venn diagram.**

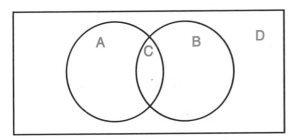

Step 2: **Identify those probabilities that you can easily find.**

THINK: The probability of a number being a multiple of 2 is $\frac{1}{2}$.

The probability of a number being a multiple of 3 is $\frac{1}{3}$.

Now find the probability of a number being a multiple of 2 <u>and</u> 3.

Multiples of 2: 2, 4, 6, 8, 10, 12, 14, 16, 18 . . .

Multiples of 3: 3, 6, 9, 12, 15, 18 . . .

> A multiple of 2 and of 3 is a multiple of 2 × 3, or 6.

The numbers in red are multiples of both 2 and 3.
Note that they are multiples of 6.

The probability of a number being a multiple of 6 is $\frac{1}{6}$.

Step 3: **Fill in those probabilities on the Venn diagram.**

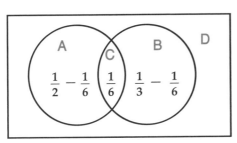

> The <u>whole</u> circle of A will be $\frac{1}{2}$.
>
> The <u>whole</u> circle of B will be $\frac{1}{3}$.
>
> Don't forget to take away the overlapping amount.

Step 4: **Use the Venn diagram to find the probabilities you need.**

a. P(multiple of 2 or of 3) $= \left(\frac{1}{2} - \frac{1}{6}\right) + \frac{1}{6} + \left(\frac{1}{3} - \frac{1}{6}\right) = \frac{2}{3}$

b. The probability of a number being in A, B, C, or D is 1.

So, the probability of a number being in D is $1 - \frac{2}{3}$, or $\frac{1}{3}$.

P(neither multiple of 2 nor of 3) $= \frac{1}{3}$.

● Probability

1. Marco works 4 days a week for a movie company, but he never knows which days they will be. It rains 1 out of every 3 days and is sunny the other 2 days where he lives. When Marco wakes up, what is the probability that it will be either sunny or a day off? What is the probability that it will be a rainy day at work?

   A. **Identify those probabilities that you can easily find.**

   Marco works 4 days a week, so he has days off 3 days of every 7 days.

   The probability that it will be a day off is $\frac{3}{7}$.

   It is sunny 2 days of every 3 days.
   The probability that it will be sunny is $\frac{2}{3}$.

   The probability that it will be sunny <u>and</u> a day off is $\frac{3}{7} \times \frac{2}{3}$, or <u>$\frac{2}{7}$</u>.

   B. **Complete the Venn diagram to show the problem.**

   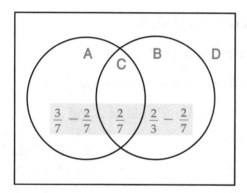

   > Use A for days off and B for sunny days.

   C. **Use the Venn diagram to find the probabilities.**

   P(sunny or day off) = A + B + C

   $$= \underline{\frac{3}{7} - \frac{2}{7} + \frac{2}{3} - \frac{2}{7} + \frac{2}{7}} \;\rightarrow\; \underline{\frac{13}{21}}$$

   The probability that it will be either a sunny day or a day off is <u>$\frac{13}{21}$</u>.

   A rainy day at work means that it is neither sunny nor a day off.

   P(neither sunny nor day off) = D

   D is the probability of every outcome (1) minus P(sunny or day off).

   So, P(neither sunny nor day off) = $1 - \underline{\frac{13}{21}} \;\rightarrow\; \underline{\frac{8}{21}}$.

   The probability that it will be a rainy work day is <u>$\frac{8}{21}$</u>.

PRACTICE

Complete the Venn diagram to solve each problem.

2. Consider the set of positive whole numbers from 1 to infinity. What is the probability of a number being neither a multiple of 4 nor a multiple of 5?

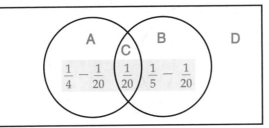

Use A for multiples of 4 and B for multiples of 5.

$P(\text{multiple of 4 or 5}) = \frac{8}{20} = \frac{2}{5}$ $P(D) = 1 - \frac{2}{5} = \frac{3}{5}$

The probability of a number being neither a multiple of 4 nor of 5 is $\frac{3}{5}$.

3. On a stretch of highway, an observer has noticed that 1 of every 5 cars is red, and that 2 of every 3 cars are made in America. What is the probability that the next car that passes will be a red American car? What is the probability that it will be a foreign car that isn't red?

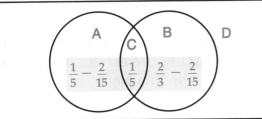

Use A for red cars and B for American cars.

The probability of a red American car is $\frac{2}{15}$.

The probability of a foreign car that is not red is $\frac{4}{15}$.

4. Of the 40 people in a club, 20 have false teeth and 10 have red hair. What is the probability that the president of the club doesn't have false teeth or red hair?

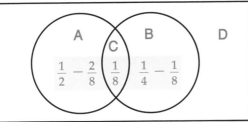

Use A for false teeth and B for red hair.

$P(\text{false teeth or red hair}) = \frac{5}{8}$; $P(\text{neither false teeth nor red hair}) = 1 - \frac{5}{8}$

The probability of the president having neither false teeth nor red hair is $\frac{5}{8}$.

● Probability

Use the information below, and the Venn diagram if you choose, to solve the problems. Choose the best answer for each problem. In the answer section at the bottom of the page, fill in the box of your choice.

Big Lee has heard 30 of the 50 songs on the jukebox in his local diner. Of the songs on the jukebox, 20 are really horrible. Big Lee walks into the diner and plays a song at random.

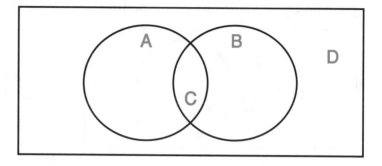

1. **What is the probability that Big Lee has heard the song before?** C

   A $\frac{1}{5}$ C $\frac{3}{5}$

   B $\frac{2}{5}$ D $\frac{4}{5}$

2. **What is the probability that the song is really horrible?** K

   J $\frac{1}{5}$ L $\frac{3}{5}$

   K $\frac{2}{5}$ M $\frac{4}{5}$

3. **What is the probability that the song is a really horrible song Big Lee has heard before?** C

   A $\frac{4}{25}$ C $\frac{6}{25}$

   B $\frac{1}{5}$ D 1

4. **What is the probability that Big Lee has heard the song already, or that it is horrible?** M

   J $\frac{1}{5}$ L $\frac{6}{25}$

   K $\frac{2}{5}$ M $\frac{19}{25}$

5. **What is the probability that Big Lee has never heard the song before and it isn't horrible?** C

   A 0   C $\frac{6}{25}$

   B $\frac{9}{25}$ D Not given

Write About It

6. **Write your own probability problem about Big Lee using the information given on this page.**

   Answers will vary.

   Check students' problems.

1. A☐ B☐ C☒ D☐   4. J☐ K☐ L☐ M☒

2. J☐ K☒ L☐ M☐   5. A☐ B☐ C☒ D☐

3. A☐ B☐ C☒ D☐

Test-Taking Skill: **Examine the Parts**

If you have trouble visualizing how a figure can be transformed, reflected, put together, or taken apart, try comparing the parts of the figure to those in the answer choices.

Here are some questions to ask yourself:

- Does the figure have the same number of sides as its net or transformation?

- Do matching sides have the same dimensions and angle measures?

- Do the sides in the figure adjoin the same sides as its net or transformation?

Example

Which net could be folded to form this prism?

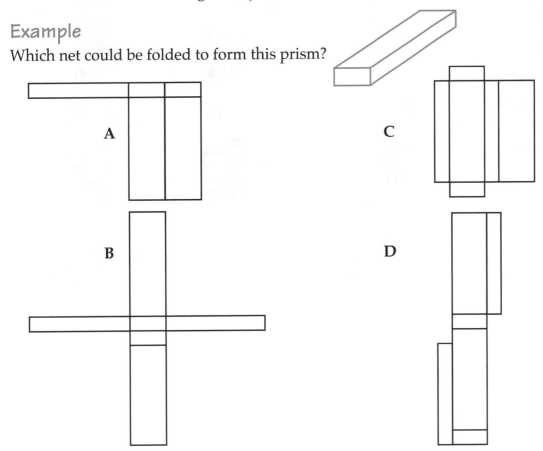

Compare the parts of each net to the corresponding parts of the prism.

THINK: Choice **A** has only 5 sides, but the prism is a 6-sided figure. I can eliminate Choice **A**.

In Choice **B**, the two smallest rectangles are next to each other, but they are not like that in the prism. I can eliminate Choice **B**.

The rectangles in Choice **C** are congruent to those in the prism. They adjoin the correct sides.

The net in Choice C could be folded to form the prism.

Choose the best answer for each problem. In the answer section at the bottom of this page, fill in the box of your choice.

1. **Which drawing shows another view of the shape on the right?** D

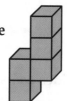

A    C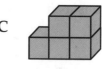

B 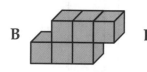   D

2. **Which drawing is a reflection of the figure on the right?**
J

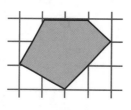

3. **Which domino is the same domino as the one below, rotated 90° clockwise?** B

A   C

B   D

4. **Which polygon forms the base of the solid figure?** L

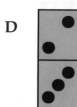

J   L

K   M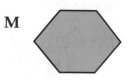

© 2000 Metropolitan Teaching and Learning Company

---

1. A ☐ B ☐ C ☐ D ☒   3. A ☐ B ☒ C ☐ D ☐

2. J ☒ K ☐ L ☐ M ☐   4. J ☐ K ☐ L ☒ M ☐

● Test-Taking Skill

Using a Function Rule to Solve Problems

Some problems can be solved by applying a function rule—an operation or combination of operations—to a given number or numbers.

Example

The table below shows the results of sending some numbers through a "function machine." Each of the numbers that come out of the machine has had a specific function rule applied to the number that went in. What is the missing number in the table?

In	27	12	6	15
Out	9	4	2	

A. Find the rule that is applied by the function machine.

Look at each ordered pair in the table: (27, 9), (12, 4), and (6, 2).

Ask yourself: What's the same about each ordered pair?

THINK: The "Out" numbers are less than the "In" numbers, so I'll try subtraction or division.

Try subtracting. $27 - ? = 9 \rightarrow 27 - 18 = 9$ Rule: Subtract 18.

$12 - ? = 4 \rightarrow 12 - 8 = 4$ Rule: Subtract 8.

The two rules are different, so try another operation.

Try dividing. $27 \div ? = 9 \rightarrow 27 \div 3 = 9$ Rule: Divide by 3.

$12 \div ? = 4 \rightarrow 12 \div 3 = 4$ Rule: Divide by 3.

The rules are the same. Once you think you've found the correct rule, try it on another ordered pair to check that it's correct.

$6 \div ? = 2 \rightarrow 6 \div 3 = 2$ Rule: Divide by 3.

So, the function rule for the table is: Divide by 3.

B. Use the rule to find the missing number in the last ordered pair.

$15 \div 3 = \underline{\quad 5 \quad}$

So, the missing number is $\underline{\quad 5 \quad}$.

1. The table shows the results of entering some numbers into a function machine. What is the missing number?

In	3	8	6	11
Out	7	17	13	

Step 1: **Find one rule that works for each ordered pair.**

Try adding. $3 + ? = 7$ $3 + 4 = 7$ Rule: _____Add 4._____

$8 + ? = 17$ $8 + 9 = 17$ Rule: _____Add 9._____

Try multiplying. $3 \times ? = 7$ $3 \times 2\frac{1}{3} = 7$ Rule: _Multiply by $2\frac{1}{3}$._

$8 \times ? = 17$ $8 \times 2\frac{1}{8} = 17$ Rule: _Multiply by $2\frac{1}{8}$._

THINK: Neither adding nor multiplying generates a rule that works for each ordered pair. I'll try two operations.

$3 \times ? + ? = 7$ $3 \times 2 + 1 = 7$ Rule: _Multiply by 2, then add 1._

$8 \times ? + ? = 17$ $8 \times 2 + 1 = 17$ Rule: _Multiply by 2, then add 1._

Check your rule.

$6 \times$ __2__ $+$ __1__ $= 13$ Rule: _Multiply by 2, then add 1._

Step 2: **Use the rule to solve the problem.**

$11 \times$ __2__ $+$ __1__ $=$ __23__

The missing number is __23__ .

2. In a computer game, the distance a ball travels depends on the setting a player selects. On setting 3 the ball goes 12 feet. On setting 4 the ball goes 16 feet, and on setting 6 it goes 24 feet. How far does the ball go on setting 10?

Step 1: **Find one rule that works for each ordered pair.**

THINK: The ordered pairs are (3, 12), (4, 16), and (6, 24). I recognize that each input number is multiplied by 4. I'll check the rule.

$3 \times 4 = 12$ $4 \times 4 = 16$ $6 \times 4 = 24$ The rule is correct.

Step 2: **Use your rule to solve the problem.**

$10 \times$ __4__ $=$ __40__

So, on setting 10 the ball goes __40__ feet .

PRACTICE

For Problems 3–6, find the function rule and the missing number in the table.

3.

In	13	18	24	10
Out	26	36	48	

Rule: _____ Multiply by 2. _____

Missing number: __ 20 __

4.

In	10	14	25	32
Out	2	6	17	

Rule: _____ Subtract 8. _____

Missing number: __ 24 __

5.

In	35	14	42	7
Out	5	2	6	

Rule: _____ Divide by 7. _____

Missing number: __ 1 __

6.

In	3	2	8	6
Out	10	7	25	

Rule: _____ Multiply by 3 and add 1. _____

Missing number: __ 19 __

Solve . . . .

7. Garth saves money from each paycheck. If he receives $12, he saves $2. If he receives $24, he saves $4. If he receives $54, he saves $9. How much will Garth save if he gets a paycheck for $60?

Garth will save $10.

8. If you hear thunder 10 seconds after seeing lightning, the lightning is 2 miles away. If you hear it 25 seconds after, the lightning is 5 miles away. How far away is lightning if you hear the thunder 15 seconds afterwards?

It is 3 miles away.

9. When Louise pulls the window shade pulley down 6 inches, the shade goes up 11 inches. When she pulls it down 8 inches, the shade goes up 15 inches. How far will the shade go up if she pulls the pulley down 12 inches?

The shade will go up 23 inches.

10. It costs $320 to turn on the coolbinkie machine at a factory. The cost of making coolbinkies is set by a function rule—the number of coolbinkies is multiplied by $2, and then $320 is added. How much does it cost to make 100 coolbinkies?

It costs $520.

Choose the best answer for each problem. In the answer section at the bottom of the page, fill in the box of your choice.

1. The table below shows the results of entering some numbers into a function machine. What is the function rule? **B**

In	15	24	7	9
Out	9	18	1	3

   A Add 9.
   B Subtract 6.
   C Divide by 3.
   D Multiply by 2 and subtract 6.

2. What is the missing number in the table below? **M**

In	14	8	6	15
Out	19	13	11	

   J 10   L 15
   K 12   M 20

3. Jules is paid $3.00 for bus fare and $5 for each hour of baby-sitting. If he baby-sits for $3\frac{1}{2}$ hours, how much money will he receive? **C**
   A $14.50   C $20.50
   B $17.50   D $28.00

4. The table below shows the results of entering some numbers into a function machine. What output would result from entering 33? **L**

In	6	10	1	4
Out	14	22	4	10

   J 39   L 68
   K 41   M 132

5. In a computer soccer game, if you "kick" the ball at setting 4, it goes 14 feet. On setting 8, the ball goes 28 feet. On setting 9, the ball goes $31\frac{1}{2}$ feet. How far would the ball go on setting 6? **B**
   A 16 ft   C 26 ft
   B 21 ft   D Not given

Write About It

6. Explain when you would try addition or multiplication to find a function rule. When would you try subtraction or division?

Sample answer:

Try addition or multiplication when

the rule results in a greater number

being formed.

Try subtraction or division when the

rule results in a lesser number being

formed.

1. A ☐ B ☒ C ☐ D ☐
2. J ☐ K ☐ L ☐ M ☒
3. A ☐ B ☐ C ☒ D ☐
4. J ☐ K ☐ L ☒ M ☐
5. A ☐ B ☒ C ☐ D ☐

● Functions

Interpolating and Extrapolating Data by Making a Graph

Sometimes you can solve a problem by making a graph.

Example

The distance from Stonegate to Harrison is 425 miles. Crowell lies between the two towns, 100 miles from Stonegate. At noon, Shelley leaves Crowell for Harrison, driving at an average of 50 miles per hour. At what time will she reach Harrison?

A. **Draw a graph to solve the problem.**

Show *Time* on the horizontal axis.

Show *Miles from Stonegate* on the vertical axis.

B. **Find two or three points to plot on the graph.**

THINK: Shelley starts 100 miles from Stonegate, and drives at 50 miles per hour. After 1 hour, she will be 150 miles from Stonegate. After 2 hours, she'll be 200 miles from Stonegate.

Plot the points on the graph.

C. **Using a ruler, connect the points you've plotted and extend the line.**

D. **Use the graph to solve the problem.**

THINK: Harrison is 425 miles from Stonegate.

Find 425 miles on the graphed line. Move your finger down to find the time that corresponds with that distance.

The time is halfway between

_____6_____ P.M. and _____7_____ P.M.

Shelley will reach Harrison at ____6:30____ P.M.

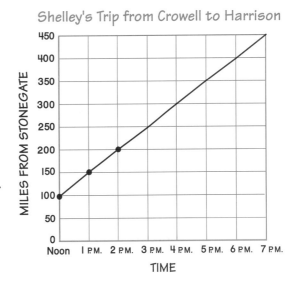

Shelley's Trip from Crowell to Harrison

● Plotting Points on a Graph

GUIDED PRACTICE

1. Use the graph of Shelley's trip from Crowell to Harrison. How many miles from Stonegate is Shelley at 5:30 P.M.?

    Step 1: **Find the point on the graphed line halfway between 5 P.M. and 6 P.M.**

    Step 2: **Now move your finger left to find the distance that corresponds to the point on the line.**

    The graph shows that Shelley will be halfway between __350__ miles and __400__ miles from Stonegate at 5:30 P.M.

    Shelley will be __375__ miles from Stonegate at 5:30 P.M.

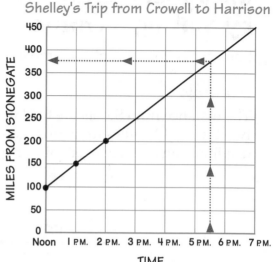

Shelley's Trip from Crowell to Harrison

Use the graph below for Problems 2–3.

2. A freight train from Pedernales to Oakville travels at 20 miles per hour. The distance between the towns is 160 miles, and at 10:00 A.M. the train is 40 miles from Pedernales. At what time will the train be 130 miles from Pedernales?

    Step 1: **Plot two or three points on the graph.**

    THINK: If the train is 40 miles from Pedernales at 10 A.M., it will be 40 + 20 miles from Pedernales at 11 A.M.

    Step 2: **Use a ruler to connect the points you've drawn. Extend the line.**

    Step 3: **Find the point on the line that corresponds to 130 miles. Then find the corresponding time.**

    The train will be 130 miles from Pedernales at __2:30__ P.M.

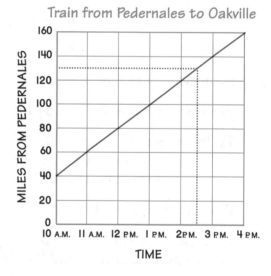

Train from Pedernales to Oakville

3. At what time will the train reach Oakville?

    a. When the train reaches Oakville, how many miles is it from Pedernales? __160 miles__

    b. What time will it be then? __4 P.M.__

    The train will reach Oakville at __4 P.M.__ .

4. **Use the following information to complete the graph showing Darlene's trip to Preston.**

The distance between Greenville and Preston is 52 miles. Rye lies between the two towns, 8 miles from Greenville. Darlene left Rye at 8:00 A.M., cycling to Preston at a speed of 8 miles per hour.

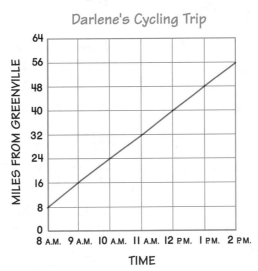

Darlene's Cycling Trip

Solve . . . .

5. **How far will Darlene be from Greenville at noon?**

   40 miles

6. **How far will Darlene be from Greenville at 10:30 A.M.?**

   28 miles

7. **At what time will Darlene be 36 miles from Greenville?**

   11:30 A.M.

8. **At what time will Darlene be 20 miles from Greenville?**

   9:30 A.M.

9. **At what time will Darlene reach Preston?**

   1:30 P.M.

10. **At what time will Darlene have completed half her trip?**

    10:45 A.M.

● Plotting Points on a Graph

Choose the best answer for each problem. In the answer section at the bottom of the page, fill in the box of your choice.

Use the following information to solve Problems 1 and 2.

Grant lives 60 miles from his son. He drove 15 miles toward his son's house and stopped until noon. Then he continued the drive at 30 miles per hour.

1. **If you labeled one axis of a graph showing Grant's trip "Time," what would you label the other axis?** B
   A Time
   B Miles from Grant's house
   C Miles between the two houses
   D Miles per hour

2. **Which of the following points would you plot on the graph?** L
   J (1:00 P.M., 15 miles)
   K (1:00 P.M., 30 miles)
   L (1:00 P.M., 45 miles)
   M (1:00 P.M., 50 miles)

Use the graph below to answer Problems 3–5.

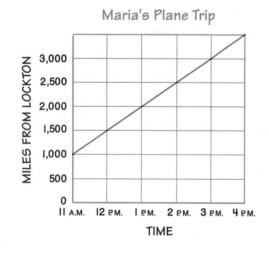

Maria's Plane Trip

3. **At what time was Maria 1,750 miles from Lockton?** B
   A 12:00 P.M.   C 1:00 P.M.
   B 12:30 P.M.   D Not given

4. **How many miles from Lockton was Maria at 3:00 P.M.?** K
   J 2,000 miles   L 2,500 miles
   K 3,000 miles   M 3,500 miles

Write About It
Write a plan for solving the following problem. Then solve.

5. **What was the average speed of Maria's plane?**

   Sample answer:

   Plot two points that are one hour

   apart from each other on the line

   graph. Then find the difference in the

   distances that correspond to each

   point. The distance traveled in one

   hour is the average speed of the plane.

   The plane's average speed is 500

   miles per hour.

1. A ☐ B ☒ C ☐ D ☐

2. J ☐ K ☐ L ☒ M ☐

3. A ☐ B ☒ C ☐ D ☐

4. J ☐ K ☒ L ☐ M ☐

● Plotting Points on a Graph

Using a Number Line to Order a Set

Some logic problems ask you to order a set—from largest to smallest or heaviest to lightest, for example. You can use a number line to order the set.

Example

The first five people to cross the finish line in a running race were Andy, Beth, Chris, Dan, and Erin. Dan came in between Andy and Beth. Chris came in between Erin and Andy. Andy was slower than Erin, but faster than Dan. Who won the race?

Step 1: **Draw a line.**
Label the right end "Fastest" and the left end "Slowest."

Slowest   Fastest

Step 2: **Use initial letters to place the runners in order on the line.**

THINK: I should start with information that tells me that one runner was faster or slower than another.

a. "Andy was slower than Erin, but faster than Dan."
Mark an *A* to the left of an *E*.
Then mark a *D* to the left of the *A*.

Slowest   D   A   E   Fastest

b. "Dan came in between Andy and Beth."
Dan and Andy are already marked. For Dan to be between Andy and Beth, Beth must be to the left of Dan.
Mark a *B* to the left of the *D*.

Slowest   B   D   A   E   Fastest

c. "Chris came in between Erin and Andy."
Erin and Andy are already marked.
Mark a *C* between the *E* and the *A*.

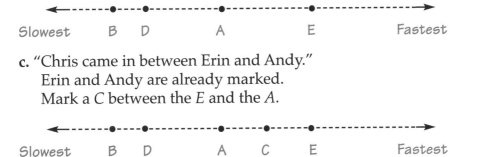

Slowest   B   D   A   C   E   Fastest

Step 3: **Use the line to answer the problem.**

The winner of the race was ____Erin____.

GUIDED PRACTICE

1. The table compares the heights of four students. Use the table to place the students in order from tallest to shortest.

Students	Who's taller?
Celine and Sam	Celine
Bobbie and Thad	Bobbie
Sam and Bobbie	Sam

Use the line below to order the heights of the students.

a. Celine is taller than Sam. Place Celine and Sam on the number line.

b. Sam is taller than Bobbie. Place Bobbie on the number line.

c. Bobbie is taller than Thad. Place Thad on the number line.

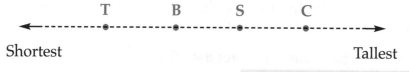

Shortest   Tallest

The order from tallest to shortest is ___Celine, Sam, Bobbie, Thad___ .

2. Which can weighs the most?

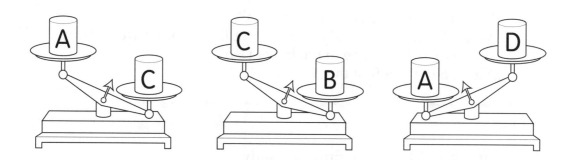

Use the line below to order the weights of the cans.

a. Can C weighs more than can A. Place cans A and C on the line.

b. Can B weighs more than can C. Place can B on the line.

c. Can A weighs more than can D. Place can D on the line.

Lightest   Heaviest

So, can ___B___ weighs the most.

PRACTICE

Mark the number lines to solve each problem.

3. **Which bag weighs the least?**

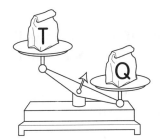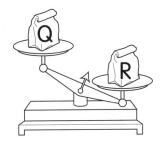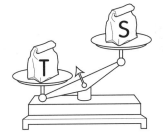

Bag S

4. **Car B costs less than car A but more than car E. Car D costs less than car C but more than car A. Which car is the most expensive?**

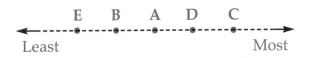

Car C

5. **Who walked the longest distance?**

Walker	Who walked farther?
Seth and Roger	Seth
Niles and Frank	Niles
Niles and Roger	Roger

Seth

6. **Five children are standing in order of height. Marco is taller than Kim. Jo is between Nora and Kim. Kim is between Marco and Jo, and Marco is between Ling and Kim. What is the order of the children from shortest to tallest?**

Nora, Jo, Kim, Marco, Ling

● Comparing on a Number Line

Choose the best answer for each problem. In the answer section at the bottom of the page, fill in the box of your choice.

1. In a cycle race, Lou, Matt, Neil, and Paul took the first four places. Matt came in second, and Neil just beat Paul.

   Which of the following lists gives the runners' order from fastest to slowest? A

   A Lou, Matt, Neil, Paul
   B Neil, Paul, Matt, Lou
   C Paul, Neil, Matt, Lou
   D Matt, Lou, Neil, Paul

2. **Which bag weighs the most?** K

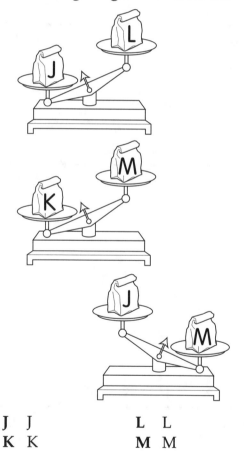

   | J J | | L L |
   | K K | | M M |

3. **Which is the largest of the four countries?** D

Country	Which is larger?
Iceland and Greenland	Greenland
France and Wales	France
Greenland and France	Greenland

   A Wales   **C** Iceland
   B England   **D** Greenland

4. At a meeting of the Fast Five, Zip was the second person to arrive. Whoosh arrived just after Varoom, but before Yikes. Who arrived before X-Ray? M

   J Zip, Whoosh, Yikes, and Varoom
   K Zip and Varoom
   L Varoom, Whoosh, and Zip
   M Nobody

Write About It

5. Write an ordering problem of your own that can be solved using a number line. Then show your solution.

   Students may come up with various

   kinds of problems. Check their

   problems and solutions to make sure

   that they correspond.

1. A ☒   B ☐   C ☐   D ☐   3. A ☐   B ☐   C ☐   D ☒

2. J ☐   K ☒   L ☐   M ☐   4. J ☐   K ☐   L ☐   M ☒

● Comparing on a Number Line

Using Logic Tables to Solve Problems Deductively

Some problems ask for a solution based on several clues. Making a table can help you solve these problems.

Example

Andie, Boo, Chris, and Drew live in the same town. One of the four is Andie's sister, one is Boo's daughter, one is Chris's father, and one is Drew's dentist. Who is Drew's dentist? Use these clues:

1. Boo is younger than Drew and Andie.
2. Drew is either Boo's daughter or Andie's sister.
3. Andie is a woman.

Step 1: **Make a table to keep track of the clues. Eliminate any impossible choice.**

	Andie's sister	Boo's daughter	Chris's father	Drew's dentist
Andie	X			
Boo		X		
Chris			X	
Drew				X

Step 2: **Use the clues to eliminate more choices.**

Clue 1 states that Boo is younger than Drew and Andie. So, neither Andie nor Drew is Boo's daughter. Mark an X in those boxes. Now look at the column for Boo's daughter. The answer must be Chris.

Clue 2 states that Drew is either Boo's daughter or Andie's sister. But Chris is Boo's daughter. Drew must be Andie's sister.

	Andie's sister	Boo's daughter	Chris's father	Drew's dentist
Andie	X	X		
Boo		X		
Chris		✓	X	
Drew	✓	X		X

Step 3: **Use each checkmark to make more entries in the table.**

THINK: There can be only one check in each row and in each column. When I mark a check, I can mark Xs in each other box in the column and row.

	Andie's sister	Boo's daughter	Chris's father	Drew's dentist
Andie	X	X	X	✓
Boo	X	X	✓	X
Chris	X	✓	X	X
Drew	✓	X	X	X

Now you need to find which of Andie and Boo is Chris's father and which is Drew's dentist. Use the third clue: Andie is a woman.

Drew's dentist is __Andie__.

1. Alice, Betty, Cheryl, and Daisy are happily married to Kevin, Leo, Mark, and Nathan, but not in that order. Use these clues to find out the name of Betty's husband:

   • Alice isn't married to Kevin or Mark.

   • Daisy and Mark are celebrating their tenth anniversary.

   • Nathan has never met Alice or Betty.

	Kevin	Leo	Mark	Nathan
Alice	X	✓	X	X
Betty	✓	X	X	X
Cheryl	X	X	X	✓
Daisy	X	X	✓	X

   a. Use the clues to mark Xs or checks on the table.

   THINK: I can mark Xs to show the relationships stated in the first and third clues. I can use a check to show the second clue.

   b. Add to the table, using the entries you've already made.

   Complete any rows or columns that have only one empty box.
   If a box is checked, fill in the other boxes in that row and column with Xs.

   Betty's husband is __Kevin__ .

2. When Larry, Mike, and Nadia eat lunch together, each orders either milk or juice to drink. They have noticed that:

   • Either Larry or Nadia orders milk, but not both.

   • Mike and Nadia do not both order juice.

   • If Larry orders milk, Mike orders juice.

   Complete each table below to find out which of the friends ordered milk yesterday and juice today. (Only one table will work for all of the clues.)

	Yesterday	Today
Larry	**milk**	**juice**
Mike		
Nadia		

	Yesterday	Today
Larry	juice	juice
Mike	**milk**	**juice**
Nadia	milk	milk

	Yesterday	Today
Larry		
Mike		
Nadia	**milk**	**juice**

   __Mike__ ordered milk yesterday and juice today.

© 2000 Metropolitan Teaching and Learning Company

PRACTICE

Complete the tables to solve each problem.

3. Mr. Brown, Mr. Green, Mr. Rose, and Mr. Tan live in four houses that are painted brown, green, rose, and tan. Use these clues to find out who lives in which house:

   - None of the men live in a house painted the same color as his name.

   - Mr. Green's house is not brown.

   - Mr. Tan's house is not brown or green.

	Brown house	Green house	Rose house	Tan house
Mr. Brown	X	✓	X	X
Mr. Green	X	X	X	✓
Mr. Rose	✓	X	X	X
Mr. Tan	X	X	✓	X

Mr. Brown lives in the __green__ house, Mr. Green lives in the __tan__ house, Mr. Rose lives in the __brown__ house, and Mr. Tan lives in the __rose__ house.

4. Angus, Barry, and Curt are performing eels. They can do only two tricks—begging and leaping through fire. Whenever they perform, each eel does one trick. The audience has noticed that:

   - Angus and Curt never leap through fire together.

   - Either Angus or Barry begs, but not both.

   - Whenever Barry begs, Curt leaps through fire.

   One of the eels leaped through fire yesterday and begged today. Use the tables to find out which eel it was.

	Yesterday	Today
Angus	fire-leap	begging
Barry		
Curt		

	Yesterday	Today
Angus		
Barry	fire-leap	begging
Curt		

	Yesterday	Today
Angus		
Barry		
Curt	fire-leap	begging

The eel that leaped through fire yesterday and begged today was __Curt__ .

Use the information below for Problems 1–4. Choose the best answer for each problem. In the answer section at the bottom of the page, fill in the box of your choice.

Abbey, Bella, Carmen, and Deidre are friends. They each have a son, a car, and a pet. The sons' names are Al, Biff, Carl, and Dan. The cars are an Adder, a Boxer, a Cobra, and a Diva. The pets are an ant, a boa, a cat, and a dog. These clues can help you find out the son, car, and pet of each woman:

- No woman's name starts with the same letter as her son, her car, or her pet.

- Abbey doesn't drive a Diva, and her pet has no legs.

- Carmen isn't Al's mother, she doesn't like dogs, and her car isn't an Adder or a Diva.

- Deidre's son is Biff.

1. **If you make a table of the four women and their four pets, which boxes can you mark with an *X*?** C
   - A the boxes in the first column
   - B the corner boxes
   - C boxes with the same inital letter
   - D boxes on the last row

2. **What car does Deidre drive? Use the table to keep track of the clues.** J

	Adder	Boxer	Cobra	Diva
Abbey				
Bella				
Carmen				
Deidre				

   - J Adder
   - K Boxer
   - L Cobra
   - M Diva

3. **Who is Carl's mother? Use the table below to keep track of the clues.** A

	Al	Biff	Carl	Dan
Abbey				
Bella				
Carmen				
Deidre				

   - A Abbey
   - B Bella
   - C Carmen
   - D Deidre

4. **Who owns the cat? Use the table to keep track of the clues.** M

	Ant	Boa	Cat	Dog
Abbey				
Bella				
Carmen				
Deidre				

   - J Abbey
   - K Bella
   - L Carmen
   - M Deidre

Write About It

5. **Write your own logic problem about Abbey, Bella, Carmen, and Deidre. On another sheet of paper, make a blank table. Fill in the table as you write clues, and change clues if you think it improves the problem. Trade your problem with a classmate.**

Answers will vary.

Check students' problems.

1. A ☐ B ☐ C ☒ D ☐
2. J ☒ K ☐ L ☐ M ☐
3. A ☒ B ☐ C ☐ D ☐
4. J ☐ K ☐ L ☐ M ☒

● Making a Table

Choosing a Strategy for Solving Problems

To solve a problem, you have to choose a strategy. Here are some of the strategies you have studied so far.

Show Information Another Way	**Decide on the Kind of Answer You Need**
• Make a Diagram • Decide What Kind of Numbers to Use • Make a Table to Generalize • Solve a Formula for a Desired Variable • Draw a Number Line • Use a Tree Diagram or a Venn Diagram • Make a Graph	• Interpret Quotients • Decide Whether to Estimate • Estimate Products, Quotients, and Mixed Expressions • Estimate Percents • Use Rates to Write Measures in a Different System
Find Needed Information	**Decide What to Do First**
• Read Information from a Table or Chart • Read a Graph • Read Information on a Diagram	• Use a Diagram to Solve Multi-Step Problems • Write a Word Equation • Write a Proportion, a Unit Rate, or a Ratio • Break a Figure into Parts • Use a Function Rule to Solve Problems

Example

Suppose you toss 3 pennies. What is the probability that all three will come up heads?

A. **Strategy: Show information another way.**
Because there are more than two events, it is too hard to show the outcomes in a table. So, make a tree diagram.

THINK: To save time, I can complete only the part of the tree diagram that shows the probability for the case in which all 3 pennies come up heads.

PENNY 1	PENNY 2	PENNY 3	PROBABILITY

$$H \longrightarrow \frac{1}{2}$$

$$H \longrightarrow \frac{1}{2}$$

$$H \longrightarrow \frac{1}{2} \quad \Rightarrow \quad \frac{1}{2} \times \frac{1}{2} \times \frac{1}{2} = \frac{1}{8}$$

$$T \longrightarrow \frac{1}{2}$$

$$T \longrightarrow \frac{1}{2}$$

$$T \longrightarrow \frac{1}{2}$$

B. **Use the tree diagram to solve the problem.**

The probability that all three pennies will come up heads is $\frac{1}{8}$.

GUIDED PRACTICE

1. Gina tossed two cubes, each numbered 1–6. What is the probability that the numbers showing on the tossed cubes will add up to an even number?

   Step 1: **There are only two events. So, show the information in another way by completing the table.**

	1	2	3	4	5	6
1	2	3	4	5	6	7
2	3	4	5	6	7	8
3	4	5	6	7	8	9
4	5	6	7	8	9	10
5	6	7	8	9	10	11
6	7	8	9	10	11	12

   Step 2: **Solve.**

   THINK: The probability that the numbers tossed will add up to an even number is $\dfrac{\text{Even numbers tossed}}{\text{Total numbers tossed}}$.

   So, the probability the numbers tossed will add up to an even number is $\dfrac{18}{36}$, or $\dfrac{1}{2}$.

2. Ms. Reeves's bill for lunch is $12.87. She wants to leave a 15% tip. To the nearest dollar, how much should she leave as a tip?

   Step 1: **Choose a strategy, and describe it.**

   > Sample answer: Decide on the kind of answer you need—an estimated answer.

   Step 2: **Solve, using the strategy you chose.**

   > Sample answer: $12.87 rounds to $13; $0.15 × $13 = $1.95.

   > She should leave $2.00.

3. The James family has 3 members who deliver newspapers each week. Each person earns $2.75 per customer per month. One has a route with 89 customers, and each of the other two has a route with 76 customers. How much in all do the 3 deliverers earn per month?

   Step 1: **Choose a strategy, and describe it.**

   > Sample answer: Decide what to do first by writing an equation.

   Step 2: **Solve, using the strategy you chose.**

   > $p = (89 × $2.75) + 2(76 × $2.75); p = 662.75

Choose a strategy for each problem. Then solve.

4. A jar contains 5 marbles that are these colors:

   blue red blue yellow yellow

   Suppose you draw 2 marbles from the jar. What is the probability that you will draw at least 1 blue marble?

   The probability of drawing at least 1 blue

   marble is $\frac{7}{10}$.

5. There are 5 crayons in a box. The blue crayon is on the far left. The pink crayon is between the green and white crayons, and the yellow crayon is between the blue and green crayons. What is the crayons' order from left to right?

   blue, yellow, green, pink, white

6. Suppose you toss two cubes, each numbered 1–6. What is the probability that the numbers showing on the tossed cubes will add up to 6?

   Of 36 numbers tossed, 5 add up to

   6, so the probability is $\frac{5}{36}$.

7. From a catalog, Jahari bought a tie for $19, a robe for $55, and a shirt for $32. He paid $120.25, including shipping and handling. How much did shipping and handling cost?

   $19 + 55 + 32 + x = 120.25; x = 14.25$

   Shipping and handling cost $14.25.

8. A traffic circle has a circumference of 439.6 feet. What is the radius of the traffic circle? ($C = 2\pi r$; use 3.14 for π.)

   $r = \frac{C}{2\pi}; r = \frac{219.8}{3.14}; r = 70$

   The radius of the traffic circle is 70 ft.

9. Neil receives 1 paycheck per month. This month, he worked for 21 days. If the total amount he earned for the month is p, how much does he earn per week (each week has 5 days)?

   Let p = amount of paycheck in dollars.

   He earns $p \div 21$ each day, or $\frac{5p}{21}$ per

   week.

10. A special packing crate has the dimensions shown at the right. What is the volume of the crate? ($V = lwh$)

    Top part = 68.25 ft^3; bottom part = 147

    ft^3; the volume of the crate is 215.25 ft^3.

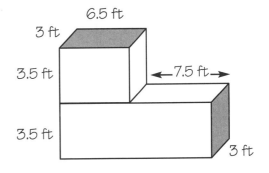

6.5 ft
3 ft
3.5 ft
←7.5 ft→
3.5 ft
3 ft

Choose the best answer for each problem. In the answer section at the bottom of this page, fill in the box of your choice.

1. Suppose you draw 2 cards from a box containing 5 cards, each with one letter: U H C M I . After you draw the first card, you put it back in the box so that you always have 5 cards. What is the probability that you will draw at least one consonant? D

   A $\frac{4}{25}$ C $\frac{9}{25}$

   B $\frac{6}{25}$ D $\frac{21}{25}$

2. A room is $12\frac{1}{2}$ ft long and 10 ft 2 in. wide. What is its perimeter? K

   J   22 ft 8 in.   L   45 ft 8 in.
   K   45 ft 4 in.   M   Not given

3. Suppose you have a drawer with 2 blue socks, 2 red socks, and 2 yellow socks. The socks are mixed up. If you reach into the drawer and pull out 2 socks at random, what is the probability that you will have 2 socks of the same color? C

   A $\frac{1}{9}$ C $\frac{1}{3}$

   B $\frac{1}{6}$ D $\frac{1}{2}$

4. If a laser printer can print x pages per minute, how many pages can 3 laser printers print in 10 minutes? L

   J $3x + 10$ L $10 \times 3x$
   K $3(x + 10)$ M $10x + 3$

5. Jane bought a quilt at 30% off the original price. She also used a coupon for an additional 10% off the sale price. If the quilt cost $200 originally, what did Jane pay? B

   A $120   C $140
   B $126   D $160

6. Ms. Parker began on the 8th floor of her building. She took the elevator up 7 floors, then down 11 floors, and then back up 3 floors. Which floor is she on now? L

   J   Floor 3   L   Floor 7
   K   Floor 5   M   Floor 8

Write About It

7. Choose a problem on this page, and describe the strategy you used to solve it. Then describe a different strategy you could have used, and write about how you would use it to solve the problem.

   Answers will vary.

1. A ☐ B ☐ C ☐ D ☒   4. J ☐ K ☐ L ☒ M ☐

2. J ☐ K ☒ L ☐ M ☐   5. A ☐ B ☒ C ☐ D ☐

3. A ☐ B ☐ C ☒ D ☐   6. J ☐ K ☐ L ☒ M ☐

Test-Taking Skill: Make an Organized Record

Some problems require you to find possible outcomes of an event. Making an organized record of the outcomes can help you.

Example

A game is played where cards with the numbers 1, 2, and 3 are placed in each of two containers. Player A draws a number from one container. Player B draws a card from the other container. If the product of the two numbers is odd, player A wins a point. If the product is even, player B wins a point. Is the game fair? If the game is not fair, which player is more likely to win?

A. Read the problem carefully and decide how you will solve it.

You'll need to find all the possible outcomes, and count how many are odd and how many are even. Then you can determine if the game is fair, or which product is more likely.

B. Use an organized list, table, or tree diagram to show all possible outcomes.

To keep track of the numbers and their products, make a table.

	1	2	3
1	$1 \times 1 =$ 1	$1 \times 2 =$ 2	$1 \times 3 =$ 3
2	$2 \times 1 =$ 2	$2 \times 2 =$ 4	$2 \times 3 =$ 6
3	$3 \times 1 =$ 3	$3 \times 2 =$ 6	$3 \times 3 =$ 9

C. Solve the problem.

Step 1: Count the odd products. There are ___4___ odd products.

Step 2: Count the even products. There are ___5___ even products.

Step 3: Compare the odd and the even products to determine if the game is fair.

There are more ___even___ products than ___odd___ products.

D. Answer the problem question.

No, the game is not fair. Player ___B___ is more likely to win.

Use an organized list, table, or tree diagram to solve the problem.

1. **Jenna, Kyla, Lenore, and Maya are playing Monopoly. In how many different ways can the four girls finish first, second, third, and fourth?**

Sample answer shown.

Let J represent Jenna, K represent Kyla, L represent Lenore, and M represent Maya.

JKLM, JKML, JMKL, JMLK, JLKM, JLMK

KJLM, KJML, KMJL, KMLJ, KLJM, KLMJ

LJKM, LJMK, LKJM, LKMJ, LMJK, LMKJ

MJKL, MJLK, MKJL, MKLJ, MLJK, MLKJ

There are 24 ways the girls can finish first, second, third, and fourth.

2. **In a club election, there are 4 candidates for president and 2 candidates for treasurer. How many different possible results are there for the election?**

Sample answer shown.

Let the candidates for president be A, B, C, and D. Let the candidates for treasurer

be E and F.

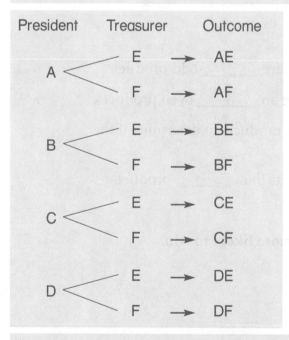

President	Treasurer	Outcome
A	E	AE
	F	AF
B	E	BE
	F	BF
C	E	CE
	F	CF
D	E	DE
	F	DF

There are 8 possible results for the election.